DEMOTIC INDUCED NEUROSIS

VOLUME VII

BY: TODD ANDREW ROHRER

iUniverse, Inc.
New York   Bloomington

iUniverse books may be ordered through booksellers or by contacting:

iUniverse
1663 Liberty Drive
Bloomington, IN 47403
www.iuniverse.com
1-800-Authors (1-800-288-4677)

Because of the dynamic nature of the Internet, any Web addresses or links contained in this book may have changed since publication and may no longer be valid. The views expressed in this work are solely those of the author and do not necessarily reflect the views of the publisher, and the publisher hereby disclaims any responsibility for them.

ISBN: 978-1-4401-6949-6 (sc)
ISBN: 978-1-4401-6950-2 (ebook)

Printed in the United States of America

iUniverse rev. date: 8/18/2009

"Neurosis is the inability to tolerate ambiguity(doubt)." - Sigmund Freud

"What progress we are making. In the Middle Ages they would have burned me. Now they are content with burning my books." - Sigmund Freud

"...for I have sworn upon the altar of god eternal hostility against every form of tyranny over the mind of man." –*Thomas Jefferson to Benjamin Rush, 23 Sept. 1800*

I swear infinite hostility against any form of tyranny over the minds of adults or children regardless of morals and norms of acceptability. Welcome to the machine.

Reasoning with rabidity requires imagination.

Rabidity: irrationally extreme in opinion or practice.

Things that have never been done, occasionally work.

Learning has to do with memorization; Understanding has to do with concentration.

Please be mindful this is a diary and it documents the mental progression I am in since the accident. I am still in mental progression as a result of the accident so nothing I suggest is set in stone. Skip around in the book because it is not in sequential order, it is in random access order. Left brain is sequential based, right brain is opposite or random access based. If I insult you and you still like me, it is because you choose to like me.

I once made a psychology chat room religious and made several religious chat rooms psychotic.

6/28/2009 5:16:10 PM- Perhaps money separates the enlightened from the unconscious perhaps. Perhaps one will kill anything for money once they believe they cannot live without money. Perhaps once one perceives money is required to live perhaps they often end up dying for it. Perhaps you can work yourself to fear or perhaps put fear to work for you. Perhaps it is better to fear life than death; it requires courage to fear neither. If you fear words, then perhaps I control you. If you fear death, then perhaps I own you. Conditioning away from fear has more to do with achieving mental clarity and less to do with running out into traffic, but it may accomplish the same thing, mentally. Perhaps stress is symptom of neurosis. Perhaps some speak lies for profit and some speak truth for prophet. Past is past is a nice way to say expect more punishment. I perceive everyone is wise, so clearly i am delusional and extremely biased.

A left brain dominate person is left brain dominate to an extreme. Unless a person has slight sense of time and slight sense of hunger and is nearly "void" of emotions they are left brain dominate to perhaps an extreme degree. Left brain has the following characteristics: verbal, logical, and analytical thinking. Left Brain is excellent at naming and categorizing things, symbolic abstraction, speech, reading, writing, arithmetic. The word sequential denotes sense of time. This is conditioning caused by the three R's. What that means is when a child is born the child has silenced sense of time or is extreme right brain dominate. This is because a child in the womb would harm the mother if it has a strong sense of time because a side effect of the 3 R's is pronounced emotions, such as depression, fear, paranoia etc. So a baby in the womb would harm the mother if it was left brain dominate. This is also why the Buddhists picked the Lama when he was 3, because at 3 he had not been exposed to the 3 R's.

The word contrary in the right brain characteristics denotes opposite. This denotes everything the left brain has, the right does not have. Left brain has strong sense of time, fear, strong desires and cravings, elementary logic, right brain is opposite. "complexity, ambiguity and paradox" What this means is , I had an "accident" and I am so far into the right brain, I cannot communicate properly with the ones conditioned into the left brain by the 3 R's. To clarify that, I had to nearly kill myself accidentally condition away my fear and "woke up". I am back to how I was mentally before the "3 R's" "conditioning". I conditioned away fear and in my case I conditioned away fear of death and all other fear evaporated and then right brain or subconscious "opened up".

What this opposite thing means is, I say things that makes you think I am on drugs, because in reality when a person does a drug, that "high" sensation is in fact them going back to right brain and they perceive they are high and feel euphoria, but they are not high, they simply are temporarily taken back to how they mentally were before the 3 R's "indoctrination." A person who gets "high" tends to talk a lot. One might suggest the fact I have written 6 "large" books in 6 months denotes I talk a lot. So I "woke up" as a result of "not trying to save myself(conditioned away from fear) and I found myself(right brain extreme or subconscious- the powerhouse of the two aspects)" I could easily suggest some comments from others to describe how I was in left brain in contrast to how I am now in extreme right brain. For example Moses suggested "Adversary", Jesus suggested "darkness", Mohammad suggested "infidel", and Buddha suggested "the sane".

1

Nietzsche said "A causal stroll through the lunatic asylum proves faith means little", or something along those lines. So in summation: Human beings were in a state of grace or Garden of Eden(right brained) mindfully and using the creative aspect of right brain, someone invented the 3 R's, and a side effect of scribe and math(demotic and Dena) conditions one to left brain. So man "ate of the tree of knowledge" the 3 R's, and fell from grace "right brain" and became the fallen angel. Left brain is very physical focused and the opposite is right brain which is very cerebral focused.6/28/2009 11:56:37 PM

Worry and stress are a symptom of the "three R's" conditioning and are simply unwanted side effects of said conditioning that can be negated by conditioning away from fear. I understand one thing for certain, uncertainty. I was deemed crazy by my peers before the accident and now I agree with them. I am the first to admit I am not and the last to understand I am.

6/30/2009 12:46:19 AM – There is perhaps an absolute time. This would be time not based on observations by a person or a tool, but an absolute time beyond the realms of observation and then there is time based on observation. So the contrast as far as me is, I used to be extreme left brain to the degree I was a nervous wreck and this means time was very powerful, and I had very little patience because time was so powerful in my mind or my mind registered time so greatly. This is typical perhaps in depressed people. They get impatient very easily because their sense of time is so strong. One thing would go bad for me and that was it, even a slight minor thing and I would panic and determine very irrational things.

I failed a class, no point in living. I lose my job, no point in living. One minor thing and I made very harsh decisions that had no logical reasoning to them. So then in real life if a man gets divorced and then kills himself or kills his wife and himself that is not a symptom that man is mentally insane, that is a symptom that man has very little patience, because of the strong sense of time that is a characteristic of left brain and encouraged by the "three R's", it is more complex than that but that's a good start.

Now my accident has happen and I am on the reverse hemisphere, to such a degree I cannot even feel stress. I find myself attempting to remember what satisfaction was like. For example, I should be satisfied I published a book. I have no concept of satisfaction or concept of accomplishment therefore I am not stressed about it. One can be stressed from accomplishment just as easily as one can be stressed from lack of accomplishment. Stress is a symptom of a strong sense of time. "I have a deadline to reach." That is an indication of stress. Stress is devastating to the body and attempting to reach these goals of accomplishment increases that stress. One who is left brain dominate cannot understand what being right brain dominate to an extreme is even like because it is completely opposite in every way. In the same regard I cannot remember what having fun is like. I can laugh from time to time but I cannot think of anything I want to do to have fun. One way to look at it is I am passive. This appears to a person with strong emotions or left brain dominate as a sad thing, but I am unable to be sad for more than a tiny amount of time. I cannot hold a grudge. I cannot remain mad for very long and I can't remain satisfied for very long. I am not talking a day I am talking seconds. So this time aspect in relation to be extreme right brain dominate means the toll of stress on the body itself is greatly reduced in contrast to ones with left brain dominate. Anything a person with the left brain dominate can think of that may cause them stress cannot cause me stress. That is a good and bad thing. There is this concept about right brain that suggests paradox. This paradox aspect and this lack of stress aspect can cause problems.

Here is a paradox. I write books and publish them for sale and the moment the copyright goes through I put them online for people to download for free. I sell my books to make money and then at the same time I give them away for free. Both statements are true but they are contradictions. If I give my books away for free I will not have money and I am okay with that. That is dangerous. I am not charitable, I simply am on the extreme right brain and it is full of complexity and paradox. Translated, that means I can be easily taken advantage of by a person who is left brain dominate because a person who is left brain dominate can use the elementary logic. For example: Make money at all costs. I cannot make such a solid judgment calls as that. I can only use a paradox. My logic is, make money if you can but also give the books away if you can. Somehow after this accident I decided I made some discovery and I wanted

3

to tell everyone in the world and somehow I decided I cannot do that unless I give the books away and also sell the books. Perhaps I did not make an important discovery, I only perceive I did. Another paradox is, I write in my books everyone should be right brain dominate and then I say one should not attempt to become right brain. Another paradox, I write people who are left brain dominate are not using the full spectrum of the mind and are not as complex in their thinking and then I say, I perceive everyone is perfect just the way they are when I look at them with the "feeling through vision" aspect that has happened as a result of the accident. These are simply contradictions and a person with left brain dominate assumes contradictions are a symptom of confusion. Contradictions can happen and a paradox can be acceptable in some situations. A person who says, " Killing people is always bad", is trapped too far in the left brain elementary logic aspect. I perceive all killing of people is bad but I also perceive we as a species may have to kill a lot of people because we are getting way to over populated. This may play out in wars or disease outbreaks, but we cannot simply keep increasing population forever, and at the same time keep trying to make everyone live as long as possible because it simply will collapse everything. Something has to give eventually. I perceive things are perhaps already starting to "give way". So the right brain in an extreme form is simply very open minded. One might suggest with extreme right brain nothing is off the table but also it makes one very cerebral and mentally focused and less physically or materialistically focused. That does not mean I make rash physical decisions, it means I consider every possibility very swiftly and keep pondering the opinions to an extreme and then I make a decision. Pondering options to an extreme does not take much time when one uses the powerhouse right brain or subconscious aspect. There are very few people in "nirvana" or right brain dominate who snap, meaning they do not get upset and go on a rampage of physical destruction of their self or others, which means nearly all rampages are carried out by ones with left brain dominate because they have a strong sense of time and thus have a greatly reduced "threshold" of tolerance. That is good and bad. A person who gets laid off work who is left brain dominate goes home, and does something physically rash and permanent, that is bad. The same person who catches an employee stealing from them and then takes action swiftly to stop it, that is perhaps good. So in contrast, a right brain dominate person would get laid off work and perhaps ponder the meaning of it and before they knew it they would make their self perceive it was proper or a "good thing" or "everything for a reason", so they perhaps would not go to that physically rash and permanent conclusion. Now, in the same respect if they caught and employee stealing from them, they also may not try to stop it, but forgive that person and perhaps keep forgiving them until it perhaps harmed them in a financial way. That perhaps is not good. Let's look at Socrates. His friend tried to convince him to break out of jail and escape his fate and Socrates suggested "where can I run?" so Socrates did not break out of jail when he could have, and thus he ended up being forced to drink the hemlock. That is perhaps bad. Jesus had the last supper and could have easily escaped instead of have that last supper, but instead he did not run. He faced the "hemlock". So both of these people were "taken" advantage of because they were first off treated unfairly because they were "on the right hand" side and that means they cannot react swiftly when making life or death decisions in some respects. A left brain dominate person would have run from that jail and run away before the last supper. That is reasonable. The truth is, this world is no longer all right brain dominate people so, the "lambs" get taken advantage of by the "lions" generally speaking. "The pen is mightier than the sword" is perhaps not an absolute. Jesus and Socrates were very clever with their words but in the end the "sword" took care of them both. So a more accurate description of that saying would be. Perhaps the pen is perhaps mightier than the sword, perhaps. This is all a symptom that being right brain dominate to an extreme has its flaws because it is dependent on the environment one is in. The same goes for left brain dominate people. In a scientific or research field, right brain dominate people do well and also, all great inventions are created by right brain dominate people. Edison, Tesla and Einstein and also many researchers and scientists in many fields are right brain dominate to a degree simply because the right brain has the tools, creativity and complex thoughts in relation to considering all options swiftly. I prefer to call the right aspect the machine. In right brain extreme the mind is just ticking away all the time pondering everything, pondering solutions to everything and it never slows down, and because the sense of time is so silent it does not get "tired". In fact that is why one in extreme right brain dominate is not prone to making money or material gain as much because the cerebral aspect has to "cancel" out all of the satisfaction and "fun" and pleasure "feelings" in order to power the "machine."

I tend to swing my opinions about this left and right brain benefits simply because I perceive I went too far to the right by accident. I did not intend for this accident to happen so I am an accident. I am simply way too far into the paradox, complexity, contradiction aspect and the left aspect is way too silent. So I am biased about this. Some may perceive what I write about is proper and accurate to a degree and they may determine they wish to accomplish this right brain dominate state of mind but I would never tell someone they should because I am, as Buddha suggested "if the string is too loose and it will not play If the string is to tight it will snap." I will use some hypothetical's to explain this. A person gets laid off and loses their job and goes home and kills their family and their self. This means they were too far into the left aspect and they snapped. Someone comes to my house and robs me of my money and I do not call the police because I determined they may need that money more than me. That means my string no longer plays. This means both people are to biased and they are not in harmony and getting proper notes out of the "string"(mind). This can be taken to deeper levels. A person owns apartment buildings and a tenant cannot pay rent because they lost their job and that landlord kicks them to the curb. That means the landlord is way too far to the left and their string snapped. This is because a material item is more important to that person, than a person. On the other hand what exactly is perfect harmony? There is perhaps no such thing as perfect harmony because it is relative to the observer. So that means everyone is simply in various states of mental disharmony. Buddha was very careful to explain why anyone can be a Buddha and they should not seek it by starving. This is because he accomplished it by starving and he went way to the right. His string was not playing because he went too far by accident. I honestly tried to suicide and I failed and now I am stuck in the extreme right. There is nothing in heaven or earth that is going to change that because it is a mentally permanent thing, I conditioned away my fear of death so all emotions were purged and I went extreme subconscious dominate or right brain dominate. So I have to be careful and make sure I do not give off the impression I am so special when I perceive I am more along the lines of cursed. I messed up and had a permanent accident. I cured myself of depression and that is because I lost my emotional capacity. I have shades of emotions at this stage since the accident of less than nine months ago but they are more like twitches, not long lasting things like ones on the left feel. I am not capable of love or hate or bitterness or sadness for anymore than a moment or two which denotes like a minute or two. So to me it is strange because I used to be very emotional. I had many highs and lows and now I have mostly "so-so" feelings. I swing back and forth at light speed, so in general I am what would be known mentally as "on the fence". I am not proud of it because I cannot be in a state of pride, and I cannot be in a state of shame, and I cannot be in a state of anguish or happiness for more than a moment. This is essentially what nothingness is. Nothingness is being many things, but being unable to be one emotion for more than a moment. This of course is the price one pays to achieve extreme concentration and complexity in their thinking. So this is a good example of "trade off's". One might suggest I do not get to eat the cake I just get to have the cake. This is along the lines of when Jesus was on the "mountain" looking over the earth and he was given a choice, you can have all the physical things and pleasure and fun and "feelings" or you can take the "machine road". One is not bad or good, whichever road they choose, it is simply a choice one has. This again is the trade off aspect. "As he increases I decrease". You simply lose a little and get a little which ironically is essentially what E=MC2 means. You're converting things from one state to another. You get strong sense of time and strong emotions with left brain or you lose strong sense of time and strong emotions and achieve right brain. So right brain has extreme concentration and complexity in thought processes and the opposite is left brain and it is not so good at concentration and complex thoughts. One may perceive that is saying left brain is bad but in reality there are situations in life it is best not to "over think" things and it is best not to "concentrate" too hard on things, of course "over think" and "too hard" are relative to the observer. This is why I am certain some of these teaching from "religious" people where not threats or "do or die" scare tactics, they were simply attempting to explain a very complex situation the best they could based on the "vocabulary" of the time. Simply put, there is no reason to get upset with others no matter which road they choose, because both roads have advantages and disadvantages. The complexity in that is in general people who are "educated" into the three R's are not given a choice they are "forced". Granted some "religious" people would have a lot of trouble perhaps in dealing with that concept but that is because they are perhaps under the influence of left brain and left brain is all about fear, meaning that is a side effect of the left brain 3 R's, strong long lasting emotions. Right brain has short lived emotions and left brain is capable of holding a grudge for a lifetime. So this again is the opposite aspects. One hemisphere has a characteristic and the other hemisphere has a totally opposite characteristic or "anti characteristic".

This is the aspect that screws everything up, "right brain thinking is difficult to put into words because of its complexity". I am a firm believer in that suggestion. Perhaps an easy way to determine what extreme right brain is like is, to think about how you are as left brain dominate and consider the complete opposite. Left brain may be very sentimental about things and prone to avoid change and difficulties, and right brain is the opposite. Right brain is all about loss of attachments but again that is complex to explain. I think in infinity so I have to be mindful about what goals I set for myself. One might suggest I would have infinite wives so I must be mindful to avoid that goal of having a wife. Jung was well known for being married and also having a few mistresses and was open about it. This of course has much more to do with the fact he saw everything as perfect.

One with left brain has the ability to find a woman attractive and fall in love or become a "lush" for her. The opposite right brain aspect means one is able to become a "lush" and fall in love with every girl they meet, not most girls, but every girl, because of this "feeling through vision" aspect. One does not "judge a book by the cover" but by the "contents" or "feeling"

6

from vision. This of course is what heightened awareness is all about. So left brain males find some women attractive and some ugly and right brain males in "nirvana" or extreme right brain, find everything about every single female attractive. One can possibly imagine that would be a problem and I assure you it is, to a degree. This is complex again. I cannot stay in a state of "lust" so to speak for more than a moment. This has a lot to do with the memory. One might suggest I can ponder my way out just as fast as I ponder my way in. So there are some misunderstandings about women in some of these "protective of women" religions. It is perhaps hard for me to even comment on this topic but one might suggest when a guy perceives every women they see if perfect, one may get protective of their wife and cover her up so these ones in "nirvana/ right brain extreme" won't fall in love with them. I perceive males in general, because of nature, are attracted to women in general, and then when one goes to right brain extreme, there is heightened awareness, and this natural attraction in general is multiplied by a huge factor. This of course is what alcohol tends to do to a male, and I speak strictly about males because perhaps it is more complex for a female in "nirvana".6/30/2009 2:27:30 AM

3:21:21 PM – If you expect to fail you will seldom be disappointed by failure. Failing at failure is rare but winning at failure is common. The depressed and suicidal are in a state of humility and meekness, everyone else is in various stages of arrogance. Saying 'Thank You" sometimes makes "them" go away. Patience is a concept few can afford consistently. No one is in trouble but all are looking for it. A physical ship sinks in cerebral waters.

7/1/2009 6:06:25 AM – What this "empty feeling" is in ones with left brain dominate is a symptom that person is aware there is something "wrong". They are aware they are not using 100% of their mental ability. This is caused by the "three R's". The three R's make them left brain dominate so they are sitting on this huge powerhouse and they are only getting about 10% of the power from it and so they feel this "empty feeling" and they desire to fill it, but they tend to fill it with physical things and they never can because it is not an aspect that can be filled, it is an aspect that must be opened up. Once one goes to right brain dominate to an extreme that "empty feeling" is gone. One might suggest that person is "whole" again. My eyes should be illegal. Relativity suggests I am relatively screwed. I have many swords to fall back on if the ones in front get dull. The sea is lonely but the depths hold many treasures.

Everything that you know, what remains the glow, everything worn away.
http://www.youtube.com/watch?v=soGiveUulT4

7/2/2009 1:48:36 PM - Emotional attachments require courage to achieve and strength to break. Loving the world to death is effortless, allowing the world to be, takes patience. Distance is relative to the desire to bridge that distance. Longing to be with something you desire is in direct relation to how long you perceive you have been separated from it. The blood seldom dries from a deep wound. A lone wolf's lover is the shadows. The more I want you the less I want me. I am enlightened but a little heavy on the end and a little light on the light. The definitions of words are far less dangerous than believing the definitions. In the beginning there were no labels or contrasts. Some illusions are convincing and some illusions are just illusions. I will tell you whatever you want to hear but that does not mean I will believe what I tell you. I am much more so now than i was so.

7/2/2009 11:54:55 PM – Doc Holiday found out he had TB. He realized he was dead. He realized he had a death sentence. Doc could have went into his room and lay down and died but instead he said one thing to himself. "I am dead so I am going to do what I want to do." Many people get deadly diseases and in the last few days of their life they make peace with the maker and they spend those few days dealing with all the things they did not do but wished they would have done. They spend their last few days in anguish because they realize they wasted their whole life pandering to rules and regulations and conformity and they never got around to living. They essentially spent their whole life serving other people and at the same time denied their own purpose. Doc Holiday faced his eventual death mindfully and had none of that foolishness. He had gun fights and he cheated, he never lost but he never played fair either. Morals and rules and laws are for people who still are clinging to life and thus they end up never doing what they will wish they had done. They will be like Mother Theresa. They will run around their whole life serving some sort of agenda that is not their agenda and then when they are near death they will write a letter to their "spiritual;" leader and say, "I wasted my whole life serving rules and regulations and I totally denied my own purpose." I never did very well in the world of rules and regulations, they kept saying I was a loser because I couldn't pass their tests. So it is just as well. I could very well be in the ground right now and they would say "He was a troubled person and we kept telling him he was." Ironically that is not the case. I am like Doc Holiday. I got the big fear out of the way and Iam sitting on my death bed and I thinking "What did I want to do with life now I have three days left to live." I can do anything I want because I only have three days left. I do not care about rules, morals, regulations , responsibility , class , justice, righteousness. I care nothing about any of those things. I only have three days left. I am not concerned about teaching anyone anything. They will wake up eventually without my help. They will wake up whether it is in the split second before they smash into a tree or the split second before they put a bullet through their skull, so I have three days left and I will serve myself because I understand I am unable to serve the "sane" in this world. The "sane" tend to assume I am stupid so I do not pander to that sort of "darkness".12:10:33 AM

7/3/2009 12:24:54 AM – I fiddle on the roof and watch the mice scurry. I have a speech impediment called clarity. I can't seem to get my blood off my hands no matter how fast I write. Anger is a symptom of correct understanding; intolerance is the absence of understanding. 3:56:55 AM

11:26:57 AM - I have decided. Welcome to the machine. Anger cannot function in the absence of control. Envy is a prerequisite of control; jealously is a prerequisite of controlling love. Foolish anger is a symptom of ignorance, being an angry fool requires concentration. Lost love leads to envious rage; Understanding one cannot control leads to fleeting elegance. Loss of control is a symptom of anticipated expectations of predictability. A sunken ship is a treasure to the depths as the woman who christened it longs for its return. Finding love is far easier than understanding love can never be satisfied. A man can spend a thousand years to find a woman he can never have.

"My hands are red, my past lives, my mouth looks black with sticky knives I might want you let me look in your eyes. Hide your soul it's very deep, I don't think I can take that leap. I never look back from where i came from, I didn't look back, I saw the angels there. Everything you try to keep, every night you try to sleep." http://www.youtube.com/watch?v=soGiveUulT4

A storm on the sea may sink a ship and a storm in the mind may build an unsinkable ship. Patience is relative to which clock the mind is running on. Patience is power but is relative to the minds sense of time, so absolute patience is not possible. Satisfaction is relative to ones perception of dissatisfaction and no two people's perceptions are identical. A poisonous snake perceives it is compassionate by not allowing its prey to suffer when it injects more venom than required. Patience is not a virtue it is a craving to avoid the appearance of impatience. Patience or impatience in infinity is relative to the patient. Whatever you do is normal relative to you or you would not do it. Contact denotes someone suggested what is proper and your whole existence is based on that suggestion. Contact denotes someone suggested what is proper and your whole existence may evolve around that suggestion. You are only as wicked as others suggest you are, for doing deeds they suggest are wicked. If I please you, you may like me against your will. If I insult you and you still like me, it is because you choose to like me. A word cannot trump a desire; a desire can encourage a deed; a deed can inspire words. A woman can sink a ship much faster than a man can bail. Not speaking your mind is a symptom you desire acceptance. I may not agree with what you say, but I am not embarrassed by watching you embarrass yourself. All are lost, but very few understand they are, and even fewer are happy about it. A sinking ship can always test the depths. A woman can cure a man of sanity much quicker than I. A submissive woman controls a man easily.

There are many people in this world right now who could not pass the English and Math tests that education insists upon simply because they were more right brain inclined, not because they are stupid. So the whole education system is biased and racist against human beings who are right brain inclined and ironically everyone is born extreme right brain dominate. A child has imaginary friends and says things wise beyond their years. That's why one seldom remember their early years simply because in right brain extreme short term memory is altered and long term memory is increased. I understand the three R's left brain "conditioning" made my emotions so strong it nearly cost me my life. I understand that so I do not have to prove that. Society neglected to tell me unless I conditioned away from fear after the education I would end up trapped in 10% cerebral power and 90% nervous wreck.

The idea to raise an army is more powerful than the ideals of an army. An idea can be silenced for a moment but it will adapt and become stronger. They cannot defeat you with swords if you first defeat them with words. I prefer to wreck my ship on the rocks of the harpy than drown out at sea wishing I had. I would rather die on the altar of dreams then live in a cage of safety. You cannot reason with me because I cannot reason with you. Being unable to achieve stress is quite stressful. I am not a good mentor but I am quite a foolish one. When i start spitting blood into my books I kill a few monsters in the video game to calm me down. I cannot save anyone but I can point out the spots where their snorkel will be ineffective. A law cannot change how you think and seldom changes how you act.

"A woman knows the face of the man she loves as a sailor knows the open sea."

-Honore de Balzac. – I quote other people at times also.

Achievement has to do with failing often enough to understand the correct path. I understand my fingers are far more enlightened than I will ever be. The water is harmless once you understand you cannot breathe in it. If I tell the truth it will harm you; tell a lie it will harm me; say nothing it will harm us both. A lie is relative to ones inability to understand the truth. The waves of a stormy sea have far more mercy on a man than the beauty of a woman that man can never have. You can make any result look like a win it simply requires gullibility, denial or extreme open-mindedness. I think I have been talking to web cam girls who want to sell me porn for most of the week. My only friend on twitter is a guy who chases rattlesnakes for fun and I am serious. If I remember the most important thing to remember i will tell you, if i remember. Since you answered my call for help I now assume you must need help. The difference between a lemur monkey and a human is negotiable. If you keep allowing me to write I will keep allowing you to read. Anyone can arrange words but a poet can rearrange them. My only friend on twitter sleeps with rattlesnakes. I am not insane I simply trust everyone.

These two songs are pre-suicide era.

"Sometimes i feel like an echo. Sometimes I feel like I'm tripping on you. Sometimes i feel the night is over. The night has just begun." – Fresh and Clean. I quote myself because no one else will.

http://www.youtube.com/watch?v=k-BnUN0-ZR0

"This is where I get off. I was born in the winter time. This is where I get lost. I was born in the waste of time. Don't be afraid. It only hurts when you think about it."

http://www.youtube.com/watch?v=7lck40czMaY

I made a psychology chat room religious once. I also made several religious chat rooms psychotic. If you need my help, I need yours. My best friends on twitter are a guy who sleeps with rattle snakes, a robot that loves pasta, and a monk that loves money. I am pleased with your humor but I am too blind to see it. The hardest part of letting go is understanding you can't hold on. Climbing the mountain of love requires strength to understand when it's best to climb down. Being alone; Being loved; the suffering is often the same.

7/4/2009 12:45:17 PM – An intelligent deed is often dangerous. Luxury is the acceptance of certainty; Wisdom is the acceptance of doubt. Peers who look at your life 100 years after you are gone will determine your fruits without you asking. Being responsible is often being unreasonable. Some horses cannot be broken so they must be set free. The lemur monkey discovery put a damper on my god complex. A comment about Washington:"Although he did not explicitly seek the office of commander and even claimed that he was not equal to it, there was no serious competition." I do not seek command and I am not worthy of command but there will not be any serious competition.

A teacher must understand the lesson plan so it does not pervert them. Common sense does not run in herds. I will trade my life for a proper deed no one will recognize. Every genius doubts he is, undoubtedly. Every proper teacher understands she isn't. A proper teacher is a dedicated student. Cutting down the fear in your eye often assists others in cutting down the fear in their eye. Madness is the cornerstone of all great ideas. One that perceives their self as nothing perceives all others as something. It is easier to assist others than it is to understand one is only able to assist their self. I submit you are wiser than I will ever be, I no longer sea. Genius is in direct relation to one's ability to be unreasonable. Being unreasonable at the perfect time requires intelligence. I will die a thousand deaths to experience the gnashing of teeth caused by a proper understanding. Great depths require excellent vision. I talk about myself because I understand the alternative. Understandings that do no trouble the spirit are called ignorance. Understandings that do not cause concern are called misunderstandings. When I leave, I take everything with me. A mind is useful when it is well used; useless when it is used less; fear in the mind decides which path the mind is on. Physical war is a nasty affair, mental war is a love affair. All paths lead to the same sink hole. Seldom does one wake up to early. Few know but multitudes misunderstand. In general humans frighten easily but often return in greater numbers. A poor fiddler can play as loud as a good fiddler and breaks far more strings. Forgiveness has more to do with forgetting than mercy. A lone wolf loves that he is not under the influence of those who love with strings attached. I do not want to know what they expect me to do just so they love me.

I will clarify this word Holy because it is clearly misunderstood. This one is going to go deep so dawn your snorkel. I am mindful not to insult some of these "preachers" of the Holy books simply because they have no clue what they are talking about. They know not what do or what they say.

Eph 5:18 "And be not drunk with wine(temporary right brain state of mind with drugs), wherein is excess(to much drugs to achieve right brain "high" may kill you); but be filled with the Spirit(permanent right brain state of mind through fear conditioning);"

The comment "wherein excess" denotes doing drugs "wine, pot, cocaine". They will certainly help one reduce the emotions and that "opens up" the right aspect of the mind, as in "spiritual awakening", but it is only a temporary fix. Other words, you will drink yourself to death attempting to keep this "right brain state of mind" open.

Act 2:15 "For these are not drunken(on drugs, crazy), as ye(left brainers) suppose, seeing it is but the third hour of the day."

In summation, "Holy" is in relation to "On the contrary, the right brain seems to flourish dealing with complexity, ambiguity and paradox." One in extreme right brain appears "drunk", on drugs, crazy, insane but only relative to ones in left brain dominate. Holy as in "holes in the head" or "crazy". They are not crazy or "holy" relative to others in the right brain but only relative to ones in the "left brain".

Moses appeared "drunk" to most of the people he was around. Jesus appeared drunk relative to most of the people he was around but not the disciples because they became right brain dominate and they appeared "drunk" or "holy" to ones they spoke to "the left brainers" so the left brainers killed them all because the left brainers are unable to tolerate ambiguity in general because they are very physically focused and also are perhaps not as "complex" cerebrally as the right brainers. So these "wise" beings were slaughtered because they appeared like they had "holes in their head" as in "holy" as in "drunk" relative to the left brainers they were speaking to. Then Mohammed came along and after his "mediation in a cave and finding God "right brain" he understood what the "left" did to the ones before him "Moses and Jesus" and he experimented with the cutting off their heads strategy, and that is very logical and he was very wise to experiment with that strategy because he understood he did not stand any better chances than the disciples and Jesus and Moses against the "darkness" the "left".

The Demotic conditioning aspect made the whole world "drowned" into the left. There was a great flood one might suggest because of the "scribe aspect". When one is outnumbered by such great odds and they look at their friends "Moses and Jesus" and see what happened to them, one tends to experiment with new strategies. Mohammed was wise because he did what humans do best, he adapted his strategy based on the situation he was facing. He looked at all the facts and determined "cutting heads off might work." I understand that is proper and a proper logical conclusion considering he did not have the luxury of freedom of speech and perhaps 1500 years ago was a bit different than it is now in relation to what one could get away with saying, to the "left", in a public forum. I find no fault with his determinations so you should not either. People do the best they can based on the situation they are facing. One might suggest you would be wise to never insult these beings in my presence if you know what's good for you. Avoid assuming I have such aspects as tolerance and mercy. In case you are wondering the simple fact that Mohammed agreed with Moses and with Jesus proves Moses and Jesus existed because Mohammed could detect the genuine article by its fruits. This has much more to do with the "heightened awareness" the "right brain" provides in relation to its ability to detect patterns and ability to detect and understand complexity. So, we know for a fact Mohammed existed and he "vouched" that Jesus and Moses were genuine and that is proof beyond all understanding they were in fact real people. If you do not grasp that you should perhaps consider achieving brain function, and then perhaps try to grasp that again. Now, before I start spitting blood into my book I will attempt to discuss something of importance.

These are some "Sacred Sayings" of Buddha.

"Anger will never disappear so long as there are thoughts of resentment in the mind. Anger will disappear just as soon as thoughts of resentment are forgotten."

The clarification that needs to be made here is, one under the influence of the "left" has quite a good short term memory and not a great long term memory and also magnified emotional capacity. This means it is very easy for them to hold a grudge or a vendetta. The comment "as there are thoughts of resentment in the mind." suggests as long as one is "left brained" they will be susceptible to the "resentment" aspects of emotions as a result of the ability to hold a grudge because of the side effect "emotions" caused by the three R's conditioning. The comment "Anger will disappear" denotes once one conditions properly away from fear and starts saying "perhaps" often the anger will at first increase because is starting to let it go, but eventually it will be greatly silenced when the "right brain" is achieved and then one will simply "forget" about an trespasses against them or they will ponder them away. One might suggest they will not go to work and mow everyone down because they were insulted because the emotions will be very silenced and essentially one will simply not give a flying "stuff" about insults, they will be in a machine state.

Another comment by Buddha:

"To be idle is a short road to death and to be diligent is a way of life; foolish people are idle, wise people are diligent."

"Foolish" in this comment denotes "left brainers" and it is not a judgment, it is a fact, but deeper still, it is not their fault because they were conditioned by the "scribe and math" aspects as a child, so it is just so. "Wise" denotes ones on the right and that is not a judgment that is a fact because the right brain is "complex". So the ones on the left tend to not "produce" as much or appear 'slothful" simply because they have much less "brain function" they tend to go through their whole life and essentially accomplish very little relative to nothing because "diligent" denotes "the machine" or right brain extreme constant thinking or pondering. This of course is not a permanent situation, being left brained, because if one determines it is proper, they can condition into "right aspect" or negate the "left aspect". The comments about "life and death" is essentially what Jesus suggested the "darkness and the life", Moses comments about the adversary, Mohammed commented about "infidels". Jung comment about the "unconscious and the conscious". This of course is in relation to the "left aspect" is the retarded brother of the "right aspect", essentially in contrast.

Another comment By Buddha:.

"A disturbed mind is forever active, jumping hither and thither, and hard to control; but a tranquil mind is peaceful; therefore, it is wise to keep the mind under control."

"A disturbed mind" is quite accurate. Early after the accident I recall my mind was doing many calculations or sorting or processing to such a degree I could hardly function in any fashion, mentally. I wondered if I would ever be able to write music or write and I essentially panicked and sought out medical advice from a neurologist. Now I am much more use to it but the "disturbed mind" comment would be perhaps better clarified as "the battle within" the mind, which denotes the right aspect is always "pondering" or thinking or processing. It is simply a powerhouse beyond description or unnamable. This comment by Buddha is very complex. A left brain person is consumed mentally with fear and emotions and these anomalies "block" the heightened awareness or right brain and this makes life in general much harder and so they suffer. One in extreme right brain essentially lose the emotions and fear and thus have great cerebral power and so they may suffer but bit mentally because they cannot maintain a mental state of sadness.

16

"I would rather die than do something which I know to be a sin, or to be against God's(right brain dominate) will."

Joan of Arc

This is perhaps out of context. I am not intelligent enough to discuss supernatural aspects. I understand this "I would rather die" denotes Joan did not fear death. First it is perhaps important to understand why. "Several local raids occurred during her childhood and on one occasion her village was burned."

Wikipedia.Com

This is perhaps why she did not fear death and also I did not read anything about her education. She grew up on an "isolated" farm and she took command at 16 and was put on trial at 19, so perhaps she was not conditioned by the "scribe and math" aspects to an extreme which is a certain way to remain as a child or in the "right" in relation to "suffer the children". So perhaps she just did not get "educated" and so she was naturally "wise". So this comment she made is essentially the mind set of one in extreme right brain. I would rather die than not write my infinite books. I do not care about elementary logical conclusions, I "woke up" and I am going to write infinite books or I am going to die trying, but there is no other option on my table. I am uncertain why I decided to write infinite books but I perceive I discovered a great truth relative to my perception and I decided to write about it, and my own life is not relevant in contrast to that, although Buddha suggested "Health is important."

"One life is all we have and we live it as we believe in living it. But to sacrifice what you are and to live without belief, that is a fate more terrible than dying."

Joan of Arc

Joan was quite the revolutionary which is a trait of the free "right brain "aspect. "we live it as we believe in living it" is essentially saying "we have the right to life liberty and the pursuit of happiness" according to what we each perceive is happiness. That is perhaps a radical concept to the isolated fear based "left brain" aspect of the mind." to sacrifice what you are and to live without belief, that is a fate more terrible than dying" this is strictly a right brain freedom comment. In general ones on the "left" are conditioned out of the complex right aspect of the mind as a child so they forgot how complex the mind can be, but once the right is opened back up, one is perhaps willing to die than to go back to the left. The right is a very powerful aspect and it is like a drug a person would rather die for than give up but that is proper because it is not a drug it is a natural compliment to human beings. So essentially Joan was certainly "holy" and she was burned at the stake by the "darkness" left brainers because she appeared "drunk" because of her "complexity and ambiguity". Freud suggested. "Neurosis is the inability to tolerate ambiguity". I will clarify that, Left brainers tend to slaughter or make outcasts of right brainers because left brainers have such slight brain function compared to the complexity of right brainers they usually end up finding a way to kill them based on "ambiguity". That perhaps leads to a great pondering. Perhaps this left brain scribe conditioning is pushed onto people to keep them "stupid" and easily "manageable", and if so who is making sure it is done? Perhaps it is a supernatural aspect or perhaps it is simply a misunderstanding by man.

In Florida we have mole crickets and they have arms or claws that cover up their eyes so they tend to not be able to see very far. They simply burrow into the ground and they cannot see where they are going because they are essentially blind beyond one step in front of their nose. Their ability to see more than one move ahead is rather limited.

"You say that you are my judge; I do not know if you are; but take good heed not to judge me ill, because you would put yourself in great peril."
Joan Of Arc

Demotic script (planned language)and dena (arithmatics)
"If you reflect back upon our own educational training, we have been traditionally taught to master the 3 R's: reading, writing and arithmetic -- the domain and strength of the left brain."

Once upon a time mankind was very right brain orientated. One day man invented scribe and mathematics using right brain creativity. A side effect of these inventions was that man unintentialy became left brain dominate and thus his emotions and physical aspects were heightened and his right brain cerebral aspects and heightened awareness were silenced. The only remedy to counter act this perhaps unwanted side effect of scribe and math is to attempt to condition one's self away from fear and use the word "perhaps" often, if one determines that they want to be an "Einstein" and determine it is a proper path they wish to peruse.

"Neurosis is the way of avoiding non-being by avoiding being."
Paul Tillich
To clarify , Left brain conditioning by scribe is a way of avoiding right brain (nothingness) by avoiding being(in the now or in the moment or right brain slight sense of time). 12:31:19 AM

7/5/2009 12:45:54 AM – Apparently Heimdall has decided it's best not to rest.

"Sin, guilt, neurosis; they are one and the same, the fruit of the tree of knowledge."
Henry Miller

All of these are traits of shame, embarrassment, guilt, hate, strong cravings and desires and addictions, stress usually kill people in one way or another because these emotions are a byproduct of this "we have been traditionally taught to master the 3 R's: reading, writing and arithmetic -- the domain and strength of the left brain.", which is what "knowledge" means in that above quite. The simple fact people continue to plug this left brain conditioning on children means perhaps some person is aware of this consequence and some person or group or entity is encouraging this left brain conditioning. One might suggest it is far too obvious someone is looking for a battle to end all battles and I eat for no reason. Let's start with addiction caused by the "three R's". Addiction is simply a person who is using drugs to simulate extreme right brain mindset. The drugs are not getting them high, they are bringing them back to how they were when they were children before the "three R's" conditioned them out of right brain into left brain. I do not know that, I understand that.

Mydeathspace.com

D. C. (23) passed away from an alleged heroin overdose

A, C. (22) allegedly committed suicide by overdosing on painkillers and sleeping pills

T. Z. (21) passed away from an alleged drug overdose

R. T. (19) died from alcohol-related causes after he overcame heroin addiction

K. E. (19) allegedly committed suicide by gunshot to the head

This is what happens when people are "educated" and the emotions are so strong they only want to use drugs to make the strong emotions go away, so they can "relax" and make the "shame, guilt, anger" subside.

K. O. (14) took her own life by an unknown method

K. A. (14) allegedly took her own life for unknown reasons

This is what happens to young kids when the "knowledge " conditioning is to powerful and they are very far into the right aspect and then get conditioned very swiftly to the left aspect and they cannot handle all the powerful emotions. The emotions like shyness, guilt, embarrassment are simply to strong so they end up making very harsh decisions to escape the conditioning. One might suggest I find it very funny you perceive you are not going back to the void.

Gen 1:2 "And the earth was without form, and void;"

You are simply mentally abusing children and so you are going back to the void, and there will not be a vote, and there will not be a choice, it is just so. One might suggest my fingers are saying that, and they became rather wise as of late. Never ever assume I am religious. One might suggest I am strictly vengeance based. I will go back to my video game now because I do not perceive the dead can hear, see, or understand my words.- 1:11:17 AM

12:26:30 PM - You can't sin against what you are. Courage to live has everything to do with acceptance of death. Thoughts and thinking is the worst invention ever created. I will pay a penny for your thoughts and infinite gold if you will stop having them.

"A casual stroll through the lunatic asylum shows that faith does not prove anything. "
Friedrich Nietzsche

The humor in this comment is very thick. "Faith does not prove anything" this denotes whatever you perceive or think does not mean it is fact. That is in direct relation to everything being relative to the observer. One might suggest they have faith one needs food to stay alive but then one has to determine what life is and what is death. Life and death are relative to the observer so they are simply not facts or provable. One first must prove there is no after life in order to prove this is life, without doing that there is no contrast. Your faith on the merits of afterlife proves absolutely nothing, means nothing, and counts for nothing. Relative to me this world is a "lunatic asylum", is absolute fact, relative to absolute facts that means nothing. $E=Mc2$ denotes 0=0 which means nothing is happening at all, illusions are simply going from one state to another into infinity. If you have emotions reality will scare you, if you have no emotions reality simply makes you laugh.

"Neurosis is always a substitute for legitimate suffering."
Carl Jung

Suffering is for the wise fools and comfort is for the fools. What you will do to others to keep the materialistic comforts is the only pondering to consider about wealth. Being satisfied by materialistic comfort is like drinking from an empty glass. Material Purpose is the craving of a mind with no purpose. Act natural so you don't taint the experiment.

I have to write some things because I am getting back logged. The story of the Prodigal son is simply showing how at times one may be perceived to be "following the rules" or expectations and appear on the "right track" and at times one may be perceived to be "bucking the rules" and headed down a "dark path", but in reality one is never intelligent enough to grasp how things may turn out. This is perhaps more along the lines of why everyone should be free to peruse their own path, their own way relative to pursuit of happiness. Here is an example, a guy becomes very depressed because he could not fit into the "norms" of society and so he isolated himself from society and attempted to kill himself for many years and finally something happened and he understood everything and wrote many books and explained these things he perceived he understood. Simply put, there is no human being in all eternity that could have predicted that outcome, and there never will be. One might suggest some are late bloomers in relation to they look like they are headed down a dark path and sometimes it does end up "bad" but sometimes it ends up at a very deep watering hole that is warm and comfortable. No one knows how it will turn out and it's best to allow people to see what kind of trouble they get into because sometimes trouble ends up being a blessing in disguise. No one can win but some have quite memorable losses. I will explain further this prodigal son story. One son went to school and got the scribe conditioning and appeared right on track and the other son quit school and avoided the scribe conditioning because he was right brain aware and did not want to be conditioned and in turn he ended up the "right"eous one or the wise one when all was said in done, so the father threw a big feast because the father assumed the one who stayed in the scribe conditioning was the wise one, but he was pleased to have misunderstood. The father gave the "lost" son what was due him which is respect to make his own decisions this is in relation to a parent not trying to force kids to their will. Letting a child make up their own mind and having the patience and maturity to understand maybe it's not best to force kids to be brainwashed against their natural right brain inclination just because that parents assumes it is best. Perhaps a parent in extreme left brain neurosis would be unable to live with that reality.

Suffering often assists one in understanding why they are suffering.

I cannot charge for my words because they are not my words. It is important that one's give away my words so that I might be able to live with myself for putting a price on the words to begin with. I am nothing because I put a price on the words, and thus I have totally failed. I have blown it because I put a price on the words. So you have to give them away so perhaps one day I might be able to live with myself for making such an unforgivable mistake.

Someone apparently assumed they understand something. One might suggest Heimdall is pleased when I detect someone has determined they understand something. I will be certain to list their web site in my book so the entire universe will be able to see their understanding are nothing but judgments from darkness, blindness, elementary logic and thus foolishness.

1:22:46 AM – I am apparently weird tonight so I will cover this aspect.

"Gen 3:1 Now the serpent(script and math) was more subtle (appeared like a great idea) than any beast of the field which the LORD God had made. And he said unto the woman, Yea, hath God said, Ye shall not eat of every tree of the garden? "

Gen 3:2 "And the woman said unto the serpent, We may eat of the fruit of the trees of the garden: "
Gen 3:3 But of the fruit of the tree which is in the midst of the garden, God hath said, Ye shall not eat of it, neither shall ye touch it, lest ye die(become left brain dominate as a side effect and silence(Crescent moon where only a sliver of the right aspect is seen(light) and the rest is darkness(left brain)) .
Gen 3:4 And the serpent said unto the woman, Ye shall not surely die(physically die):
Gen 3:5 For God doth know that in the day ye eat thereof, then your eyes shall be opened(become self conscious, shy, embarrassed, physical focused), and ye shall be as gods(gods of physical aspirations as opposed to cerebral aspirations as they were), knowing good and evil(good and evil is contrast which is LABEL(left brain excels in naming and categorizing things) and labels are relative to the observer, contrary to seeing(perceiving) everything as a whole or as one thing which is right brained).

Gen 3:6 And when the woman saw that the tree was good(looked like a good idea this scribe and math) for food(knowledge food), and that it was pleasant to the eyes(scribe is pretty as in hieroglyphics), and a tree to be desired to make one wise(wise as in education or understanding), she took of the fruit thereof, and did eat, and gave also unto her husband with her; and he did eat.
Gen 3:7 And the eyes of them both were opened(Became left brained), and they knew that they were naked(pronounced or strong emotions such as shame, shyness, embarrassment which are side effects of left brain as a result of the scribe and math conditioning); and they sewed fig leaves together, and made themselves aprons(they started judge a book by the cover instead of by the contents, they became self conscious and physical based.)

The comment in this text about women is in reality an inside joke. It was not women who invented scribe and math it was men, but if Moses said the men ate the apple "they" would "hang him high", so he said the women screwed up and ate the apple because he knew the women would not butcher him.

This is all the proof you will ever need.

"The Mesopotamian scribe, or dubsar, received his or her early education in the "tablet house," or é-dubba. As in Egypt, he was generally male and belonged socially to an elite class."

Wikipedia.com topic: scribe

This was apparently the first written language:
Archaic Sumerian - 3100 ¬ 2600 BCE
Classical Sumerian - 2600 ¬ 2300 BCE
Neo-Sumerian - 2300 ¬ 2000 BCE
Post-Sumerian - 2000 ¬ 100 BCE

So Archaic Sumerian was 3100 years before Christian era. So that was about 5000 years ago. So this means the script conditioning was happening for about 2500 years before Moses and Buddha came. So this is why the story of Noah suggests the world "drowned". The scribe aspect looked like a good idea, looked like light, look like a tasty apple in relation to " And when the woman saw that the tree was good(looked like a good idea this scribe and math) for food(knowledge food), and that it was pleasant to the eyes(scribe is pretty as in hieroglyphics), and a tree to be desired to make one wise(wise as in education or understanding), she took of the fruit thereof, and did eat, and gave also unto her husband with her; and he did eat."

So we all got very "wise" and as a side effect we have very pronounced emotions, very pronounced sense of time, very pronounced attachments to physical things, very pronounced sense of hunger, fatigue and in general we achieved the "wisdom" of a brain dead mole cricket (silenced cerebral awareness), and the only "anti-venom" to this is to say "perhaps" a lot and condition one's self away from side effects called "emotions" namely fear. Simply put, keep the language and math, but be aware you have to do some things in order to counter act the unwanted side effects so you keep the heightened awareness aspect of the right brain dominate so you can make Einstein look unwise or to make sure the right brain is not veiled like a crescent moon, if you determine that is wise and that is what you want to do, and if you do not want to do that, you are not evil or bad, it simply is a personal choice, so no pressure. Now I will discuss something of importance.- 2:00:40 AM

5:57:43 AM – I submit there are times late at night I crave to delete everything I have written and burn all of my books and my only chance to avoid doing this is to keep writing because I understand these moments of extreme doubt (ambiguity)are perhaps to see if I will listen to my intuition or my emotions.5:59:40 AM

9:10:31 AM - When the ship is sinking the competition revolves around who goes under with the greatest difficulty. If I cared about my writing I wouldn't bother to publish at all. Women give men something to shoot for; Men give the women something to be grateful about. Men have all the graces women decided they didn't want. The majority of women I have known have shown me a great deal of "left" tolerance. Although shocking, some women

22

have done just fine without me. A woman's tolerance of a man is relative to her sense of humor. Failure is often a winning strategy. Failing sometimes, leads to dedication, failing often, leads to mastery. My only flaw is my inability to count them all. It's better to be perfectly flawed than have spotty perfection.

4:34:21 PM - Uncertainty troubles the fearful and delights the climbers. A good man would rather face death than cheat it; swim to a bottomless ocean just to avoid the shallows. Mental attachments and fear may hinder one's ability to consider all possibilities. I write about what I perceive is proper in order to understand it was not. Hatred, friendship, anger, fear and pity are the cornerstones of most misguided determinations. Liberty is quite lonely as slavery is often luxurious. One who sees things properly often has rage afterwards. Life is long stretches of wickedness dotted with moments of bad judgment. Harmony is relative to the imbalance of the observer who seeks it. It is harder for one to become angry with their own deeds than to be pleased with others deeds. In my darkest moments I often ponder fates sense of humor. Misunderstandings are far easier to clarify than stupidity. Money cannot assist one with mental struggle but it often assists one in avoiding it. A big fish often overlooks its wake. People tend to be angry at the world because they perceive they are not a part of it.

7/7/2009 1:15:03 AM – I am mindful this heightened sense of awareness or extreme right brain dominate aspect is perhaps unwanted. I am mindful human beings invented scribe and thus achieved silenced sense of awareness as an indirect result for a reason, perhaps a reason unknown to anyone. One see's what they want to see. Apparently because of this accident when I see the face of any woman I feel this sensation from the eyes even in pictures and old movies and it is a more powerful sensation than any physical sensation. I am unable to describe it beyond perfection ,love, lust, joy, delight. That is not anyone's fault but my own fault. Somehow I accidentally conditioned my mind so that my sight is "too powerful". I detect things even through pictures that I am unable to explain. Feeling through vision is how I would describe it. This feeling through sight is only increasing. This sensation is strictly in relation to the eyes and not nudity or facial features. One might suggest I would marry every woman on the planet without hesitation and I would neglect my infinite books. One might understand why I must isolate myself in my room. One might have a slight understanding of what self control is if they had "love at first sight" with every single woman they encountered. One should perhaps be very cautious to not underestimate this reality of heightened awareness or extreme right brain dominate. This sensation is not about "sex" because the sensation from looking is in fact sex, and this relates to just looking at the picture of a woman's eyes. I would advise one to not seek such an extreme state of heightened awareness. I submit I made a mistake and had an "accident", went too far to the right, and now I am doomed. - 1:28:13 AM

1:59:56 AM - The darkness only detects the light after the light is gone. I am the first to submit I am wrong and the last to understand I am not. I understand no person would intentionally condition another person into left brain dominate using scribe and math. I understand scribe and math are a very attractive form of "knowledge" and they perhaps are simply unaware of the side effects of teaching these methods. I have faith it is not intentional.

"A casual stroll through the lunatic asylum shows that faith does not prove anything. " Friedrich Nietzsche

When everything is relative to the observer, faith and intuition confuse things further.

When everything is relative to the observer, faith and intuition is all that counts.

The reason these comments are paradoxes is because for example a police officer might be looking over a crowd and he might see a person is nervous or worried and that cop might decided to search that person, so that cop is doing something based on observation but also a cop uses his intuition to make the final call on that. What is known a gut instinct. This gut instinct is not always accurate it is simply an intuitional feeling. This intuition is rather tricky because at times a male might be certain a female likes him from an intuitional feeling but then that female might surprise him and reveal his intuitions are perhaps slightly biased. This is perhaps what is known as "wishful thinking".

4:14:06 AM – The meaning of life is simply to use fear conditioning and "perhaps" mental conditioning methods in order to negate the left brain (strong emotions and physical focus) conditioning caused as an indirect result of the "three R's" or the "tree of knowledge" to go back to right brain dominate as everyone is when they are born. This increases awareness and unlocks some interesting cerebral aspects that are lost as a result of the "three R's" conditioning. The language and math aspect remain, only the heightened awareness aspect increases. This of course is ones free will or choice to achieve and it perhaps does not make a bit of difference in the long run if one achieves this or not.- 4:18:55 AM

5:27:53 AM – It is much easier to understand than to forget understandings. An understanding
is like a thorn that hurts more, the deeper it goes. Ignorance is like a lover that always says yes. Clarity is the ability to ponder darkness; Darkness is the inability to detect clarity. It is perhaps best no being ever understand what I speak of. Things with true value cost you everything. At a depth of six feet oxygen is not required.

I had an accident and discovered how anyone can go "subconscious" dominate very easily and it takes no longer than a few months of conditioning to start this "mental cycle". I am not suggesting making one on the "left" slightly more intelligent I am talking "Einstein" intelligent. This may affect the entire species in many different ways so I am careful to make sure everyone understands it is your choice only. You are not good or bad because you do this. It is a choice you have. I am obligated to talk you out of it as well as talk you into it. That is the paradox.

3:22:22 PM –
"If you're not ready to die for it, put the word 'freedom' out of your vocabulary. "
Malcolm X
"Beauty is a short-lived tyranny."
Socrates
Joh 15:13 "Greater love hath no man than this, that a man lay down his life for his friends."
"I don't even call it violence when it's in self defense; I call it intelligence."
Malcolm X
"Deu 28:20 "The LORD shall send upon thee cursing, vexation, and rebuke, in all that thou settest thine hand unto for to do, until thou be destroyed, and until thou perish quickly; because of the wickedness of thy doings, whereby thou hast forsaken me."
One with "left brain" must first avoid looking at the name of the people who said these comments because the time stamps in relation to the names and the labels associated with the names will hinder their ability to grasp the words.
[("Many of the beliefs traditionally attributed to the historical Socrates have been characterized as "paradoxal" because they seem to conflict with common sense.")
("the right brain seems to flourish dealing with complexity, ambiguity and paradox.")] = the complexity when one is extreme right brain denotes the "processing power" is so extreme, one at times can find contradictions that are both true so they are a paradox. To the ones in Left brain they may appear confused determinations but that is an illusion. I am only confused about why I tolerate a society that would do this to the offspring," 8 U.S. soldiers dead in 2 days in Afghanistan". I submit I am not warmed up so I am still at the stage I can tolerate slightly, but I submit the "garden of Eden days" will not be lasting much longer. On one hand that is good news for some and on the other hand that is not good news for some. So the wisdom

comment one may obtain from this is: If one wishes to drink blood they must first learn how to breathe in my red sea.

Beauty is mental anguish one experiences when they mentally wake up to the fact they never were awake.

Perhaps Lord of all denotes lord of all living thing perhaps. Perhaps Death is lord of all living things because all living things die. I defeated death when I was convulsing after taking many Paxil in my final suicide attempt and I said "I want to die" and did not "try to save myself", so somehow I defeated my fear of death and then, when the fear was gone I had an "ah ha" sensation mentally about four to six months later, so it was delayed, not instant.

Perhaps Love the lord means do not fear death or Fear not.

"1Jn 3:14 "We know that we have passed from death(fear of death which is a side effect of the "scribe" aspect") unto life(right brain dominate to the extreme or subconscious dominate and go back to how we were before the scribe aspect "drowned the world in the flood"), because we love the brethren(right aspect of the mind for it is a cerebral powerhouse and less prone to physical focus) . He that loveth not his brother(ones who are right brain extreme(ones who put them on crosses or makes them drink hemlock, or poisons them with mushrooms or poison lamb chops or burn them on stakes) abideth in death(the left aspect of the brain, because they are in neurosis and cannot tolerate ambiguity.)"

We all ponder ourselves into the light eventually.

God (death) loves us all no matter we do. One might suggest God has a plan for everyone and it's called impermanence. Perhaps god is love of money, and greed, and making money off of others, and physical focus. THAT IS NOT MY GOD. I am the first to submit I am wrong and the last to understand I am not. Anger is a gift given to the ones with clarity for their efforts. Mental gnashing of teeth is the first indication one has mental function.

"There is no coming to consciousness without pain."

Carl Jung

"Show me a sane man and I will cure him for you."

Carl Jung

  Peter was crucified head down in Rome, 65 A.D.

  Andrew was bound to death. He preached until his death in 73 A.D.

  James , son of Zebedee, was bchcaded in Jerusalem by the knife. (Acts 12:1-9).

  John was banished to the Isle of Patmos, 94 A.D. (Rev. 1- 9).

  Phillip was crucified at Heirapole, Phryga, 53 A.D.

  Bartholomew was beaten, crucified, then beheaded by the command of a king, 53 A.D.

  Thomas was run through by a lance at Corehandal, East Indies, 53 A.D.

  Matthew was slain by the sword in the city of Ethiopia about 61 A.D.

  James son of Alphaeus, was thrown from a pinnacle, then beaten to death, 62 A.D.

  Thaddeus was shot to death by arrows, 73 A.D.

  Simon was crucified in Persia, 72 A.D."

You are perhaps asking "Oh wise author of infinitely poor books why are your eyes black with rage?"

My eyes are black with rage because I am mindful the ones on the "left" cannot handle the "complexity, ambiguity and paradox" of the ones on the right so they tend to slaughter them. The ones on the left are simply brain dcad mole crickets and should not be allowed to keep their head because they cannot use their head. I am mindful Mohammed was truly wise when we understood what the "left" had done to all these wise beings and he started cutting heads off. I find absolutely no fault with his wisdom. What causes my eyes to go even further black is I used to be "left" or "lost" and I understand it is no ones fault , it was simply an good invention by man(demotic and Dena) and it had unintended side effects. So I cannot justify my rage so I have to let it go because my mind "right brain" cannot be fooled. I have to let all my rage out in words because I cannot justify lifting a finger when I understand it was perhaps no one's fault, it was just a good idea that had unintended consequences mentally speaking on the species.

"One day mankind will invent something and it will have unintended consequences." And that happened about 5000 years ago or more. So I can't blame anyone. So I will implode or let go of my rage. I submit I look at the razor cuts on my left wrist and it is hard for me to let go of my rage at times. I can only try to let go of my rage. I do understand I am trooper no matter what happens.

Rev 18:24 "And in her(the left brainers) was found the blood of prophets, and of saints, and of all that were slain upon the earth.""

Rev 17:6 "And I saw the woman(the ones on the left) drunken with the blood of the saints(ones of the right), and with the blood of the martyrs of Jesus(ones like Jesus, ones on the right) and when I saw her, I wondered(pondered as in said "perhaps" often) with great admiration(as in how stupid can they be, since these "saints" were only trying to wake people up from the "neurosis the demotic and Dena caused). "

Rev 16:6 "For they(ones on the left) have shed the blood of saints and prophets(ones on the right), and thou hast given them blood to drink; for they are worthy." (The saints died while doing a right/"right"ous thing , which is trying to "wake everyone up". I think if you reach heightened awareness and lose your sense of time and think about this (without time stamps on your thoughts)it is going to make you very meek at what we do to ourselves sometimes.)

Rev 16:4 "And the third angel poured out his vial upon the rivers and fountains of waters; and they became blood."
Do not ever assume I am religious. I am strictly on a vengeance mission. The rivers of blood is theblood of the ones on the right the left has slaughtered down through history. - 9:03:33 PM

Rev 22:10 "And he saith unto me, Seal not the sayings of the prophecy of this book: for the time is at hand."
This is very straight forward, "for the time is at hand." denotes after the "flood" which made everyone left brain dominate because of the "scribe" aspect, peoples sense of time was very pronounced as well as emotions like shame and embarrassment which is why Eve and Adam put fig leafs on after the ate from the "tree of knowledge". So the time is at hand denotes people in general have a strong sense of time or are on the "left hand" as opposed to the "prophets" who are on the "right hand" aspect of the brain = (nirvana/slight sense of time). So this comment is saying make sure you get the word out and tell everyone the scribe

aspect somehow made everyone conditioned into the left aspect of the mind and they have to condition away from fear as in "fear not" and the proof is everyone has a strong sense of time or "the time is at hand" in relation to the world in general. What I find extremely funny is no one has a clue as to what I am saying. I am blessed with a speech impediment and the inability to notice it.-11:54:44 PM

7/8/2009 1:05:13 AM – The food from a dead horse's mouth has more flavor. I will have to write a book to clarify that last comment. This extreme right brain dominate state is very complex and one tends to be able to assume any identity they want because they have extreme creativity or they have a vivid imagination, this is in

relation to how some creative people such as artists like Edgar Allen Poe did some drugs to reach his state to be a creative writer. Many painters and musicians also use drugs to achieve this creative state of mind. The problem with that is simply the drugs work but they tend to kill you eventually. There is no question beer, pot, cocaine, crystal meth all kinds of "euphoria" drugs will enable one to achieve a certain state of right brain dominance but it does not last, so one ends up taking it often and in time they become addicted and it harms them. Simply put a person who is inclined to do drugs is attempting to reach the state of mind they were at as a child, or the state of mind one is naturally in before the "scribe" "educational knowledge" is forced upon them. So people go through their whole lives, after the "scribe" indoctrination, looking for a way to get back to where they were as a child. They are not evil or bad because they do drugs. People are not evil or bad because they like material things and like money. These desires and cravings are simply a side effect of the left brain conditioning "scribe" causes. The left brain aspect gives one this sensation of "emptiness" and these material things and drugs tend to fill that emptiness. That emptiness on one hand is simply a need to feel satisfaction. The need to fill satisfaction is abnormal and is strictly a left brain aspect caused by "scribe". Right brain state of mind has no concept of satisfaction so one tends to not desire to be filled or satisfied. Satisfaction leads to "pleasure" and when satisfaction is not achieved there is "displeasure". That alone is the source of nearly all problems a person can have in life. Ones on the "left" are looking for a way to be satisfied but these cravings tend to be physical focused. So that alone drives the entire "consumer" based capitalistic civilization. People will kill each other for material things, from shoes, to a watch, to a bit of money, in order to be satisfied. That is not because those people are evil or bad, that is because they have been conditioned by the scribe aspect or have been around people who have been conditioned by the scribe aspect or both, too much, and they have assumed that "lifestyle" or mind set. It is not what a person will do for a million dollars it is what a person will do for 10 dollars that is the problem. So one might suggest in the extreme right brain aspect money has no power and this need to be satisfied has no power anymore, simply because one is so cerebral, they spend much of their time pondering things.

I am mindful you may assume I have this script I write from or perhaps some "goal" in mind to write these books but I do not. I operate strictly in real time. That is the opposite of left brain totally, left brain is very "plan" orientated. A person makes a plan, for example for the weekend, and when that plan starts to fall apart they get upset and angry because their "satisfaction" desire appears to be in question. This is on one hand a time based, left brain concept. The memory is so different in extreme right brain state of mind things like planning for a weekend is nearly not possible. Perhaps I am too far into the right aspect because I conditioned the hardcore way away from fear, but that perhaps is not an absolute for everyone. I have a slight idea of what I wrote about yesterday in the thick pamphlet, but outside of that I remember nothing. I do not perceive I could go out in public and perform music and "remember" the lyrics. I can adlib or perform in verbatim but it is nearly impossible for me to actually do short term memory things. I suggested in earlier diaries something along the line of "absent minded professor". This memory adjustment is simply the result of the right brain shutting many things down so it can focus all of it energy on concentration and that increases ones awareness to the "now". It is too early into the accident to suggest absolutes in relation to memory. I do not detect supernatural hocus pocus. I do not detect spiritual unseen forces. I do not hear voices. I do however detect a great amount of "pondering", mentally speaking or "the machine" is ticking away.

I prefer to call it the machine state of mind. It is as if all forms of what a person considers "emotions and feelings" are simply muted. I cannot sum it up perhaps any better than this simple comment.

Joh 3:30 "He must increase, but I must decrease."

Left brain "strong emotions, attachments, strong sense of time, strong need to be satisfied, fear" MUST decrease so that right brain "machine state, heightened awareness, extreme concentration" CAN increase. It is one or the other. If one tries to have both they will not be very good at either, they will be lukewarm. Lukewarm denotes they will be trapped in between the two. They will rest on the edge of the "worlds". One way to look at it is, everyone knows it is impossible to be pleased with material things. One can never have enough drugs, money, food, power so the left aspect state of mind is doomed to be dissatisfied. The right aspect is unable to be satisfied and thus dissatisfied for

more than slight moments simply because the machine is pondering them into another thought so swiftly they are simply unable to "rest of their laurels".

One thing I am quite certain of is some of these people who are tied up in material drives to be satisfied are very prone to be afraid. I was very afraid of scary movies and the dark, the entire time I was depressed. So people who like drugs and like money and like material things and like food, all of these problems are a symptom of the fear aspect. I understand fear is not what most think it is. Fear is a mental abnormality that is a side effect of the "scribe" conditioning. If I had fear I would never publish my books I would be afraid I might get embarrassed, or harmed, or attacked, or abused for what I write. I have no fear. I try to find things to make me feel fear. I try to write things that will make me feel fear and then I publish it and then a day after I send it to the publisher I totally forget about what I wrote. I totally forget everything I wrote the day before so I am unable to "worry" or be "concerned" about what I write. Lack of fear and thus lack of worry is in fact very healthy for the body in general. This has much to do with the altered memory. People on the left tend to allow short term memories to fester them into stress. Perhaps the whole world will show up at my house and take me out back and harm me for what I write, but I certainly will not stress about that because I am unable to. I cannot remember what I write exactly in the thick pamphlets and I cannot live forever anyway.

So there is a definite trade off going on here. One can have the cake (right aspect powerhouse, concentration, heightened awareness) or one can eat the cake (left aspect , satisfaction, physical based, strong feelings and emotions). I am not allowed to ever suggest one or the other is better because both are totally different. One cannot compare the two because they are opposites. Perhaps a very mysterious thing is everything I write are things everyone already knows. To clarify, every idea and concept I write about are things every person already knows. I did not learn what I write about in school. I learned what I write about because I conditioned away the "fear" the hard way, and then the fear went away from my mind and then I could think clearly, and everything was like a crystal day. I simply did not learn anything I just cleared the "fear" fog away and everything now makes perfect sense. It is not hocus pocus, it is simply the right aspect of the mind once fear is gone is "beyond understanding" meaning it understands everything in relation to texts and ideas and concepts. I have no clue how, but I certainly did not know any of this stuff nine months ago, and it was a very rough battle mentally to get this far.

Somehow I at times can understand the future and so it is even beyond the ability of the person who has extreme right brain to figure out. Everyone knows the subconscious or the "veiled" aspect of the mind is powerful in relation to one who has "strong sense of time", very powerful. One can go on and on about religious and supernatural aspects but that is not my place to comment on. I am still trying to adjust and come up to full power. There are ones in nirvana who suggest a "hocus pocus" aspect. One may suggest that once the fear is gone and the "machine" turns on, a person has their entire life to try to figure out the extent of the power they have "unveiled". Forget about all that physical based crap. You have this "kingdom within" your mind that is going to keep you quite busy. One might suggest you will be very happy in a small house, with just enough money to buy food and you will be happy. You will have silenced hunger so you will eat much less and that is in fact healthy. One does not need three meals a day to live. One can eat one meal a day and eat a vitamin or not eat a vitamin. It is perhaps difficult for one to grasp that idea when one is in the left, because they feel hunger. So on the left one feels hunger and gets hungry and feels weak when they don't eat often and one the right does not feel hunger strong at all, and does not get weak when they don't eat often. That of course is a generalization based on contrast. In contrast to how hungry I used to feel, I am seldom hungry. One might suggest my food is my pondering and my understandings. So my physical hunger has decreased and my cerebral hunger has increased.

One might suggest I publish my books and people read them and find out perhaps they do have a choice to achieve right brain "lifestyle" and that pleases them and perhaps they may determine to go that path and so I "feed the multitudes" with my words, but the catch is, I feel no satisfaction because I am in the "machine" state. One might suggest I feed people with my words, but my true intention is to feed myself or "focus on my own log" because I am not an authority, I am simply attempting to adjust, and my form of adjustment, is to keep talking to myself. I do submit I do not perceive my ability to use language is getting better as far as literary mastery, it in fact is getting worse. I have great difficulty using past and future tense words and even present tense words. This is why I am certain this "scribe" aspect is what it is mostly about, the "tree of knowledge". I never was very focused on math but now I do have an aversion to math but the "scribe" or written words are very obvious to me as being a problem. So when a child is very young they are thrown into school and they appear "dumb" because they have trouble adjusting to "scribe" and then they slowly start to "learn" "scribe" and what that is really doing is silencing the right aspect of the mind. So when a teacher says to a child "You get an A on your essay because I saw no grammar flaws" they are in reality saying "The killing off of your right brain aspect is coming along nicely." I will go up against the smartest being in the universe and convince them of that swiftly.

Perhaps the trick is to balance the anti-fear conditioning starting at a young age with the "scribe" teaching. Now, if this in fact has nothing to do with physical aspects in relation to the brain and in reality I am some "spirit" and no person can ever achieve this state of mind without facing death the hard way, then everything I write about is not going to work for anyone ever, unless they mess up on suicide but come very close to dying. I tend to lean to the psychological aspect. I tend to understand this is simply psychological conditioning and I perhaps went to the extreme by accident. The archeologists suggest I am a lemur monkey and no amount of complex pondering is going to ponder that way, in relation to me. In fact it is quite liberating to understand I am a lemur monkey because all the stress is off. Of course I am an idiot, and I cannot write, and I am vain, and I am a loser, because I am a lemur monkey. Can you blame me? I am after all a lemur monkey. Lemur monkeys are not even supposed to be able to type thick pamphlets, so if I can type one sentence that makes sense to anyone else in the universe, I have accomplished the impossible. So I accomplish the impossible every time I spell a word correctly. If I get very lucky sometimes I form a full sentence. On very rare occasions and perhaps because of "super natural powers" I type something that is wise relative to other observers.

I got goose bumps and that is a symptom I am shifting in an out of reality. I am unable to even explain that one. I can only suggest I near this state of mind where I can feel the "matrix" or the "vacuum" at this point since the accident. It is simply unexplainable because I am not use to it and it is some sort of new occurrence. One might suggest I try my hardest to be angry and vengeful in my books because I am trying to slow this state down. Simply put, as my "scribe" or grammar ability decreases the "other" powers of the "right" are increasing and this is the "progression" I have been aware of since the "D-day" on OCT 31st, 2008 when I got the "ah-ha" sensation. I am not saying it is supernatural. I am the first to submit I am wrong and the last to understand I am not. It better not be supernatural. I will go play my video game before I eviscerate myself. I am certainly beyond the realms of insanity at this point. That is a fact. I speak with ones in the "know" or in "nirvana" and we just crack jokes and speak freely and then I try to speak to the ones on the "left" and they just assume I am a freak of all nature, and I ponder, I certainly must go to India to get away from these people on the left, and then I recall I am an American, and I am not running from anyone, ever.

I am quite certain I went from the extreme of left brain, and deep depression and deep anger and being harmful to myself, and went one inch further and ended up on the extreme of right brain, as if these aspects of the mind are a circle and not a linear shape. It could also be somehow due to the accident my left brain aspect just turned off or became extremely silenced but not in a physical trauma kind of way but somehow my brain just kept the left aspect functioning like normal but turned off or no longer registered the signals coming from it.- 3:09:41 AM

"Nonviolence is fine as long as it works."
Malcolm X

This is true wisdom. What if Washington would have tried the nonviolent approach? Ones who preach nonviolence above all else are certainly being taken advantage of. The complexity is having the cerebral aspect at full power so one is able to determine properly when peaceful methods can work. This again goes into the "spooky" aspect of relativity. Patience is relative to the observer. Paranoia is relative to the observer. I am aware something's I write perhaps gives one the impression I am not patient and I am paranoid. The reality is, in the extreme right brain state of mind, I am capable of being anything from second to second as far as mental states. That is why one must determine carefully if they even want this "right aspect" mental state. One day with no sense of time is a very long time so patience is very important. The clarification here is, ones on the "left" tend to rest on their laurels. The ones on the "left" can go through their whole life paranoid. So one the left can actually say Mohammed was bad but Jesus and Moses were good, even after Mohammed said he agreed with Jesus and Moses. That's a symptom of silenced awareness of the left brain. Any argument one might have that Mohammed was not in direct accordance with what Jesus and Moses were saying, you write a book about it and I will read that book and then wrap my fish heads in it. I lost my train.

I am unable to have one set state of mind for more than a few minutes because the "machine" is pondering so fast I simply reach different states on a minute by minute basis, this is how the concentration stays so high, or the heightened awareness stays so high. I can feel all the emotions but I am unable to rest on them for more than a minute or two, no matter what. So the accurate emotional state I am in on a daily basis is nothingness which denotes the color black and black is a combination of all colors. So to be accurate, I have no emotional capacity which means I am not affected by emotions because I fall out of their "grip" swiftly. This is perhaps why, in some respects, marriages fail, simply because one of the people lose the attachment. "Eyes wander" so to speak. That's the strange part about the right aspect, when a person gets married the right aspect feels that is attachment or being "chained" and it is a miracle the marriage lasts at all and if it does it tends to be a failed marriage in respect to, the "magic" is lost. It becomes a marriage of connivance because the right aspect is always looking for something new or is looking to remain free. I am convinced Jung certainly had a leaning to "right aspect". I will verify that if I can fit him into my schedule. "The marriage lasted until Emma's death in 1955, but he had more-or-less open relationships with other women. The most well-known women with whom Jung is believed to have had extramarital relationships were patient and friend Sabina Spielrein and Toni Wolff."

Jung was not evil to have other relationships I understand he was perhaps simply a "lush". People on the "left" cannot stand that reality because people on the left are generally control freaks, contrary to people on the right. One might suggest it is like a person who has a few drinks and get tipsy and then becomes a "lush" but multiply that by about a million and then factor in one has extreme clarity and it never wears off and one can understand why at least one of these wise beings in history had many wives. This of course needs clarification, "As he increases I must decrease." This denotes "sex" as in physical intercourse is not the same on the right as it is on the left. "Sex" as in intercourse on the" left" is all there is, when that gets old, it is over for the relationship. So, then there is the "right aspect" "sex", its far more "telepathic" or cerebral. A single look in the eyes is quite powerful one might suggest. I do not know why.. Perhaps it is best to say, all the characteristics of the left are magnified when one is extreme right brained and also something's are lost, and also some things as a result are added. That was perhaps the most vague statement in the universe. It is perhaps just nature's way of keeping us procreating, so this whole concept of marriage is based on generally a "left brain" focused world. It fits right into the "control" aspect of the left brain and it goes against the "freedom" or "free spirit" aspect of the right brain. The Catholic church has this, no condoms rule, or only have sex if you want to procreate, and I am quite certain this is a tradition based on the fact, when one is in the extreme right, they are "having sex" without the "intercourse" aspect anyway. I could sit here and say when I see a picture of any girl and see her eyes it does nothing, but in reality I "feel" this "perfection" and I do not know what it is, but it feels like a drug I want, but I cannot figure out exactly what it is.

One might suggest it would interfere with my pursuit of infinitely poor thick pamphlets, if I decided to follow that drug. I am not suggesting I am some chastity freak that's not reality at all. I am saying this "cerebral or telepathic" aspect of sex is increasing. That is not good or evil, it simply is. I submit I am using commas but I understand most are probably improperly used. I just cannot tell often where commas go anymore. I perceive my sentences are organized properly but sometimes, I reread them, and they are certainly "way out" of sequential reality. It is also difficult for me to proof read my thick pamphlets because I have to relive the understandings again. It is perhaps like reliving a memory that has been forgotten. Granted my train to Clarksville has derailed.

I was watching a documentary and it was discussing fearlessness. It explained how some people like bomb disposal and test pilots genetically inclined to fearlessness, Genetically inclined to fearlessness. That is simply impossible. Fear and many emotions are a side effect that is instilled in children when they are "educated" with the "scribe" concept. The reason it is impossible it can be a genetic inclination is because I use to be very afraid and very shy and very embarrassed easily, and now I have none of that, and the proof is I publish these horrible books and say things, no being with fear or shyness would ever say. I accidentally conditioned myself away from fear, as in fear of the "big fear" and lost all the aspects that were tied to it. Fear of embarrassment, fear of judgment from others, fear of the dark, fear of death, fear of ghosts, fear of ridicule. I am simply immune to your consultations. If I was inclined genetically to be afraid, I could not have ever accomplished that because it would simply be in my genes.

I will clarify.

Pre- Left brain "scribe" mental conditioning:

Gen 2:25 "And they were both naked, the man and his wife, and were not ashamed.(NOT AFRAID OR SHY OR EMBARSSED)

Why did they decide to have the conditioning?

Gen 3:6 And when the woman saw that the tree was good for food(NEW KNOWLEDGE), and that it was pleasant to the eyes(SCRIBE LOOKED LIKE A GOOD IDEA), and a tree to be desired to make one wise(YOU WILL BE RICH BECAUSE FEW ARE SCRIBES RELATIVE TO 3500 BCE), she took of the fruit."

Post-Left Brain "Scribc" conditioning

Gen 3:7 "And the eyes of them both were opened, and they knew("they knew" they were naked which means they started judging a book by the cover instead of "feeling" the contents, which is right brain, right brain is seeing the whole , not the details, and we can all only hope that it was not cold that day, relative to Adam) that they were naked; and they sewed fig leaves together, and made themselves aprons." This is simply saying they gained emotions like shame and embarrassment and shyness and fear. That is not good or bad, but it certainly is fact.

 Here are some more symptoms after the "knowledge" or "scribe effect" or eating of the apple.

Gen 3:8 "And they heard the voice of the LORD God walking in the garden in the cool of the day: and Adam and his wife hid themselves from the presence of the LORD God amongst the trees of the garden."

This is a bit of humor "cool of the day". Clearly Adam was not pleased to understand the cold effects in relation to the fact Eve just started seeing "tiny details' instead of "the whole".

Perhaps no one ever gets my humor. The clever aspect of this comment is this:" Adam and his wife hid". One only hides when they are afraid or they are fearful or ashamed. These are "side effects" of the left brain scribe conditioning. They were not ashamed before they ate the apple ", the man and his wife, and were not ashamed." And now they are ashamed and hid so they are afraid also. I also detect this wife aspect is simply suggesting Adams mate. I am also certain this entire story is not reality as in a real Adam and Eve but simply a parable explaining how this "left brain "scribe" conditioning happened. I am certain of that and if Heimdall suggests certainty, one is wise to ponder it carefully.

Gen 3:17 "And unto Adam he said, Because thou hast hearkened unto the voice of thy wife, and hast eaten of the tree, of which I commanded thee, saying, Thou shalt not eat of it: cursed is the ground for thy sake; in sorrow shalt thou eat of it all the days of thy life;"
Be mindful this comment is not insulting women because I have already understood Moses had to use women as a "scapegoat", because if he said men created the scribe problem, or ate off the tree of "knowledge", he would not have lasted very long. So he had to lie. He simply lied, because he understood the men would slaughter him, and I recall I have already explained why women are the dominate gender in the species in the last volume. If you doubt women are the dominate gender in the species, you are simply in denial.
This is perhaps very profound " in sorrow shalt thou eat of it all the days of thy life". I got goose bumps reading this aspect of the comment and when Heimdall gets goose bumps it is because of something that the "spirit" of the words does to me. I get the spirit of the comment and it effect's my body.
That is not good or bad, relatively speaking, so to speak, what have you. So "in sorrow" denotes depression, sadness, hate, shame, misery, fear, shyness and it is simply saying after you get the left brain conditioning "scribe" aspect you will be like that "all the days of thy life." And in the last few days you are alive if you get lucky and get a terminal disease, you will wake up after you face the inevitable death, or if you live to be old age you will start to wake up from the "conditioning", and you will perhaps understand you were robbed of your life by the shiny red apple called "(demotic) script and dena (arithmatics)" because no one told you, you have to condition away the "emotions" that are a side effect of this "knowledge". I will pause for now because I just became aware mankind has brought so much hurt on himself because of this invention called "script" and "math" and I am aware of all the people who have died needlessly because of this invention, that if I did not pause, I would be reduced to just spitting blood into my thick pamphlet. You try to just focus on this. Perhaps every war fought for control of any kind is a war as a result of this "scribe or script aspect". Perhaps every time someone kills their self because they are depressed or sad or shy or embarrassed or angry or harms someone else because of that, it is because of the "script" and "dena". Those are side effects of that "knowledge". They alter the mind from its natural docile, cerebral state to a violent physical state. That is not good or bad, but it is perhaps dam sure fact. The only true logical solution is to let everyone out of prison, pay them money for making them like they are with this "education", and attempting to explain to them methods on how to "reverse" this mental side effect of the conditioning called "out of control" emotions and physical focus. Then help everyone who is not in prison with the same methods because nearly everyone who is not in actual prison is mentally in prison because of emotional issues, in one way or another as a result of the conditionings. I am not talking in America I am talking worldwide. That is

perhaps an absolute fact. If you cannot grasp that, it is simply because you have are not using 100% of the right brain power because of the 'Demotic" conditioning. so go sit a cemetery at night until you feel better.

Perhaps the abused are having ideas in relation to lawsuits. One might consider a "stress" related lawsuit. All the stress you may have in your life is a side effect of the conditioning, that is fact and stress is relative to the observer. The proof is, if I had stress I could not be pumping out books this fast. I would simply be to mentally frozen to pump out thick pamphlets like this constantly. It would perhaps be impossible. On the contrary, I have zero stress. I think with extreme concentration to the degree, all these books I write take no effort and do not stress me out even slightly. One might suggest writing these books is effortless. I am mindful no being can even understand anything I say and that means I must write effortlessly faster. To clarify, no being in the universe writes thick pamphlets as poorly or as swiftly as I do. Perhaps if the college I tried to get into when I was 18 had a bit more sympathy and gave me a C instead of a D on my final exam comma test I would not have had this accident and everyone would be much more blissful from here on out , relative to my perception. I bet you think I am kidding. Past is now. 6:50:35 AM

"We cannot defend freedom abroad by deserting it at home. "
Edward R. Murrow

7/8/2009 6:00:41 PM – I just got the proof from volume 6 and it has many "errors" and then in that volume I read "Neurosis is the inability to tolerate ambiguity" and I told the publisher to send it to the printer. I realized I make no errors in my diary unless I perceive I do, and as of right now I do not perceive even one single error in volume six. If you perceive errors in any of my books, perhaps you will get over your neurosis in time and of time. I am mindful I am the artist of my thick pamphlets and if I am pleased with them that is all that matters in all reality because: Beauty is relative to ones lack of neurosis. If everyone painted the same picture there would be no point in having so many people. When you judge yourself you understand why you judge others. I am a racist against myself or I wouldn't publish these stupid books. If I had decency I wouldn't publish these idiotic, stupid, retarded, evil books relative to some on the left. I wouldn't publish these books if I wasn't the god dam devil because I am in fact shattering people's entire mental worlds of understanding. Maybe if people like me I will do anything so they will keep telling me they like me.

"The powers not delegated to the United States by the Constitution, nor prohibited by it to the States, are reserved to the States respectively, or to the people." "To the people" denotes the people are the bottom line outside of the constitution. The constitution states all people are equal and have a right to freedom and their own pursuit of happiness relative to what they perceive is their purpose. This means there is no law that can infringe on a person's pursuit of happiness or that law in fact denies that person pursuit of happiness. So the only valid law is perhaps, Do not harm other's physically. Maybe do not steal from others, but stealing is very relative to the observer. Society steals peoples intelligent aspect of their mind because they condition them BY LAW into script and Dena and then they don't tell them about fear conditioning so the people won't end up with 10% cerebral function, that is stealing and harming and in some cases murder. If person gives someone a "drug" and that person dies then that person is responsible for murder. So if society "teaches" children this script and Dena and that child gets depressed and shy and embarrassed and kills their self, the society is a murderer because the emotions are a side effect of FORCED education. Some people certainly do not want that to be truth although it is truth. It is not the language or the math it is leaving out the fear conditioning aspect that is the problem.

The "powers that be" certainly will put their best minds on this aspect and they will say I am insane and crazy, because if I am not, they are going to have infinite law suits into infinity. They will have to burn my books. After this book is published someone is going to read this because I give them freely. So now you see, these laws, and truth, and justice for all will be put to the test. I understand they perhaps were not aware but a judge usually determines ignorance is no excuse. I do not hold grudges and I do not accuse anyone. I cast no stones in this matter. I lost my train.

Outside of these two rules, no killing or harming and questionably no stealing, anything goes because if that is not the case then it will only be a police state robbing people of their pursuit of happiness. The laws are simply a symptom of the control mentality encouraged by the "script" conditioning that is in fact forced on people at a very young age as perhaps a fear instilling tactic. The fear tactic is, if one does not get the script conditioning they will not be able to make "good" money and so they will be in discomfort, working slave jobs, because the entire society is based on money. So it is a carrot on a stick, so to speak. A person 5000 or more years ago invented script and found it was a type of magical invention and they were thought of as wise and so many desired to learn this script. So from that point on human beings have had this notion that without this script education one is not intelligent and thus society in general is a mental racist against anyone who they deem is not "intelligent" and does not have this "script" education. So the core of society itself is a racist against people who are mentally different. This alone negates society as being an impartial jury. This also negates society from being an unbiased observer to being a one sided slave master.

What this denotes is Amendment 13 of the constitution is in fact being violated.

"Neither slavery nor involuntary servitude, except as a punishment for crime whereof the party shall have been duly convicted, shall exist within the United States, or any place subject to their jurisdiction."

"Involuntary servitude" is evident because the powers that be force children and adults alike to get this script and math education by force of law and by "carrot and stick" tactics. This in fact hinders one's mind and in turn alters their "pursuit of happiness" on one level and it also puts them in a position they have to adjust their "pursuit of happiness" in order to conform to being "educated" involuntarily. So a person is a child and before they can determine their purpose they are forced by law into the "script" education and thus are push into a life of involuntary servitude to the "powers that be" because their mind is turned from right aspect to left aspect and this in turn blocks their mental capacity. This in turn puts this "stone around their neck" because they are then force to seek further "script and math" education in order to make "money". This again denies them their own purpose and "pursuit of happiness". This is also extortion because ones who do not desire to get the "script and math" education are deemed "not intelligent" and are relegated by society itself to low paying jobs and are in turn deemed "stupid" by society as a whole because they do not conform to the "script" conditioning. So this means any being who resists the "indoctrination" by the script is considered an outcast and thus laws are passed against them. A person without a "proper script" education is forced to remedial jobs and if they try to make money other ways, those others ways are in general against the law, so they are essentially doomed by the society to either, a life of "crime" based on the biased opinion of a biased "slave master" society or they have to withdraw from society and attempt to survive away from society.

In America, African Americans in general are right brain dominate denoted by their in general creative abilities, as a result of not being educated into script in the slavery Era, and thus they tend to not do well in the "script and math" indoctrination and so they are outcasts in relation to a biased societies judgment of them, and are forced to attempt to make money in fashions that are deemed "criminal" by that biased society, that is again knowingly or unknowingly. So the society as a whole creates the "game" and anyone who does not fit within the limited confines of the "game" are deemed to be outcasts or relegated to "criminal 'activity because they did not want to become indoctrinated by the "script and math" aspects or were not good at it. Therefore they are relegated to "involuntary servitude". " "Neither slavery nor involuntary servitude"

They are simply locked in prison and deemed to be threats to society because, they could not "pass" the indoctrination of the 'script" aspect and thus are deemed to be unworthy. It is impossible one human being can be less than another human being when both are equal to begin with, so this denotes that society as a whole is a racist against beings with right brain dominate in general, knowingly or unknowingly, and simply passes laws that are racist and biased against them, to ensure they are at a disadvantage, by making sure the "rules" of society are "demotic and dena" favored and not in the favor of right brain people. This also applies to any human being who does not "pass" "demotic and dena" schooling. So society as a whole is racist, and biased, and invalid as a whole, knowingly or unknowingly, because it denies a person their freedom to peruse happiness, relative to what that person perceive is happiness, so society is sham, contrived by control freaks, which is a left brain dominate characteristic, which denotes they are very "high" on rules and regulations, in order to control others. Which means they are very prone to "make slaves" of others or make people bend their own desires to such an extreme they simply are relegated to involuntary servitude. What this denotes is all of society as whole, are slaves and prone to be slaves and are pleased to be slaves, because they perceive they are not slaves but "productive members" of the society, which forced them against their will to be indoctrinated into scribe which altered their minds to begin with. So the people in general in this whole society in general, are not even valid unbiased observers, they are in fact unable to think clearly because they have been mentally altered to the extent, they cannot mentally make decisions properly. It is impossible to indoctrinate a person into the lesser complex aspect of the mind as a child, by force of law and by force of "norms of society," and then suggest they are unbiased in their determination capabilities, unless "society" does it unknowingly. Once the well is poisoned the water is undrinkable until the well has been drained of the poison. I am only leaving this aspect of my thick pamphlet intact because a dead horse does not mind a repeat performance.

Amendment 14:
"No State shall make or enforce any law which shall abridge the privileges or immunities of citizens of the United States; nor shall any State deprive any person of life, liberty, or property"

This "nor shall any State deprive any person of life, liberty, or property" denotes the moment a state passes a law and says a child MUST become "scribe and math educated" they deny that child the right to liberty, and thus the entire law, judicial, and government entity, is simply a tyrant and thus totally and completely biased and invalid. When a state passes a law that say one must be "educated" into scribe and it is the law, they in fact abridge that person's liberty because the scribe aspect changes that child's mental faculties to such an extreme, it robs that being their ability to think properly and it is in many cases permanent and forever, so they turn that person into a slave of the state , under the state, and under the "rules" of that sate, and thus the entire society structure is nothing but an indoctrination of mental altering on children and adults so they cannot think at full mental capacity.

It is not relevant whether this is directly or indirectly done. The robbery of one's mental liberty is evidenced by the fruits of their mental outcomes. What this means is all bets are off, one cannot trust the society that mentally harms children and makes it against the law to not mentally harm children at a young age. What the entire society is right now is a direct symptom of the forced indoctrination by the state and control structures. The entire society has been robbed of their mental liberty because the control structures in the society "force" people by law to hinder their minds while they are child, so everything in the society goes back to the initial indoctrination as child by law into the "scribe and math" indoctrination. So the entire control structure in the entire society in not only not valid it is in fact a "slave making" machine. It kills people's minds so they can be controlled easily with fear tactics and threats of being outcasts, so the control structure is simply the destroyer of liberty on every level. Once the mind is "damaged" by the scribe and math aspects, all the fruits from that mind are damaged fruits. Keep the people extremely dumb and make sure you pass laws that makes every child is forced indoctrinated by 'education" to be very 10%ish "left brained". Make laws that make it impossible for a person to be a "norm of society" unless they have major doses of "scribe and math" indoctrination. The more schooling they have, the farther to the left brain they go, and the more silenced the right complex creative aspect of the mind becomes. "As he increases, I must decrease"Left Brain = fear and scare tactics work easily.

Do not assume I have even started to write.11:43:33 PM

11:52:01 PM – So now that calmer minds prevailed, I am to understand that I am supposed to have compassion even though I fully understand, the reason I could not do well at the prescribed education promoted by society is because I was very right brain inclined, or I was unwilling to kill my right brain natural aspect just so I could fit in to the prescribe norms of a society, that is a control freak and a destroyer of freedom of thought. And this in turn made me feel like an outcast of society because I could not do well enough at these prescribed education models, and that in turn made me hate myself because I could not take the brainwashing as easily as others could, and so that led me to want to kill myself, and in turn try to kill myself for 10 plus years, and take a razor to my arm and slice it until I was covered in blood, and take many pills and try to harm myself, because I could not take your brain washing "education", and you presume I am going to have compassion on you? Is that what your brain dead mind presumes I am going to have? I cast no stones on this matter.

7/9/2009 12:20:08 AM – Oh look, It's a brand new day. Let's get on with the drowning.

"In all criminal prosecutions, the accused shall enjoy the right to a speedy and public trial, by an impartial jury of the state and district wherein the crime shall have been committed."

"by an impartial jury". Do you perceive I am going to tolerate being at the whim of a person the control structure has mentally conditioned with their "scribe" aspect, so that person is in general in a mental coma? A jury that is extreme left brained as a result of the "education system, and forced into that mental state by law, is only partial to judgments and sadism, and masochism. It is generally all a poisoned well because of the "education" indoctrination. You can go on into infinity with your elementary logic but "jury of my peers" means people who are extreme right brain dominate that are thus capable of complexity in their mental processes. That denotes in a trial if anyone on the jury has a strong sense of time, strong sense of hunger, and has sense of fear and shame and guilt and shyness, they are in fact not a jury of my peers but they are in fact a partial jury. They are biased against me. I am not concerned what they have to say about me because they have 10% brain capacity which means they have 10% mental complexity because they were mentally raped and robbed of their mental liberty by force of law by the control structure called society. So you can go on and on about morals and justice and what is right and what is wrong but at the end of the day, if you have been indoctrinated by the "scribe and math" aspects which you perhaps have been because it's the law, you simply do not have the brain complexity to even speak to me let alone, judge me.

Exactly when do I get my justice in this great law structure that is concerned about justice and quality and freedom and ones right to pursue happiness? You do not have enough material wealth in this universe to give me justice nor the ones you mentally raped by force under the guise of law. Just keep your mouth shut about justice, and freedom, and equality, because if you don't I will hang you with every word you say. Do you perceive you have enough money to compensate all the families of children who killed their self because they became shy or embarrassed or upset because their emotions were so strong due the "scribe conditioning"? Do you think you have enough money to compensate all the people in this society that are struggling mentally on a daily basis because you robbed them of their strong mental aspect of the right brain when you passed a law and said every child must be "educated" and then you don't have the clarity to understand what "fear not" means in relation to conditioning away the unwanted side effect of the education? Do you perceive there is enough money in the universe to fairly compensate those people who have drug addictions and overeating problems and emotional problems all the result of the script and Dena conditioning? Do you perceive "slave master" your chances of longevity are increasing or decreasing, at this very second in reality? Do you perceive all out revolution to the core is more likely or less likely at this second in reality? I cast no stones on this matter.

"We the People of the United States, in Order to form a more perfect Union, establish Justice, insure domestic Tranquility, provide for the common defense, promote the general Welfare, and secure the Blessings of Liberty to ourselves and our Posterity, do ordain and establish this Constitution for the United States of America."

I don't see anywhere in here where you have a right to mentally rape children by forcing your education indoctrination on them. Perhaps you interpreted "promote the general Welfare" to mean you get to destroy everyone's mind with your "education" so they have no brain function so they can be easily manipulated with fear tactics. "We hold these truths to be self-evident, that all men are created equal, that they are endowed by their Creator with certain unalienable Rights, that among these are Life, Liberty and the pursuit of Happiness. — That to secure these rights, Governments are instituted among Men, deriving their just powers from the consent of the governed, — That whenever any Form of Government becomes destructive of these ends, it is the Right of the People to alter or to abolish it, and to institute new Government,"

So you take peoples "unalienable Rights, that among these are Life, Liberty and the pursuit of Happiness." by indoctrinating then by force with your laws and make them get 'educated" or you are biased against them and so that means "That whenever any Form of Government becomes destructive of these ends, it is the Right of the People to alter or to abolish it,".

So you rob people's mental capacity with your forced "slavery" tactics and that means you have become destructive to the ends of "(Mental)Life,(mental) Liberty and the pursuit of (mental)Happiness)" and so that means "is the Right of the People to alter or to abolish it". So that means you are either going to get altered or abolished much swifter than you ever dreamed. I simply do not pander. Do you perceive I am kidding or do you perceive my eyes are black with rage? Simply put nothing you do or say, and none of your laws are valid, because you are simply a mental rapist, directly or indirectly, knowingly or unknowingly. I do not care how many "involuntary servitude" mental slaves you have on your side because if I needed an army I would have one. Everything is going to change or you are going to be burning books. I cast no stones on this matter.
Do you understand the definition of "The big fish has arrived."?

The correct answer to all my questions is, Perhaps.- 1:03:43 AM

1:08:22 AM – Perhaps, you perhaps, will perhaps, wish I perhaps, died perhaps, from that handful of Paxil perhaps, when I perhaps, get warmed up perhaps, because when I perhaps, get warmed up perhaps, you perhaps, will not perhaps, be able to perhaps, do much of anything, perhaps, psychologically speaking, so to speak, what have you, perhaps. Perhaps, that is perhaps, proper comma usage, perhaps. All of America is collapsing because someone keeps forcing the people to get indoctrinated into the left aspect due to "scribe" and then it has now nearly killed America. We can't come up with good inventions because no one has creativity, which is the right brain aspect of the mind, because the scribe aspect kills that off. Therefore I have no other conclusion but to suggest, something wants America and freedom to die, and therefore they are going to get what is known as, a reality check, as in checks and balances, and there is no morals, laws and no rules in said endeavor. There is no mercy, and there is no quarter given, nor expected, period. All bets are off.
Let's get back to reality. I am perhaps convinced in reality is it absolutely no one's fault for the unwanted side effects of this scribe invention. It simply was too good of an invention to not pursue. Once people started writing down things they started to lose long term memory

and gain short term memory. This is why some cultures keep verbal records of their history or one person is deemed the "story teller". In "modern" society there is no need to keep mental records of events because everything is in books and thus the long term memory is not very valuable because if one forgets they can simply look it up in a book. This is perhaps quite funny that the education system bases many tests on short term memory and at the end of the year a student does not remember anything they learned. How many non-math professionals still remember how to do algebra? The answer is, perhaps none. This is in direct relation to the comment" learn from your mistakes." If you only have a strong short term memory which is left brain then you are unable to essentially learn from your past mistakes in relation to "those who forget the past are doomed to repeat it", and that is essentially all civilization has been doing for 5000 years or more is repeating the mistakes of the past because they only have essentially a strong short term memory as a result of "writing". That in fact is hilarious. We are our own worst enemies. That is also hilarious. We bring it all on our self. That is also hilarious. We get what we asked for. That is beyond hilarious. We asked for "knowledge" and "wisdom" and we certainly got it, but that is of course relative to the observer. Script has certainly made us wise as long as you do not compare us to anything other than a lemur monkey. We still kill each other and our offspring over dirt, we are truly wise. You can write infinite books and explain how wise we are in general as a species and I will wrap my fish heads in them and my fish heads will be pleased with your wisdom. Even I have moments of clarity. - 1:46:08 AM

3:23:26 AM - I have pondered myself into a pondering. Everything I have ever written is in relation to this. I will write some more as soon as I can get a tourniquet on my wounds. Now the tourniquet is on, the blood is only pouring out of my mouth. So I was around 14 when I first decided to check out. This is complex because one may suggest I was depressed but in reality I was not. That is why it is important you stop feeling for a moment so you do not harm yourself. I was inclined to creativity. I was in gifted classes but I asked to be taken out of them because I wanted to just be normal or in with normal kids, or treated like everyone else. So in the US there are gifted classes but unfortunately ones who determine who is gifted are not in nirvana or right brain extreme. The reality is every single child is extremely right brain dominate and genius until the adults get their hands on them. Consider how Lama was chosen. He was three years old and the monks showed up at his "house" and said he is reincarnation of some god and let us take him and school him. The inside joke is every child has the mental faculties of a god compared to the ones that have been "educated" with scribe and even the ones educated with the scribe have Einstein intelligence if they just apply "Fear not". This is why the monks take someone who is very young. Remind yourself I am not religious I simply understand this. So when an adult has a child and that child has imaginary friends and lives in their own little world, that is in fact right brain dominate traits. Jesus was in the temple when he was child and considering he was a carpenters child, he may not have had much "education". In the land of the "sane" a person who has not been educated with scribe and math is deemed stupid but in the absolute reality world that is a good thing. It is good not to have that scribe and math crap because it kills right brain. So in reality adults see a child and say my child is strange so please medicate my child so they don't have imaginary friends. This means the adults cannot stand to see something so complex perhaps, because they are reminded they were raped mentally and it harms them, so they seek to "kill it". Don't try to argue that point because you will only harm yourself. So, by 14 I was ready to die because the script and math made my emotions very strong. I was already aware I was an outcast. That is why young kids kill their self, because they are aware they are not taking to the mental rape of the scribe aspect very well. Some kids take to it okay and sometimes they actually have what is known as a productive life, but that is only relative to productive in relation to a person with 10% cerebral function. I recall I told a friend I want to take a bunch of pills and become a ghost, when I was 14 and I was not sad or depressed I just wanted to get the hell out of here. I felt unwelcomed. That is why kids check out at a young age, they show up, see what is going on and say, I am out of here. This is because the script or math aspects start to do their work, the strong emotions are already kicking in, shame, embarrassment and fear of shame and embarrassment. Then you have children who are very depressed and the pharmacy and psychology "people" make a killing in relation to money. To hear them tell it, every single child in the universe needs their drugs. The pharmaceutical company makes the drugs and the psychology people push them and get kickbacks, and then children are ruined and these "people" have the balls to say, "Your child has a mental condition." When all they have to say is "Fear not" but then they would not make so much money.

I cast no stones on that matter.

So an adult see's a child who is acting ambiguous and determines that child is not normal and must need sedation and must be "evil" or "bad' or "sick" because that child is not like they are. So the adult is completely unaware they are neurotic as a result of being mentally raped by the scribe and math aspects of education. That is extremely funny. Apparently all of civilization to me now is an incredibly bad B rated horror movie. The monster shows up and the people all run, and separate, and all get picked off one by one. Perhaps it is best society mentally rapes children since society would perhaps be unable to handle so many geniuses at once anyway. Society as a whole still cannot figure out what the hell beings who were here 2500 years ago were saying. Society as a whole cannot even grasp what beings said 2500 years ago so it makes perfect sense they should not allow such beings to be. I read an article that said, Scientists still cannot figure out exactly what Einstein's theory of relativity means completely. Ignorance is very funny. Einstein was saying what Moses was saying, and Buddha was saying, and Jesus was saying, and Mohammed, Socrates and also what Freud and Jung said. Perhaps it is best to allow the dead to bury their dead. The "sane" are perhaps best left to their own devices. It is perhaps wise to just let them slaughter their selves because that is about all they are capable of doing. They simply destroy everything in their path, like a virus, that is not like them, perhaps . They have no ability to look more than one step ahead. They are simply blind to the fact they are blind. I will write infinite books and the greatest comment they will say is, "He misspelled the word cat, so he is dumb."

Perhaps compassion is, I just sit here and write and be very harsh in my words and in reality they never have a clue what I am even talking about. They come to conclusions like, "Maybe he needs to be medicated." They can never figure out exactly what it going on so they try their hardest with their elementary logic and come up with conclusions like, he must be a god, because they cannot grasp that I am simply a normal human being that woke up or snapped out of the neurosis caused by the script conditioning by getting over, or conditioning away from fear. It is perhaps difficult for me to put myself in the position of how I was when I had strong fear. I have no fear and no sense of time so it seems like I have been like this for many years but it has not been over nine months yet. I have no ability to grasp what fear is, so when I say, "Go sit in a cemetery at night alone to get over fear", they perhaps assume that is the most dangerous unreasonable suggestion in all reality. Being afraid of ghosts is not going to change anything. I cannot win no matter what I say so I just tell the truth as I see it. If I detect spirits and supernatural aspects I would suggest that, but no luck so far. If there is a supreme being no matter what you do, it is not going to make it blink. Scientists say we are lemur monkeys. Can any of these religious beings explain that one away? They cannot, that is why they keep their mouth shut when hard facts are revealed. They rely on elementary logic. That means nothing in contrast to how a normal human being not in neurosis thinks. Perhaps the delusional ones assume I am the devil now even though I explain what all their religious books mean.

On the other hand I perceive I do reach some people. This is a comment from a person who downloaded for free volume 2 off the pirate site I put my texts on and give them freely.

slackOR at 2009-07-06 07:08 CET:

"Is this VOLUME 1...and VOLUME 2?

When will your others be released?

These are all interesting reads, and I thank you and would encourage others to read and pass along....tnx"

This is what is known as feeding the masses and in Buddhist terms it is perhaps known as a seeker. This person overlooked all the horrible grammar and overlooked the fact I had no page numbers, and overlooked my inability to sequence sentences properly, and he just wants to know more. I personally do not remember exactly what I wrote in volume 2 but this person is a seeker. They will climb any mountain to read more. They are finding mental release. They sense something about the texts. "When will the other be released?" that is why I write infinite books and it is not for the dam money. So I decided to write myself to death because there is one person in this universe who has enough brain function to listen before judging. I do not care about the "logical" or the "reasonable" beings who attempt to convince a rock they are not a rock. I am quite certain there are ones in neurosis who will certainly proclaim I am evil and bad and harmful but they are not aware who they are dealing with. They perhaps perceive I play by their rule book because they cannot grasp right brain is the rule book. There are authors and there are thinkers and what separates the two is money. I don't write for money, that's why I can write. I don't write so someone will like me, I write so someone might think. I am far past the stage of needing someone to like me. I fell for that scam one too many times. One might suggest I catch more lost cheep as a lone wolf. That is all I need is some being to tell me what I can and cannot write in my diary. They publishers have suggested to me they do not publish books with grammatical errors. They are truly quite laughable. They are more concerned with making money than with content. They seriously do not even care about content, as long as the pile of shit smells sweet and they might make a few bucks. Perhaps money is in fact, in society today, far more important than a human beings or even six billion human beings. Six billion human beings are not worth a dollar because their combined brain power is still 10% because of the scribe. Leave well enough alone, is perhaps the greatest humor because it is saying, you have perfect offspring and then you ruin them by about the age of 14 with your "knowledge" schools because you don't apply "fear not". I laugh even harder when I signed off on volume six today and somehow when they converted the text file to "print ready", it made some of the worst "errors" in the universe, and some of these "beings" will look at that book and say "This book is horrible. I cannot even read one page, this is so bad and evil and ugly. This author is a total idiot." That is in fact exactly why I leave my diaries like they are. I do not want an abomination laying their hands on my diaries, I prefer they stay brain dead. I prefer they stay blind. I prefer they take their child to a shrink and fill it with pills until one day they come home and find their child hanging in the bedroom and then they can say to their self "I don't know what I did wrong. My child must have had mental problems." I prefer they experience that.

K. A. (14) allegedly took her own life for unknown reasons

What do you mean unknown reasons. The truth is you do not have the brain function to understand what the reason is. The reason is, you ruined that child and you killed that child by your actions when that child counted on you to keep them out of harm, you forsaken them. They counted on you to protect them and you have no brain function so you killed them, and you are unable to understand you did that because if you did understand you did that, you would kill yourself. So you just keep telling yourself you do not mentally rape children and you do not mentally destroy children, and you are not mentally raped yourself, and you are not mentally destroyed yourself. It is impossible a child of 14 would kill their self because they have no problems at 14 that would make them want to die, unless they got just enough script and math education to make those strong emotions start kicking in, and some children cannot handle all of those emotions.

Gen 3:17 "cursed is the ground for thy sake; in sorrow shalt thou eat of it all the days of thy life;"

Everything you touch is cursed and you will be cursed for all the days of your life, and you will suggest a child of 14 kills their self for unknown reasons because you will never say," I forced my child to kill their self because I did not protect them like a proper adult should protect their offspring", "I did not tell them to apply "fear not.". So now you understand why you never get to talk to me, you never get to see my picture, you never get to hear me speak, you never get to find out who I am.

One might suggest I do not ever want anything to do with you. One might suggest you are cursed and you are not aware you are cursed, but I am certainly aware you are cursed. You can break the curse but you are too afraid to do anything of value, and that is the curse. The curse is metal blindness and fear and you are too blind and fearful to ever break the curse. You are mentally blind and mentally fearful and the remedy is to face your fear, and you are to blind to do that, because the fear itself keeps you blind. You can have the entire universe, but you have to sit in a cemetery at night in the dark and fight the fear away, and you will say, "That is unreasonable and dangerous and I will never do that and would rather find my child hanging when I get home from work and then explain it was for unknown reasons." Certainly you may go insane from sitting in a cemetery at night all alone fighting you fear, but that is just as well. The cage you are in mentally right now is far worse than going insane. Granted that was harsh. If you wish to go to right brain to an extreme attempt some fear conditioning. I cast no stones on this matter.

I'm not coming to your rescue. I'm not going to help you see it through.
http://www.youtube.com/watch?v=kZzTJyt8m_0

So now we have established you are cursed because of the scribe and math education. The curse is you have 10% brain function relative to heightened awareness and mental clarity. A curse hinders normalcy.

So Moses said "Gen 3:17 "cursed is the ground for thy sake;" so everything you do is cursed and everything you touch is cursed, and everything you say and think and do is cursed. You had a curse put on you and it was not something you deserved but none the less you are still cursed. The first thing to understand now you understand you are in fact cursed is, "fear not". Firstly you are cursed so I want nothing to do with a person who is cursed. That is logical and a reasonable request. You stay away from me because I am mindful you are cursed and that means I have a right to defend myself from cursed people if they get near me. That is somewhere in the bill of rights apparently, under self defense. The second aspect of that rule is, if by a miracle of god you do break the curse, you will have extreme heightened awareness and become aware and you will become aware you are not ever allowed to speak to me because of who I am. Do you think I am arrogant or serious? Now that we have established you are cursed and that you are never allowed to talk to me, we can go on to the fun part. The remedy to the curse, apparently all curses have a remedy. Perhaps if a curse did not have a remedy it would be more along the lines of "you're doomed", so in that respect a curse is a good thing. So since you cannot understand anything I say I will recap.

Man invented written language.

It looked very good. Gen 3:6 "saw that the tree was good for food, and that it was pleasant to the eyes, and a tree to be desired to make one wise, he took of the fruit."

You got a good taste of the fruit of written language and it made you wise as long as the definition of wise is cursed. You have to decide to remain cursed or break the curse. You cannot rely on me to help you and you cannot rely on me to assist you, and you cannot rely on me to come to your rescue. You may die in the process of trying to break the curse, so you may just want to remain cursed. You are not allowed to suggest I told you how to break the curse. You are not allowed to tell anyone I tried to assist you, and you are not allowed to assume I am trying to assist you. I am not trying to assist you because I do not talk to you anymore. One might suggest your privileges have been revoked. You are simply on your own. One might suggest you are pretty far from being considered my friend, to put that in a math equation. You + apple + fear = cursed < Me − fear = not cursed.

To prepare yourself for the remedy you may have to say the word "perhaps" often and do a few practice sessions of watching a scary movie in your house alone and then turning off the lights and seeing how long you can sit there before you piss yourself like a frog does when it is picked up. In case you are wondering if I can sit in the dark after watching a scary movie, I in fact beat my fear of death itself, so I certainly do not piss myself like a little frogs does when it is picked up.

You have your entire life to prepare for the cemetery aspect of the curse breaking or you can seek the hottest coals and start with the cemetery aspect. Any one of these methods, even saying perhaps a lot, may cause you to become insane, and may even cost you your life, and all of your friends, and everything you have. You very well may literally go insane and die. Since you have slight brain function because you are in fact cursed, you may try to use your elementary logic and extreme fear retardation to choose a proper cemetery or haunted house, to use as a fear conditioning tool. This is a delicate part because you are cursed and so everything you determine is cursed. On the other hand I cannot advise you because I no longer speak to you. To get around that absolute reality I will monologue to myself and if your eyes glance over it and it reminds you of something you already knew you can determine you already knew this and so it will mean I did not assist you. If you do not get that reaction then just lie to yourself and pretend you already knew this. First off, this entire curse breaking aspect may seem rather harsh, but I assure you, in contrast to how I broke the curse, it is a walk in the park.

When I detect spirits with this heightened awareness I get goose bumps but I do not get scared. I am mindful they are there but I understand they wish they were me. Said spirits are attempting to steal my glory, one might suggest, psychologically speaking, so to speak, what have you. Granted those comments were infinitely out of context.

You must pick a cemetery that is reported to be haunted or a house that is reported to be haunted. Before you get to making a selection, you have to understand you probably will go insane and you may even die, depending on how dangerous the spirits in that place are. So now you can start to back away and accept the fact you are cursed and be "Gen 3:17 " in sorrow.. all the days of thy life;".

So if it is possible for you, attempt to use your elementary "cursed logic" and understand you have two choices in all of reality. You can remain cursed and in sorrow for the rest of your life, you can attempt to break the curse but that will cost you perhaps your life and definitely your sanity. You cannot understand anything I say so I will make it into a multiple choice.

Remain cursed and in sorrow for the rest of your life.

Attempt to break curse and possibly die but defiantly go insane.

Those are your only options. So the word "attempt" denotes you may not be able to break the curse. I certainly do not know. There may be no way to break the curse. I am not an authority and I do not talk to you anymore. I may just be dead and so I am just writing to no one. People suggest I am not dead but that is what death would be like. In death the illusions around me are not going to say, "Yes this is the afterlife." That would certainly kill my buzz, psychologically speaking, so to speak, what have you. This of course is in relation, well not really, but this is relevant, well not really, but this is something, perhaps. There is a comment. "The wise walks with their head bowed, humbled like the dust." Dust is in relation to dust to dust, humbled means they are willing to give up everything to have a chance to achieve nothing. Humbled denotes you have to be willing to die to break this curse and even then you may not break the curse so you will perhaps die for nothing. The police will find you in the cemetery or the haunted house and they will just assume you killed yourself or had a heart attacked because the spirits do not like people invading their privacy and graves. So simply expect to die and if you get lucky you will just go insane and everything you have will not matter after that. So now you can understand that you have to pay the piper to break a curse that was put on you even though you did nothing wrong, you got abused as a child and got a curse put on you as a result.- 6:15:57 AM

6:30:08 PM - If I cover one eye when I look at the world I will only be half blind.

"Four people face felony charges after authorities discovered that hundreds of graves were dug up and allegedly resold at a historic African-American cemetery near Chicago, Illinois, authorities said Thursday."CNN.COM

This is a complex situation here. "Let the dead(ones on the left) bury their dead(ones on the left)." That suggests physical attachment and also coveting which is a physical concept. So punishing people for digging up bones is perhaps a symptom of a society that covets physical things which is a left brain concept. Mohammed explained this when he said "The Jews and Christians are cursed because they make gave sites as places of prayer" something along those lines. That is coveting. So you see Mohammed was understanding that Jews and Christians in general did not get what Moses and Jesus was saying, They heard but did not understand, in general. Some certainly did get what Moses and Jesus was saying but in general very few did. Very few got what Buddha was saying and very few got what Mohammed was saying but that is the name of the game. I am suggesting to people if they have a strong sense of time and strong hunger they are in fact cursed by the script aspect, I am quite certain they will not take that very well even though it is beyond all understanding a total absolute fact beyond all facts. So my strategy is to not tell them that, I write to myself in my stupid diaries because they don't understand a dam thing I say anyway. I call it my "Don't even try because they won't get it anyway" strategy. The reality of the situation above is, society makes everyone left brain dominate which is very physical based thinking, with the scribe aspect, then touts physical things like materialism, then arrests them when they try to make money. People on the left are going to try to make money since they are conditioned into being very physically focused because they perceive they can be happy if they have enough money and that will fill that "void" they feel inside, which is in reality the "void" of their awareness that something is not right, in relation to they are no longer on the "right aspect" of the mind because the scribe aspect killed it.

So you see I am not trying to impress anyone with pretty books and well spelled books and pleasing words and love and happiness in my books because I am doomed because I am talking to the living dead. Granted that is out of context so I will write another book to clarify all the clarifications I clarified in this clarification. "Lunatic asylum" is simply far too compassionate. Nezchez or whatever the hell his name is, was infinitely more compassionate that I am. It is far worse than a lunatic asylum Nezchez. It is far worse than the "dead" as Jesus suggested. It is far worse than the "sane" as Buddha suggested. It is far worse than "infidels" as Mohammed suggested. I am unable to find a word to fully explain it beyond suggesting brain dead mole crickets. The word grasshopper would be far to compassionate . One might start to think if I say grasshopper that there is a chance in hell of making a dent in the situation. Brain dead mole crickets suggests I am unable to fix a mole cricket that has a dead brain, so I am mentally in a situation that I cannot win against that. A dead brain denotes I cannot fix it and that is a proper mental state to be in because if I tried even slightly I would destroy myself because I cannot ever win in this situation ever, into infinity. It is impossible to win when speaking to brain dead mole crickets. And that is how it is, how is was, and it how it always will be, into infinity.

Gen 15:1 "After these things the word of the LORD came unto Abram in a vision, saying, FEAR NOT... "

Fear not denotes, don't be afraid of the dark , don't be afraid of your body, don't be afraid to cuss, don't be afraid to break rules, try not to physically harm others, but don't be afraid of anything ever. DON'T HAVE FEAR BASED MORALS. DON'T HAVE PETTY RULES because if you do you will simply be afraid when you break them. Then your mind will be a little scared fearful pinprick. GOD FEARING is a bad thing. You fear god? Adam and eve were walking round naked and god did not strike them down. You just hang yourself in your little world of fear and being scared and that means I am going to take over everything because no one can compete against my cerebral abilities. So to all the holy rollers who have more rules and regulations to keep safe that the grains of sand in the sea, you stand no chance into infinity of ever reaching the right hand side that I sit on. You are afraid to blink wrong. Do you think your little morals rules are going to give you sight? You are delusional beyond all understanding. Your little moralistic stupidity rules are going to keep you blind for all eternity. Don't cuss. Don't say that. Don't be like that. You have no concept of wisdom because your mind is so full of fear because you are ashamed of the very thoughts that go through your head. You are ashamed of thinking things and so your mind has just shut off the "machine" aspect. You kill the "machine" aspect of the mind with all of you little vain "moral" head games you have collected over your lifetime. You feel evil if you say the word shit in public. You feel you will go to hell and be tormented by god if you say the word shit in public and in turn you "fear" as opposed to "fear not" so you do not understand a dam thing about the religious texts so never ever, ever speak of them again because you insult me, when you speak one word from the religious texts. I will sum that one up.

Rev 1:17 And when I saw him, I fell at his feet as dead. And he laid his right hand upon me, saying unto me, Fear Not; I am the first and the last:

I AM ON THE RIGHT ASPECT OF THE MIND BECAUSE I LOST MY FEAR WHICH IS A SYMPTOM OF THE SCRIPT BRAINWASSHING AND I AM THE FIRST AND LAST BECAUSE I HAVE NO SENSSE OF TIME SO I AM IN INFINITY AND INFINITY IS FISRT AND LAST STATE OF MIND.

Simply put, I do not care what your little pinprick logic thinks about what I write. I don't care what your pinprick logic suggests I am. I don't care what your pinprick understandings convince you I am because I do not pander to the dead on the left. I do not play your little pinprick moralistic word games because I do things you can never do. I don't try because if I tried even slightly, it would be far too easy. So I do not even correct my spelling or my grammar or even lift a finger to write these books because you might get the impression what right brain is capable of is something more than effortless.

Heb 13:6 "So that we may boldly say, The Lord(the machine, subconscious, right aspect, clarity) is my helper, and I will "not fear" what man(the left, fear based, infidels, darkness, vipers) shall do unto me."

Essentially my cerebral function due to the fact of the heightened awareness and the power of the right aspect of the mind in contrast to ones on the left, is god like, but in contrast to a human being who is not "cursed by fear", it is simply normal. I am a normal human being in relation to cerebral function because I faced my fears and got over them. I fear not so I have been blessed with being a normal human being. So you think very carefully about that. I am not hocus pocus, I am simply a normal human being now that I woke up from the curse of the scribe aspect as a result of getting over fear, namely fear of death or of perceived death. You are not bad if you wish to remain cursed and it is not improper if you wish to remained cursed. I was cursed also, and I accidentally broke the curse.

I won't be messing it up like the others did.

Minor adjustments depend on whether you understand infinity properly. My goal is to sound as arrogant as I can, and then publish the words, and perhaps that will shock me back into fear and sense of time so I can get the hell out of this place I am trapped in. I am simply experimenting with ways to get out of this place I fell into. If I can just say the right combination of words arranged properly I should be able to perhaps "get back to where I once belonged."

This is my take on laws. A law said I had to get educated into scribe and math. What that means is every single time the ones who passed that law and enforce that law and encourage that law breathe, it proves beyond a shadow of a doubt, I have infinite compassion beyond all understanding. Do not kid yourself. The Buddha of the age would not say arrogant things like that nor would the Messiah or the Medhi but Heimdall would easily say arrogant things like that because Heimdall is the go between, which means Heimdall is not on anyone's side. The "gods" and "man" want Heimdall to be on their side but Heimdall is in the middle or in limbo, so Heimdall is not something, or attached to the labels but is in fact nothing or nothingness. This of course is the characteristics of subconscious or extreme right brain. It is a chameleon or the role player. Now in order to maintain my "not on anyone's side" I will discuss how ones who likes war can create an army that can seldom be defeated.

I will do this because if you want to make war and kill people you should know how to do it properly so you don't look like the jaw bone of an ass. First the Generals have to have no fear because if they have any fear that means they have no brain function so the whole army is pointless or at the mercy of a retarded general. An army with a fearful General is an army in a lost cause. So every General in an army has to go sit in a cemetery and the most haunted cemetery and the darkest cemetery all by their self with no chance of getting help when the spirits start to attack them and if they show any fear during this entire night in the cemetery, they have to do it all over again. That's the only test of a good general everything else will come naturally after that test.

So then you get to soldier training. The point about a soldier is once they sign the dotted line they are the armies slave and the army can get them killed if they want to. So forget about basic training physical fitness insanity. You just put one soldier in a cemetery over night and leave him there and make sure there is no way he can get help if something happens. Give him no water or food or a radio or a phone. Leave him there overnight. They cannot talk to their self or whistle, they have to just sit. Once they pass that test they are a trained solider. Their heightened awareness will start working in about 3 months or so. This heightened awareness will be so great they will be aware of the enemy and know where the enemy is, that's just for starters. When you try to make a strong army using physical aspects like weight training and physical fitness, that is all wasted when the mental aspect is not 100%. When one become extreme right brained or subconscious dominate their body loses a sense of time and with it goes a sense of fatigue. This means a soldier will be wide awake much longer than a soldier with left aspect dominate. To put it in perspective. The Taliban says "We love death" which means they no longer fear or have fear so they have Allah on their side or "right aspect or subconscious aspect" which is exactly why they can use crappy guns and walk around in sandals and hold off the "most advanced" army in the world for going on nine years. Perhaps you can no longer grasp anything I say. What that really means is, 9/11 was simply a well laid trap as I recall mentioning in earlier crappy thick pamphlets and the allies have zero chance of ever winning because the allies do not have "allah" on their side as in right brain dominate aspect. You know that "god made man in his image" aspect of the mind. So you go ahead and keep sending our offspring into that death trap and you keep them in the left retarded aspect of the mind and keep the generals in the retarded left aspect of the mind, and all you are really doing is sending them to a certain death for no reason at all. You might as well just kill them here in the US so you don't have to waste money shipping their bodies back in cargo jets because there is no way in hell you are ever going to win against an army that has "allah" or right aspect of the mind on their side. Taliban may not take over the world and convert everyone but they certainly will never lose to the likes of some left brained fear based, 10 percent mental power, "being", that's a fact. I don't care who you think you are, you're mistaken if you think have a chance against them, just like you're mistaken when you thought you had a chance against the Vietcong. They did not fear death or lost their fear of death so they had "allah" on their side or right aspect of the mind or at least their generals did, that's why they just sent droves of soldiers at the US. So if you want to kill other people you do it and make sure you kill everyone and no emotions or feelings or mercy, of course you can't pull that off unless you have "GOD/subconscious" on your side, so you don't look like the half ass jaw bone of an ass. I will publish this and every single person who likes war will read it and if they use these methods they will have an army that can hardly be beaten ever and they will get a nice telepathic aspect through visions as a parting gift. So how important are the secrets the government keeps from everyone now? They have no secrets compared to the secret I give freely, they just perceive they have secrets but they only have foolishness. I will now discuss something relevant.

http://www.youtube.com/watch?v=EoYN0A0K-zY

In summation. Say the word "perhaps" a lot, condition away from fear, seek to be humiliated in non physical ways and between these three techniques that should mess you up plenty, psychologically speaking, so to speak, what have you, and you will always feel high so you won't need drugs to get high, and you won't eat too much food, and you won't have stress, and you will say things like Lama says when they ask him what reality is "North, South, East, West, Up and Down.", and when you look at the eyes of women even in pictures you will notice some sort of beam thing that makes you a total lush and then you will be so mentally and cerebrally freaked out you won't want to fight wars in the first place. If you detect any grammar errors in that last run on sentence please call me and let me know. See the reality is, somehow I was so hard core in conditioning away from my fear of death I ACCIDENTALLY went so extreme subconscious dominate, there won't be anyone who is going to be able teach me, and I do not care what you think may be able to teach me, you are simply delusional in your understanding about what you are capable of when you are extreme right brain dominate. I am. If you get a bit hardcore in your fear conditioning you can be the same way, you will understand everything you read and you will be very creative. Do you perceive the author is: a) Nothing b) Something c) Perhaps Something perhaps d) Perhaps Nothing perhaps. E) Perhaps perhaps, perhaps

The correct answer is: Perhaps indivisible, so to speak, psychologically speaking, what have you, such and such, and so forth, perhaps.

You get partial credit if you guessed: 2112

Gen3:10" I heard thy voice(words) in the garden, and I was afraid(Demotic & Dena side effect), because I was naked; and I hid(shame-knowledge side effect) myself. "

So you just go on with your delusions and fear, but never assume I am on your side, sunshine. I don't charge you properly for my words because your soul wouldn't cover the fee. If I needed your advice I wouldn't be Heimdall? 3:29:58 AM

4:10:09 AM – Due to the time I am spitting up many curses at this moment so I will try to pretend that calmer tempers can prevail and discuss foolishness.

The Neolithic Revolution happened perhaps 10,000 BC. So this is when man made things like irrigation and started forming cities around these inventions and started settling. Sometime in this period man invented "script" and "math". So mankind was around for all this time (maybe 200,000 years) without script and did not "record" history and then script came along and we started recording history because we no longer had the need to keep events verbal as in story tellers. We killed off the need to verbally communicate history when we figured out how to scribe things on paper and thus we had to teach everyone how to scribe, and of course that is very detailed focused in relation to many rules and a proper way to scribe and an improper way to scribe, and thus that is all left brain characteristics.

This is a comment I found about the Cherokee Indians attempt to make an alphabet and it is quite an interesting comment because the women mentioned is very close to what the Adam and Eve story suggests.

"Sequoyah's wife destroyed some of his early work on the syllabary because she thought it was "the devil's work," according to the New York Times article."

She thought the "letters or alphabet" work was the "devils work". One might suggest males should perhaps give the dominate gender of the species a bit more respect. I am mindful you have no idea what I am talking about because I have a speech impediment and the wisdom to not notice it. Someone said recently that I think too much and I fell out of my chair. In reality I understand I write so swiftly because I am trying to reach myself in relation to people who are at the mental stage I was at for 10 years, a very dark place and I recall I did not want to read any "self-help" stupidity. I did not want to read about god. I did not want to read about people who simply say love over and over and perceive that makes a dam bit of difference considering the state of mind I was in. So I am uncertain how fast I must write or what I must say to reach myself but I know one thing for a fact, saying "pray about it" or "have faith" or "take a couple of these pills" sure as hell aint going to reach me. So never assume I write my crappy books for the 'sane'. I write my crappy books for the only people in this universe who are in a mental state of humility and meekness, the suicidal and depressed. I do not know how I am going to reach them, in fact it is impossible because I didn't want to read any books when I was depressed and I didn't want to do anything but sit in my room and ponder the next way I was going to kill myself. So all you people who are just peachy keen, I don't even know who you are but I certainly know what you are.

http://www.youtube.com/watch?v=-r_wK7PG8YM

The human body is very resilient, and when it is not, it is good at decaying. Perhaps the great mystery is what am I supposed to do, if not write books? Apparently I am supposed to be teaching this great truth I have discovered, and if you figure out what it is please do not remind me because I seek ignorance at this stage since the accident.

7/10/2009 5:21:10 PM –
"A fool is wise in his eyes."
King Solomon
This comment is essentially suggesting relativity. You are wise if you think so but avoid taking a consensus. A person does not generally do things they perceive is foolish. Wisdom in your eyes may be foolishness in another person's eyes. I perceive the spirit of the things I suggest in general is wise but that does not mean it is wise on the scale of absolute wisdom. So many assume King Solomon had these vast mines full of gold but that is simply relative to the suggestion Buddha was fat. Buddha was fat with wisdom, King Solomon had vast riches of wisdom. To suggest a being in the extreme right or subconscious dominate is a collector of material possessions is perhaps an impossibility. Perhaps there are people looking for King Solomon's mines of gold just as there are people looking for the fountain of youth and the Holy Grail. These stories are simply contrast stories about ones wealth in the cerebral aspects not in the physical aspects. Solomon's comment alone proves to me he certainly was far more cerebral focused than materialistically focused. "It is easier for a camel to go through the eye of a needle than for a rich man to reach the kingdom"(subconscious/right aspect) dominate. This is strictly because one who reaches the dominate right aspect has the "physical focused" mindset silenced to a great degree. It perhaps has nothing to do with great self control in avoiding material things, it simply the mindset. Because of this aspect it is very difficult for me to ever suggest one on the left is evil or bad because it simply does not work that way. One on the left simply tends to be a bit more physically focused and one on the right tends to be more cerebrally focused. I am perhaps very biased against left aspect mindset because I was so left aspect focused it nearly cost me my life, so no other human being in the universe is going to be able to make an argument to convince me otherwise, no matter what they say. It is in the realm of possibility my mind simply turned off my physical satisfaction "sign posts" because my inability to achieve many physical material things was causing me to be depressed. Mentally I simply no longer "care" about my physical aspects like I use to or "care" about money or "care" about physical valuables. This goes all the way to the extreme where I am nearly "numb" physically. My taste is so altered I can hardly tell what I am tasting, my pain sensitivity is to the degree I no longer feel fatigue in any absolute way. Almost as if my body is just "numb" and anything beyond that is discomfort. The main problem with this wisdom concept is who is the high roller of wisdom? Who gets to determine what is wisdom and what is foolishness? That's the entire problem with relativity or perhaps that is the entire mystery. How does one determine what is absolute wisdom without coming across as arrogant and haughty. The answer is you cannot. Relative to me a person who fills a child with pills just because that child is slightly ambiguous or complex but not literally medically ill is a child abuser but relative to that person they may perceive they are wise to do that.

So there are two opposing viewpoints and one has to be wise but that is the problem. Relativity suggests both view points are wise relative to each observer and also both view points are foolishness relative to each opposing observer. So this means a society has to have a dictator of wisdom. That is perhaps what KING in King Solomon is suggesting. King Solomon is the "buck" as in the buck stops here. Eventually a society has to decide who has absolute wisdom and that is impossible because wisdom is relative to the observer and that means it is not possible to have absolute wisdom or a person who has absolute wisdom, so that negates the possibility of leadership.

A leader is not an authority they are simply a societies attempt to have an authority but in general even the people who elect that leader have issues with many things that leader does, because there are six billion points of view on the planet and they are all wise views "in the eyes" of each individual. So if one tries to elect me a wise man I will remind them, I am only wise based on my perception and they are a fool to assume I am wiser than they are. People essentially are their own King Solomon in their mind.

The comment "they know not what they do" is an accurate description but only from the point of view of that observer. One person is cerebral based mentally and one person is physical based mentally so the observations or conclusions are going to be opposite but not evil or bad but simply they will not align. So the comment "money has no power over me" is simply suggesting when a person with the right aspect dominate see's a bag of money their heart does not start to race and their mind does not start to come up with dreams of what they would do with that bag of money, and that is in contrast to one who is on the left and physical based who would start dreaming how what they would do, or what kind of satisfaction they could achieve with that bag of money. So the whole physical/cerebral "battle " is not about good or evil it is simply to contrasting mindsets than can never see eye to eye. For an author to write a book and the day it goes live they put it on a pirate site so people can download it freely is foolishness in contrast to one who is physical or materialistically focused because they are on the left. To a person on the left that would appear to be quite unreasonable and self defeatist. To one on the right it's not about the money so that action would be reasonable or logical or wise. Both people are correct in their perceptions of that scenario relative to the comment "whatever floats your boat." Your mindset determines your fruits. In this case I am in extreme cerebral mindset or on the extreme right aspect of the brain so my mind does not see money and start getting illusions of grandeur, on the contrary my mind see's money and has an aversion to it. One might suggest it reminds me of my past and so I do not have a desire to covet it or to accumulate it. That is not suggesting I am some wise man that is in fact suggesting my mindset is not physical based. This can apply all over the physical spectrum, to clothes, and looking "pretty" and even deeper aspects, as in looking to be accepted, and looking for medals, and looking for peer groups to associate with. So the left aspect of the mind is looking for a "herd" to run with and the right aspect is contrary and a "lone wolf". The problem with that is the left aspect likes to be a part of herds so they tend to elect that lone wolf to lead them. One can think back in history at all these "great leaders" and they can understand they were perhaps lone wolfs and people on the left allowed them to "herd" them. Washington is a good example among others. At the end of the day Washington went back to his farm. So Washington became this great leader and lead the revolution but in the end he went back to his farm because he was a lone wolf. Many artists and creative thinkers are like this because right brain is the creative aspect and that means these people tend to want to be alone, by the nature of their mindset. So this creates a problem because Washington was this great leader but then he suggested you are free to peruse your own happiness. If you are free to pursue your own path to happiness then why have a leader at all, because a leader is supposed to make decisions for you. That is exactly why Washington was not very high on government.

"Government is not reason; it is not eloquent; it is force. Like fire, it is a dangerous servant and a fearful master. "

George Washington

One could also replace government with authority figures. So Washington leads this revolution and establishes this nation and then suggests there should be a government to run the day to day aspect of the nation and then he says government is bad. He says Government of authority is not reason and that means crazy or insane, simply because, one cannot have freedom to pursue what they perceive is happiness if they have an authority figure standing over them telling them what they can and cannot do.

And that is why Freud said this.

"America is a mistake, a giant mistake."

Sigmund Freud

The whole concept of Freedom is negated once you start have a powerful authority figure as in a government. It is essentially saying, You are free relative to the power of the authority that keeps you a slave. You are free relative to your inability to see the bars of the cage you are in. The whole concept of a government is a contradiction to freedom. It is a paradox. It is true we need laws and it is true we need freedom. Both concepts are contrary to each other. Basically the premise of freedom is a delight but applying it to reality is impossible because freedom is relative to the observer. My freedom is relative to the mental mindset of the majority which is in the left mindset. The left mindset is all about fear. The left mindset is afraid of the dark, so it is impossible there could be anything less than tyrannical laws passed based on the premise that we need to be in a cage to be safe from the monster outside the cage. So I am a minority at the mercy of the majority that is afraid of the dark, and passes laws based on the fact they would rather be safe than free. So America at a stage it is not freedom at all in any concept of freedom it is just a well disguised tyranny and people convince their self the tyranny is better than being unsafe.

Essentially it is more along the lines of, screw liberty I want security. Then to combine the script and math side effects which create a person very prone to fear tactics and one essentially is unable to ever suggest this is the land of the free at this stage because freedom is scary and unsafe. Freedom is chaos and anarchy; Tyranny is security and predictability. So we have this balancing act going on here called checks and balances but the reason that is not real anymore is because the population is "educated" into the left aspect of the mind and so the entire nation is simply very scared and willing to give up freedom when a pin drop's in a dark room. It is as if a single word spoken by an authority can make the population so afraid they are willing to give up all freedom to make that authority figure stop saying that scary word.

This authority figure understands what the fear words are that work the best. The authority figure suggests "terrorist" and all the little scared left brainers sign away all freedom, privacy, and all vestiges of freewill instantly in their mind, to make that word terrorist go away. I will clarify what Freud said. America is as free as the fear the education system instills in its citizens. So in general to even suggest America is free is insanity.

These tribes that live in the Amazon, that is what freedom is and America is not even within light years of that freedom and so freedom is just a big joke. America used to be free about 200 years ago but America today has nothing to do with freedom it is simply a fear based, money making opportunity for the elite. People on the left attempt to use their elementary brain logic and suggest America is the freest country in the world. They do not even have a concept of freedom anymore. Here is what the reality is, you are born and by law forced to get educated and that in turn turns your mind into a fear based pinprick of thoughts, and then if you do not jump on the wheel to make the elite rich, you are an outcast and deemed a threat. If you get in "line" or you are treated in an unbiased fashion, your whole entire life means nothing to you or to anyone around you. That is what America is today, if you doubt that, you simply are not longer among the mentally living. You are a sheep because the education made you a sheep and you are too blind to even believe that, so never say the word freedom again because the only thing you know about freedom is how to spell it.

One in America is reduced to a set limit of professions and all of the them are essentially based around this "script and math" education system. I could suggest the powers that be are not aware the education system is making everyone brain dead but I understand that is a delusion. The book 1984 is simply suggesting that the powers that be operate best when people are afraid and fearful and the best way to make people afraid and fearful is with education. Once a person is educated into the left hemisphere of the mind the powers that be only have to do one thing. They just say "boo" and everyone jumps on the wheel. I am quite certain the powers that be are perhaps going to "find something" to lock me up for because of these books. Certainly I have broken some sort of law by this stage in the books but the reality is, I am the bait, I am not late, I don't hesitate, I seal fate. Perhaps the only wisdom that can be counted on is: Your freedom is relative to your fear. - 7:22:23 PM

"The highly controversial no-warrant surveillance program initiated after the September 11 terrorist attacks relied on a "factually flawed" legal analysis inappropriately provided by a single Justice Department official, according to a report to Congress on Friday."

You can go on and on and tell everyone everything is just fine, but the reality is, you do not have the brain function to determine anything relative to what is fine and what is not fine, thanks to your education indoctrination, so you just keep your mouth shut because I am already embarrassed enough you are allowed to speak at all.

"Pakistan's military has declared that not only is it in contact with Afghan Taliban leader Mullah Mohammed Omar but that it can bring him and other commanders to the negotiating table with the United States."

This is a test. If the US does not speak to this leader of the Taliban it is definitive proof the US is not America but simply a tyrant that only desires to keep the wars going so that it can have a premise to keep everyone scared and have a premise to keep passing laws, to cancel out any remaining freedoms. In reality there are no remaining freedoms it is all tyranny from this point on. The very fact I write stupid books and suggest humanity as a whole ruined itself mentally because it embraced "script and math" to tightly and has not used anti-venom to conditioning to negate away the bad side effects of this invention is perhaps the most far flung sinister assumption in the history of mankind, bar none. And that is what separates me from all other human beings in the universe, I understand that script aspect ruined us mentally as a species, unquestionably, and Heimdall does not need an experiment to prove it because I understand it has ruined us as a species mentally and there is perhaps no way to ever go back to how we were before that invention. The comment: " Some things you can never take back.", perhaps explains my sentiments exactly. Sentimentality is a symptom of the script neurosis. Buddha called it attachments and the bible called it coveting and idolatry. Heimdall calls it brain dead mole cricket sickness. You build a cemetery to the ones who have been killed in a war and then you tout it as if you care, and then a child see's that cemetery and that parade for all the dead offspring that got hoodwinked to die in a stupid war, encouraged by the powers that be, and that child thinks, "One day I will die in a war and people will idolize me." Perhaps you base your whole existence over a god dam corpse in the ground, but people who are conscious understand that's a part of the deal, so there is no point in even marking the grave, because they get over the attachment the moment that person dies. The conscious do not spend the rest of their life crying over spilt milk. Someone dies and the whole country goes into mourning, which only proves the whole country is in neurosis, because they are all so full of attachments and idolatry, they perceive the dead are more important than the living. Are you starting to get a slight idea why Jesus made dam sure no one would ever find his body. Do you really think he rose from the dead? Perhaps you are so stupid you think a physical creature rose from the dead and flew into heaven. Apparently my faith in your intelligence means nothing.

The last thing in the universe Jesus would do is come back to the world of neurotics that killed him. You do not get anything because your brain is turned down to .00001 power. Granted it's not your fault but none the less you will defend the ones who mentally raped you because you determined you probably deserved to get mentally raped to begin with. You probably think you are not as smart as Moses and Jesus and Mohammed and Einstein because they had special genes. Is that what the brain dead retards told you? You should avoid listening to brain dead retards because they are brain dead retards. You let the dead bury their dead, you pay no attention to the dead. They are dead and gone so they mean nothing and never will mean anything but a coveting tool for the brain dead. You should not feel sad when someone dies, can you even grasp that? If you feel sadness when someone dies it is proof you are not conscious but in fact unconscious and in neurosis from the script conditioning. That is a fact. Can you grasp that? I will clarify, no matter who dies ,no matter how close they are to you, if you get sad and lonely and start crying you are in fact in neurosis and mentally unstable. Can you even grasp that? Am I so far away from you I sound like a god? Do you think when someone died early on in our species development the whole clan just collapsed in tears and misery and everyone started crying and their whole life was ruined? Do you think people in that clan killed their self when another member died?

You are perhaps so far in left field you need to first just consider yourself damaged goods. That is your only hope. You are damaged goods and you may be able to recover some brain function in your life time maybe. That is about as good as it gets. That is a symptom of how powerful this script aspect has damaged your mind. You cry over dead people, that is how damaged your mind is. You do not cry when you step on an ant yet you cry for years when a loved one dies, that is not logical that is neurotic. You are in total neurosis and there is nothing in the universe that is going to help you get out of neurosis but you. I am certainly not going to help you because I am wise enough to not get near people who are cursed. I got myself out of the neurosis in a way that you are unable to imagine and no one was there to help me. No one was there but me. I had to climb out of the pit myself and so do you. So you like challenges and you think you are tough shit, well, I love people who think they are tough shit. You are not even in the ballpark of tough in you neurotic state of mind, you cry over dead people. You are a joke. You can quote me on that. The machine doesn't pander to neurotics.

I am either the devil himself or I am god himself in contrast to the neurotics and whichever you think it is, makes no difference at all, because your still in neurosis. You are still in neurosis no matter what you think about me. I heard a lot of crap from proposed wise men who preach the merits of mercy and compassion and I realize they are still in neurosis. They say "but don't ever cuss cause that's evil." So you see, consciousness is the absolute extreme of right brain and that means no morals and no class. That means a person who understands the definition of "Sticks and stones may break my bones but words will never harm me." Do you understand what the word NEVER means? Did you brain washing teach you what never means? I do not think you know what never means. But words will NEVER harm me. There are six billion people on this planet who have no idea what never means, because they go around passing laws against saying words, so they are in full blown neurosis caused by the script apple they ate off of, forced by law of their "governments" that are only there to protect them.

Maybe you understand why I do not give a rat's ass about anything you say ever. Everything you ever say to me means zero to me. I let it all go in one ear and out the other. You just think real hard about what cemetery you are going to go sit in overnight all alone. You may die and you certainly will go insane, that is a fact but there is a 1 in a billion chance you may wake up if you are infinitely lucky. That is how deep the neurosis you are in is. Do not ask your friends what they think and do not ask your psychologists, and do not ask your clergy, and do not ask your mother, they are all in neurosis. I will repeat that. Everyone you know is in neurosis and so their advice is simply "cursed". Now you know what I mean when I say, you are on your own. I do not want anything to do with you because you as Moses explained are cursed. Can you blame me for not wanting to go around someone who is cursed? Would you go around a rabid animal? You are cursed and I cannot break that curse for you, so I have no reason to speak with you. I just write my books for me because I cannot help you. I have to focus on the log in my eye because I cannot take the log out of your eye. The proper way to look at it is, taking the log out of my eye almost killed me. It may kill you trying to take the log out of your eye, it most certainly will drive you insane, so your only chance is to let go of life all together, mentally. It is like the prodigal son story. You have to tell everyone you know you are going to the cemetery over night and you may die, and goodbye. And when they try to stop you, understand the dead want you to remain dead with them because misery loves company. Better yet. do not tell anyone because they are as Moses explained "Gen 3:17 "in sorrow …. all the days of thy life;". They love you so you will stay like they are. I am not talking about a couple of your friends, I am talking everyone you know in your entire life. You can quote me on that.

They do not want you to wake up because they do not want to wake up. I will keep writing my books but I cannot help you. If you get lucky and wake up your heightened sense of awareness will enable you to detect the ones on your side but you must be careful because some of them are also not fully awake. The ones who wake up fully tend to go temples because they cannot handle living among the dead. Perhaps you are starting to understand breaking the curse is a bit more complex than breaking a curse in the movies. Once you break the curse if you get infinitely lucky, you discover you are surrounded by insane people in neurosis. I find that quite funny. I am quite certain on the scales of the norms of society I am defiantly the most insane person in the universe. I have been in Nirvana for eight months and I cannot go any further back in history to find more things to understand. I understand everything there is to understand about civilization and where it went wrong. Life itself is just a bore now. So now you understand what I mean when I say "I messed up big time in my last attempt to kill myself." I screwed up royally. I am not the blessed one I am the cursed one. I am cursed with understanding and the rest of the world is cursed with ignorance. One might suggest that creates an epic battle. Me against six billion and all I can use is words and the six billion can use physical weapons. And the reality is, they do not stand a chance in the hell they are in. They are in mental hell and they have no chance in hell. Perhaps that would make good plot line for a book. I am going to go play my video game because I just forgot why I even write books anymore. My words get a little bloody after midnight, one might suggest.-7/11/2009 2:05:43 AM

You give Caesar what is his and you give me what is mine. Vengeance is mine. I will now discuss something of importance. I just keep "seeing" this same comment in my head over and over. I am not sure who said it but it's along the lines of : One day man is going to invent something and it is going to have unintended consequences. I just have to laugh because one day was about 5000ish years ago. So clearly this is all a joke and it is on me. This cannot be real. It is as if all of civilization has all these clues about what went wrong right in front of its nose, and everyone essentially is blind to them. It is simply far too funny that we could have messed ourselves up so badly from a seemingly harmless invention called script and math. You may not even believe that those two inventions screwed up all of civilization. That is even funnier that you would even doubt that for one second. It is all just the biggest joke anyone could ever imagine. We are truly our own worst enemy. All of these problems from stress to drug addiction to hate and war, killings and murder, stealing and anger, bitterness and religious wars , we brought all of that on ourselves because of this one invention called script and math.

One can't come up with a better joke than that in all eternity because it proves that we can destroy our selves, because we can make tools that appear to better ourselves but deep down they have side effects that can destroy us. All the wars in the last 5000 years are because script was invented and made people control freaks and coveters, in need to control land and resources and control others because control is a left brain aspect and that left brain aspect is encouraged when one learns script and math.

Perhaps your mind is so closed and warped and in neurosis you cannot even imagine that let alone understand that is absolute fact. Think about all the people who are in jail because they used drugs so they could experience the right aspect of the mind they were robbed of because of the laws that make script mandatory, and think about all the kids who are mentally shy and afraid and have a host of emotional problems because the script conditioning isn't taking very well. Think about all the people who are stressed out to the point they have heart problems, and they over eat, and they get their faces cut so they feel like they are important. That is what that one invention 5000 years ago did to mankind. You probably do not even think I am a human being at all. You probably think I am a god of some sort to understand all of this effortlessly. Do you think I have notes? Who do you think my teacher is? Do you feel like you are being toyed with like a cat toys with a mouse? You would be wise to feel you are being toyed with like a cat toys with a mouse, before he eats it. One might suggest infinity is extremely boring so I have no choice but to pass my time. I just make some casual drop ins from time to time and give the mice something to try to figure out for the next 5000 years or so. Life doesn't care if you cannot keep up with my logic and more importantly death doesn't care either. Let's face the facts here. How do I know what I know? One might suggest I am interested in what your opinion is in relation to how I know what I know when I didn't know these things before the accident. What's your hypothesis? I am dying to hear your complex logical opinion. Perhaps you have just the prescription in mind for me. Perhaps you will fix me right up with a one hour therapy session. I have to write about something so I might as well just toy with you a bit. To be honest I am out of shit to write. Perhaps I will go back into converting wise quotes from dead people. Converting wise quotes from dead people makes good filler. I don't really have to go past the story of Adam and Eve because if you don't get that parable you won't get anything after it. If you do not get the meaning of that parable you become what is known as "they hear but do not understand". So it is rather pointless to even discuss the religions tied to the Torah because one has to remedy the problem indicated by the story of Adam and Eve. Perhaps it is best you do not understand what I am saying. Perhaps it is best I have a speech impediment and I am unable to detect it. I am only left with two options. I can fill my thick pamphlets with cuss words or I can crack jokes and toy with the mice. That is my only two options. I mean those are my only two options. Who really knows, it is quite impossible for me to use this defunct time based language anyway. It is not even important I correct any of my grammar because all the proper grammar in the universe is not going to wake you up. I do not even know if I want you to wake up. I have grown fond of reading about all the killings that happen each day that are totally avoidable if only people had brain function and were not in such a deep neurosis. If you want to slaughter everyone that will give me something to write about because at this stage in my thick pamphlets I have pretty much exhausted known civilization. Perhaps I will go into detail in the books of the dead by the Egyptians, of course that is just explaining what the parable of Adam and Eve is explaining. So that is rather pointless. I am kind of trapped here to write infinite books and no one has hung me on a cross yet, but I have already covered everything one needs to know about everything. Everything is a symptom of the tree of knowledge incident. All the lemur monkeys are asleep. That pretty much sums it up. I will now discuss something relevant.- 5:27:39 AM

It's very hard for Todd to sound arrogant since he already admitted he tried to kill himself 30 times and failed, in his previous very poor pamphlets. So perhaps the wise quote from that is. Failure is no justification for arrogance. I'll try that one again just for kicks. Arrogance and stupidity are often lovers but seldom friends.

Ecc 11:9 Rejoice, O young man(a child who has not yet had the script conditioning), in thy youth(pre brainwashing); and let thy heart cheer thee in the days of thy youth(be happy before the adults mentally rape you with their "knowledge training"), and walk in the ways of thine heart(right aspect the heart of the brain), and in the sight of thine eyes(feeling through vision): but know thou, that for all these things God will bring thee into judgment(eventually the adults are going to force you into education and rape you mentally and ruin you for the rest of your life with the script and math inventions).

7/11/2009 9:03:06 PM – A message to ones after I am gone.

I have determined I cannot reach the ones who are alive while I am alive. I have determined I cannot reach them because the neurosis they are in is far too deep seeded. This generation will pass and is determined to be a lost generation. So I am leaving this message for ones who come after my generation or after the generation when I was alive. I will attempt to sum up what I understand about our species. Human species is simply an animal. We developed strong brains and learned how to make tools a bit faster than other species. These tools worked out and many were great inventions which assisted our species to progress in positive fashions. We lived relatively peacefully for many thousands of years and the tools we invented progressed and became more efficient. Much of the tool making came from the right aspect of the mind or hemisphere because that aspect of the brain is denoted by its creative ability. It is perhaps important you are able to detect a sorcerer.

Act 13:8 "But Elymas the sorcerer (for so is his name by interpretation) withstood them, seeking to turn away the deputy from the faith."

A sorcerer is a person who makes money or peddles influence by creating or suggesting supernatural aspects as their cornerstone.

Act 13:6 And when they had gone through the isle unto Paphos, they found a certain sorcerer, a false prophet, a …, whose name was Barjesus:"

This is suggesting a person on the "left" who was peddling supernatural suggestions as a foundation to influence others. A psychic may hold a séance for money and then suggest they can communicate with the dead, so the showmanship is for the money. A "religious" leader may throw around the word god and afterlife and then suggest they need your money to continue their "teachings". They are false prophets because they do not understand the religious texts they are making all their money off of. They are yes men and they are sugar coaters. They will say whatever they have to say to get their cult members to fork over the dough. So they are easily detected because they tend to be authorities on the afterlife and even more profound they tend to be authorities on god. So they tend to thrive on ones in extreme left brain because ones in extreme left brain tend to want to attach to things and covert things and idolize things. Pushing supernatural beliefs and god belief is in fact idolatry. The kingdom is the right aspect of the mind and that denotes that is your focus and that is the "log" that needs to be conditioned. So all of these "teachers" who suggest supernatural aspects are simply sorcerers and false-prophets attempting to take money from people with their words. They will say whatever they have to about supernatural aspects for a few dollars more. They essentially use supernatural aspects as fear tactics. "Give me more money and you will be saved.""Give me more money and you will be okay in the afterlife." That is simply extortion so they are in fact false prophets because their fruits reveal them as false prophets. One aspect to consider is they will never say they are wrong because that would hinder their money making potential. They will never say bad words or cuss words because they are aware that might impact their money making scheme. So in fact they are simply hiding behind supernatural aspects to make a living and this is strictly left brain thinking. They have many rules and laws and are afraid to ever say the wrong thing because they are unable to grasp, no words can harm anyone ever, and there is no such thing as a "sin" because a sin is simply an attribute of the ones on the left aspect of the mind.

These false prophets tend to exhibit many of the "sins" greed, hate, bitterness, idolatry, envy, lust for money. Ones on the right aspect understands no one is allow to be a teacher, let alone charge to communicate because ones who are properly on the right, understand they are simply in dialogue with their self which denotes they are working on their "log" or their mental condition, and sometimes that is around other people but to charge money for it denotes they are no longer assisting their self. I publish my books and they are for sale but I remind reader they can get them for free and I make sure I have them on places they can get them for free. So you see that is a paradox. I sell the books. and in the books I explain where to get them for free. The moment a person starts charging for their "comments" is the moment they stop progressing mentally and begin speaking for attention or acceptance of others so their thoughts are censored. They simply no longer think for their self. They are simply speaking what they perceive other people want to hear, so those other people will accept them. The important thing to remember once you get on the right side is, there are no rules set in stone because that may hinder one's own progression. That is what it is all about, mentally climbing the mountain all the way to the right. Its mental conditioning and one has to try very hard to remind their self others are simply tools to test out words on to assist the initial person to climb a little higher to the right aspect of the mind. One way to look at it is every rule is on the table and every rule is off the table, this allows one a wider variety of options.

Gal 5:20 "Idolatry, witchcraft, hatred, variance, emulations, wrath, strife, seditions, heresies,"

Gal 5:21 "Envyings, murders, drunkenness, revellings, and such like: of the which I tell you before, as I have also told you in time past,7that they which do such things shall not inherit the kingdom of God."

Idolatry is simply coveting material aspects and ideals. this is strictly a left brain characteristic. Lefters will idolize a grave, a grain a sand, gold, power, rules, regulations. These are simply symptoms of ones on the left. Witchcraft is someone who says "God will send you to hell for that." They tend to use supernatural suggestions to inflict damage on others and also to manipulate favor from ones they wish to impress. Drunkenness is suggesting drugs use which is a symptom of left brain because when one is extreme right brain they are "drunk" all the time, but that doesn't mean they wouldn't get drunk, so they tend not to need drugs. Being high on a drug is going over to right brain for a limited time, one who is right brained to the extreme tends not to need drugs, because drugs cannot get them high like they can to ones on the left. So these are more symptoms of left brain characteristics than actual laws or rules, they are sign posts to detect ones on the left. Hatred is a state of mind that can only be achieved by ones on the left. I am able to become angry but that is caused by the extreme gnashing of teeth from the extreme concentration of understandings I come across. I am unable to maintain hate because hate is a state of mind and the processing of being extreme right brain will not allow one to settle. Ones on the left can go through years and years hating things. They hate certain people or hate certain ideals and they hate these things for their whole life, and that is a symptom they are on the left, one on the right cannot maintain these concepts for very long because the processing is so fast, one can only achieve phantom emotions such as hate for a small period of time.

Variance denotes quarrel or argument. This is a complex aspect but it falls in line with hate. One on the left may suggest something and the one they are talking to may not agree with it, and so that initial one may hate that person. This is in relation to the left brains "herd" mentality or need to attach to things. On the contrary one on the right can argue with another person but they are unable to achieve hate, and many times they argument ends with both people who are on the right saying "perhaps", instead of hating the contrary argument to theirs. This variance is in line with the Torahs suggesting the "adversary". The ones on the left do not like people who do not agree with them. They may act polite and act pleasing but in their mind they hate people who do not fall within their understood beliefs. One on the right has a mindset that, everything anyone says to them is a possible emotional conditioning comment so they tend to see everything for a reason. Someone who disagrees with one on the rights comments may in fact give that person on the right something to consider, so they would never achieve hate but only a chance of further understandings.

There is clearly a strict double standard but it is not on a shallow race, creed, religious aspect but on which aspect of the brain is dominate. And left and right aspect of the brain are total opposites in characteristics so it is not racist because it is true. There would be no right aspect of the brain if it did the same thing as the left aspect. So thus there is certainly a double standard, people on the left act differently than people on the right, that is fact and unquestionable. I am not pleased with how I treated myself when I was on the left but as far as other people, I have much difficulty determining who is on the right or the left because when I see people or I read their words, they are all wisdom or perfection so I tend to have to ask people, "How long have to been in nirvana?" so I am what is known as a blind man. I can detect wisdom in every comment every person makes so I am a very poor judge, so to speak. This is why my mindset has to be "I assume everyone else is crazy" because I see everyone is wise and perfect. I see everyone is exactly the same as me, mentally, but that is an illusion because a vast majority are in fact on the left from the scribe neurosis. Left Brain simply needs to attach, needs to covet, needs to be accepted into groups, or a herd mentality. One person on the left says "I know there is god and my concept of god is righteous" and then another person on the left tends to emulate that person and the next thing you know we have world wars and we are slaughtering each other because one person on the left convinced another person on the left that they would be accepted if they subscribed to that their personal ideals. Basically emulations denotes one who does not think for their self, and left brain denotes one who tends to attach as opposed to be a lone wolf, in relation to their understandings. It is far easier for ones on the left to let others do their thinking for them. They tend to want to be controlled. In contrast ones in the extreme right tend to not want to be controlled or are very high on freedom.

Wrath is a complex aspect but it is similar to hate in relation to one on the left may have been trespassed against and they will desire vengeance mentally and reach a state of vengeance mentally. Ones on the right can pretend to be angry and wrathful but they can only have passing states of mind because they process or have thoughts so swiftly they tend to forgive and forget not because they are humble but because their mind will wander away from wrath swiftly. Simply put, the left is capable of holding a grudge and one on the extreme right is unable to hold a grudge. I can write in my thick pamphlets how angry I am and wrathful and then I go out to eat and look at people and I say, everything is perfect and past is past, and I can do that swiftly and then work back to being angry and wrathful but only for moments.

There is simply too much brain processing going on to remain in any one state of mind like wrath or holding a grudge. The processing will not allow one's mind to rest on its laurels thus no real chance of holding a grudge and so no real chance of holding onto wrath.

Strife is in line with wrath, it is a sustained or vigorous conflict, essentially a grudge. Seditions is also in line with a grudge, it is simply a scheme that tends to be against others in relation to say one religion against another or one group against another group. This is complex but what is important is the wrath and grudge aspects are maintained in ones on the left. This is a symptom of the left brain "knowing" anyone who is not like they are is bad or evil. Ones on the right tend to not be able to form such seditions because they tend to want to have a lone wolf mentality, or freedom, or they are pleased to be with their self so they tend not to form packs or sects or cults.

Heresy is simply intolerance of other religions or other races or other belief systems. For example the Christians do not approve of Muslims and Muslims do not approve of Jews and neither of these religions approve of Buddhism. That is what Heresy is. Everyone who is not like me is evil. That is strictly left brain because left brain is all about labels and isolation, and right brain see's everything as a whole. I see all of the mentioned religions are speaking the same message and that is in line with seeing everything as a whole, so one who has wrath against any of the these big religions or beliefs systems is clearly on the "left hand side of "god" " and the Torah, New testament, Quran suggest those beings who wrote those books were on the "right hand side".

This is exactly why Mohammed said Jesus and Moses' teachings were proper and he went on to improve on those teachings. So that proves he saw everything as a whole. Some may suggest Mohammed's teachings are better than Jesus and Moses' teachings and that proves they certainly are not on the right because all three teachings are saying the exact same thing. These teachings are not better or worse they are simply different attempts to say the same thing. Moses had his strategy and so did Jesus and so did Mohammed but the spirit of what they said, was exactly the same. This is simply because the right brain is too complex to put into words easily. There are many contradictions and many different things to cover. Mohammed said do not have wrath, and this passage above says do not have wrath, but it needs much clarification because right brain people can have wrath but only for a moment at most and left brain people can have wrath for their entire lifetime, so both can have wrath but wrath is different in both. It is simply too complex to explain even in infinite books.

Envying is simply idolatry and idolatry is simply coveting and coveting is simply attachment. This is a left brain characteristic. A left brain person see's someone they envy and then they start to covet them in their mind and then they start to act like them and before you know it they dislike their self because they wish they were that person. One on the right is a lush, they are pleased with everything they see but they cannot hold onto that state of mind for very long so that envy does not fester in their mind and thus they tend not to covet things. So in some respects this right brain dominate aspect is very dangerous because a person longs to attach to others and pretty much anyone they see, but it tends to fade swiftly, so it is not a slow progression to envy, it is a instant progression to envy but then the mind forgets and move on swiftly. So to end these traits is the comment "that they which do such things shall not inherit the kingdom of God." Is simply saying these symptoms are indicative of ones on the left as opposed to ones on the right which is the man upstairs which is "god" aspect of the mind. I tried to harm this state of mind with drink and I got very drunk but mostly motor skills were harmed but not so much the mental clarity, so I essentially just got bad motor skills. I went to sleep but the clarity was not harmed and I did not feel the euphoria because I am in right aspect. Simply put, drugs do not get me high, but when I talk in chat rooms many people say "What drugs are you on." Because I am naturally high as a kite, I am wide awake and I very alert, I have many "spiritual journeys" in my mind 24/7. So these comments are more in relation to symptoms of people who are not right brain dominate. Drugs do not work when you are all the way to the right because drugs are taken by people on the left to go further to the right but its only temporary and to make it permanent one needs some hard core fear conditioning so to speak. So if one has a drug addiction go sit in the darkest scariest cemetery over night and if you survive within a few months or so, you will no longer need drugs because you will be high all the time. That is a fact, but it perhaps is more difficult to do than I perceive because I have no fear and so that does not seems very scary to me, but I am certain I would perhaps not do that if I was in the mental left state I was before the accident.

I recall I used to be very afraid of the dark after I watched a scary movie, and that is what is so difficult about this fear conditioning, because the fear in the mind of left brain people is very real to them and so they probably will not condition away from it and so I am reduced to talking to myself in my diary because I am suggesting things no person on the left would perhaps even consider, because they perceive it is "dangerous". Simply put, I suggest things only a space alien would suggest in contrast to people on the left. It will be very scary in that cemetery but in reality that is because you have much mental residue from the scribe and math conditioning you have to clear out. You simply are not going to get to the right and into the light for free in fact it is going to cost you everything you have emotionally speaking. That's a nice way of saying you do not know what tough is and what a challenge is, you just perceive you do. The price is everything you mentally have. You cannot do it half way and once it is done you aint going back. The kingdom is within, that denotes the hardest battle you will ever fight in your life is between your ears and you have to do things you perceive you cannot do, and you should not do, because they appear unreasonable when in fact they are reasonable. They appear insane when in fact they are sane. Many illusions in your head are tricking you and harming you but you may perceive they are safety or right when they are unsafe and dark. The last thing I remember is I took a handful of pills, started to convulse, and decided I wasn't going to call for help, so avoid assuming I am some sort of authority, I am simply and accident the world is not ready for. Granted I feel off the track.

2Ch 33:6 And he caused his children to pass through the fire in the valley of the son of Hinnom: also he observed times, and used enchantments, and used witchcraft, and dealt with a familiar spirit, and with wizards: he wrought much evil in the sight of the LORD, to provoke him to anger.

Hinnom is a valley near Jerusalem and is associated with a place people go in the afterlife so it is essentially hell. And "he" caused his children. This is saying the "society" forces the children to eat the apple from the tree of knowledge and their minds go into hell or the left aspect. "HE" observed time. This is a left aspect trait, I am on the right and have slight sense of time, so I am mentally what the holy grail and fountain of youth is. My mind and thus my body is not aware of time so I am ageless because I cannot perceive how old I am. So when the children get the education they go to hell mentally because the emotions are all very strong and sense of time is very strong and hunger is very strong, and so they are in "sorrow for the rest of their life". It says "He" used witchcraft and enchantments and wizards and made the ones on the right very "angry:" and in waxing of anger. Jesus said it clearly, "Suffer the children" he said "Do what you want but stop mentally raping the children with your scribe and math or at least condition them away from fear after you teach them scribe and math so they are not in Hinnom, mentally. And the ones on the left did not like that idea so they butchered him, and they poisoned Mohammed and they butchered Moses and they poisoned Buddha and they think they are wise. So they "know not what they do." Jesus said, "forgive them because they know not what they do" because the scribe and math has put them mentally in Hinnom or hell, those inventions ruined their mind completely. I have to laugh because I cannot ever win because every 9 months the powers that be pump out millions of kids from school who graduate into mental Hinnom. I cannot complete with that kind of slaughter so I talk to myself into infinity, in vain. "Used enchantments" is saying "if you get good grades in the education you get lots of money and we will like you." "used witchcraft" is saying "If you do not do as we say god will strike you down and you will go to hell after you die so you do what we say or you will regret it, so get in there an study that math and script." "Familiar spirits" is one who say " I know god is on my side and I know god is with me and so whatever I do Its okay because God is with me." If you want to talk about god from a religious point of view, if you have a strong sense of time and strong hunger and strong sense of fatigue, you are the anti-christ religiously speaking. It perhaps would very unhealthy for you to ever realize I am telling the absolute truth because you perhaps would not be able to live with yourself. One might suggest if a person on the left realized I am telling the absolute truth they would be having what is known as an emotional breakdown right about now. If I am the devil and have a perfect grasp on the religious teachings, what would that make you?

1Sa 15:23 "For rebellion is as the sin of witchcraft, and stubbornness is as iniquity and idolatry. Because thou hast rejected the word of the LORD, he hath also rejected thee from being king."

This comment is simply suggesting people got the scribe conditioning and it killed the king, in relation to the right aspect of the mind, "the kingdom". It is tricky because one does not really reject the "king" because they are indoctrinated into the left aspect by law, force and by their parents. King is denoting the right aspect has all the power or is the "wiser" of the two aspects. That is fact. The subconscious aspect in relation to a person who has gone through the script conditioning, is the powerhouse. There are not many people in extreme right brain simply because they are forced to get the scribe conditioning as a child. They are forced by law to become "dumb". That is a fact and it is not good or bad, it just is. Be careful what you ask for, we invented scribe and math and asked for wisdom and we got it, as long as your definition of wisdom is strong emotions, elementary logic and the "not so King" aspect of the mind. The man upstairs is the right aspect or hemisphere of the brain. That is also a fact and education in general kills it or makes it veiled. One might suggest after the education the mind goes from a full bright moon to a veiled crescent moon, which denotes one silences all their mental processing power, and then they get a degree to mark the event. I will now discuss something pertinent.- 7/12/2009 6:33:49 AM

If I was capable of mercy and compassion I would have "put you down" by now, but since I will not "put you down" it is proof I desire you live in the sorrowful state of mind the scribe aspect has put you in. The fact you breathe is proof that I am in fact nothing because I do not have the compassion enough to put you out of your misery. I simply have no morals and have no class. Imagine a horse with four broken legs and you have to stand there and watch it try to get up, and when it does its broken legs snap further. And I just sit there and watch that creature torment itself in agony with the understanding it may never be able to stand on its own. That is why Mohammed cut people heads off because it was harming him to see them in such misery, perhaps.

Gen 3:17 "… cursed is the ground for thy sake; in sorrow shalt thou eat of it all the days of thy life;"

Ones on the left are simply in sorrow for their whole lives. Their happiness is empty happiness and they are simply in sorrow for their whole life and there is no exceptions, there are just ones who understand they are in sorrow and ones who are in infinite denial they are in sorrow. Your mind is simply unable to ever grasp such deep understandings. I do not need your help, I understand too much already. Being mindful of who cannot lose often reveals who cannot win. Detecting the enemy is easier than detecting their weakness, detecting its weakness often reveals its strength.

7:04:26 PM – The Inca's saw the Spanish as "gods" because they were extreme right brain dominate and "felt the perfection" when they saw the Spanish arrive on their shores, they "trusted" and they had thousands of men so they certainly could have taken care of the Spanish but you know, they gave the "darkness" the benefit of the doubt and the Spanish simply had dollar signs in their eyes which is classic left brain characteristic, or the "left" are not cerebral but physical based in their thoughts. So once again the left brainers slaughtered the right brainers, because the right brainers give the "darkness" the benefit of the doubt. This is why I take the Churches advice when dealing with the "darkness" "Never try to reason with it." This denotes I never want to talk to you, and I never want to speak with you, and never ever try to contact me.

In case you are attempting to have brain function, the Incas used a system of knots in a string as a form of memory building , so you see they had no language or script, so the Spanish arrive and say "Look at these savages" and took advantage of them as left brainers always do. So you see this is not relative to a certain part of the world it is universal. There are ones on the right and ones on the left, and ones on the right tend to be "right"ous because they are docile and they think properly and they tend not to take advantage of people. That is why I am going to change everything or die trying because I have already given up on trying to function in a world full of vipers. I will now discuss something worth mentioning.

I can hardly write a paragraph without spitting blood through my black eyes. Of course the Americans did the exact same thing to the American Indians. So this whole concept of a superior race takes over an inferior race is not a proper way to look at it. The proper way to look at it is the left brain barbaric demons take over the right brain docile wise beings because the wise beings understand the barbaric vipers know not what they do. Essentially the ones on the right have compassion on the "sane" aspect of the species. Once in a while one wakes up and starts cutting heads off and that is proper because no one has it perfect, and when dealing with vipers its best to cut the head off so it does not infect the others. So I am not really talking about human beings I am talking about things that have been mentally altered through force to the degree they are mentally in fact less than human beings. They have been mentally altered and are no longer considered the living but in fact mentally considered the dead. It is rather foolish of me to worry about spelling and grammar when I am dealing with mentally dead creatures. I find just assuming they are illusions assists me in tolerating them for another second. An illusion is lower than dirt because an illusion is not even real at all. Less than nothing is a proper way to look at it. Please avoid assuming I am a racist because in reality I do not even acknowledge you are here at all. I almost killed myself because of this script and math conditioning, so I will never go back to the left, and because of that I have deep seeded issues because I "woke up" and found out why I was trying to kill myself for a good part of my life, so I have an infinite log in my eye, and I will never get it all out.- 7:15:41 PM

Here is my thought process on this matter of left and right brainers.

Slaughter all the left brainers because they are sick animals.

They are only sick because they were mentally abused as children by the script forced on them by the adults. They will never understand that because their pride and ego caused by the script will not allow them to admit they are ill. Write it in your books and take it one sentence at a time and if all else fails you can go to the cut their heads off strategy. That is my thought process on that matter so you see it is wonderful I tend to ponder things very carefully because if I did not my armies would be filling the rivers with blood at this very moment. One might suggest when I give the signal to attack it is all over for the vipers, there is not enough weapons in the universe to save them this time. Granted this book is perhaps my most sinister book but the reality is, the understandings are very harsh on the mind and I try to keep in perspective I am sitting in my isolation chamber and just writing books and there is no need to panic because there is a good chance this is the afterlife and there is no point in doing anything but laughing at the whole situation, because I really do not even feel sadness or sorrow, I just feel so-so about everything. I have shades of anger and shades of sorrow but I simply cannot hold a grudge especially when I see people and I feel that perfection aspect thorough vision, all my anger is silenced and I try to figure out how can I possibly be upset with such perfection. So I just keep typing because I cannot seem to remain angry enough to take physical action. It is all about mindset. I have to write everyone is retarded because I only see them as perfect and that helps me to maintain. That gives me some harmony because I already see myself as nothing or I cannot see myself in a mirror so for my mental safety I have to attack thin air. Simply put, if I saw any redeeming qualities in myself I would not have taken all those pills, so now I am stuck in that mindset. Everyone I see is perfect when I look at them in contrast because I see myself as nothing. Only a master can convince the universe to stop expanding with his words. When human beings start to think money and material things are more important than a human being they tend to eventually assume they are not as important as material things and money and then they are doomed. There are human beings that kill their self and kill others on a daily basis over material gains or material control and kill them directly and indirectly, but the reality is, it always comes back to haunt them because eventually they will determine their very life means nothing if they do not have a certain amount of material wealth. This is the problem with the left brain mindset that is encouraged by the scribe conditioning. A person tends to perceive material gain is relative to their well being and that is in turn is that beings purpose in life, material gain, and when material gain is not achieved they become depressed, and that depression leads to making rash decisions that eventually may lead to their own death.

69

So a man loses his job and comes home and determines he cannot pay his bills so then he kills himself and perhaps his family and perceives that is a wise decision when in reality debt is meaningless. There is no debtors prison, and if worse comes to worse you can go fishing and live in a homeless shelter or build a shack in the woods to live, and all of those options are in fact a billion times better than killing yourself because you are in debt. Debt means nothing because no matter how much debt you have, you can always just ignore it and live without credit. Living without credit is a billion times better than killing yourself and your children and wife because you lost your job. Credit ratings mean nothing. It does not mean you are wise, and it does not mean you are smart, and it does not mean anything except, the ones who are essentially loan sharks and live off charging usury rates are more likely to charge you usury rates to loan you money. Credit rating is a nice way for the loan sharks to determine who the suckers are and who the intelligent humans are. You are not wise to pay 18% interest on a monetary purchase you are in fact a sucker because people will suggest you have bad credit if you do not pay such loan shark rates when in reality, you are in fact wise to not allow others to rob you blindly. This is exactly why so many people are defaulting on their mortgage payments , they are waking up to the fact, the carpetbaggers have gone too far and have become too greedy. There is no debtor's prison. Nothing is going to happen if you have a bad credit rating because the entire economy is collapsing and people will make sure if you want to buy a car or a house you will get the loan or get the credit you need because if they do not sell these cars and houses they make nothing.

But the problem with that is, people are becoming wise and doing more with less because of the internet. This means the burden is growing greater for ones who try to "play by the rules" or the ones who try to keep a good credit rating. They are going to have to pay higher interest rates to make up for all the wise beings who have thrown off the yoke of the carpetbaggers and thus they will become wise beings and also in time throw off the yoke of the loan sharks and their usury rates. The carpet baggers make this credit rating system and then make it sound like you are less than a human if you do not have a good credit rating, when in reality all that says is you are more likely to pay 18% interest on a purchase, so in fact you are everything in the universe except intelligent to pay such an interest rate. The truth is you do not need a credit card and you do not need a credit rating to breath air. You are a human being and you can adapt to any situation as long as you have brain function and that is tragically not the case due to the scribe side effects for many. Life is perhaps very hard if you only use 10% of your brain power. Life is effortless if you use 100% of your brain power. That's the main difference between right and left brain, it is not good or evil but it just is. Many of these thoughts that are encouraged in the mind by the scribe aspect are simply roadblocks that turn quite an easy existence into a nightmare existence. Granted I have to write about something so I am just fiddling at this stage in my infinitely poorly written thick pamphlets, psychologically speaking, so to speak, and then there were none. Only a crazy person would publish this book.

The strange thing about this accident is I understand there are ones who will "get it" and they will seek the hottest coals and attempt to cancel out the scribe aspect by conditioning away from fear and then they will not need me anymore because they will become their own army, and they will attempt to explain it to the ones near them and then there is this domino effect I am aware of. It is as if I have to keep mentioning don't you dare assume I am something special and don't you dare assume I am anything but what everyone else is, they just perhaps have not woken up to the extent I have, but they can, and it is quite effortless to do so, once one realizes these fear aspects in the mind are not real, they are simply side effects of the script conditioning. It is as simply as a person ate off an poison apple and in order to get the poison out of their system they have to do some safe fear conditioning to get the fear poison out of their mind and then they are well. That is it. Nothing complex, don't try to make a mountain out of a mole hill. Don't try to read supernatural things into this, don't try to look at it as bad and good or wrong and right, it is simply a poison that has an antidote, one simply has to apply the antidote and they are not good or bad if they do not apply the antidote, it is their choice whether to apply the antidote or not. One might suggest some people like the physical attachments and some people like the telepathy. Some people prefer vain attempts to fill the void inside, and some people prefer to make peace with the void inside. Some people prefer to be drama and emotional centered and some people prefer the machine. Some people prefer to act on illusions in their mind and some people prefer to manipulate the illusions in their mind. Neither is good or bad, they are simply mental lifestyle choices. I could perhaps make a very good argument that people are being robbed of their choice when they are forced by laws to accept the scribe and math conditioning but I understand that as Moses suggested, the apple appeared like wisdom and appeared good to eat, so it is a very tricky and convincing trap. Certainly the apple of knowledge looks like light from every angle except from the side effects on the mind angle. It is perhaps like a drug that makes one feel very good but in the end it kills them mentally and thus completely. One day man will make an invention that will have unintended side effects. The humor in that comment is thick. A deep truth about all of these ancient religious texts is simply the founders are Moses in the west and Buddha in the east and the ones who are unmentioned are the Hindu's in the east and the "tribes" in the west. To clarify the American Indians were aware of what Moses was saying and the Hindu's were aware of what Moses and Buddha were saying or aware of this thousands of years before they said it. Another way to look at it is, some of these "tribes" even today are looked at as "3rd world" or "uncivilized" but relative to absolute truth, that is an infinite compliment. They are not under the influence of the "snake" or "apple" or "tree of knowledge" so they appear ambiguous to the "sane" who are under the influence of the "snake" or "tree of knowledge" and so the "sane" tend to suggest these "tribes" are "stupid" because the "sane" are in neurosis and unable to understand they are in fact "insane" due to the poison from that apple. Perhaps that is why I have to keep a very good sense of humor.

I have been aware of this "reverse thing" since the start of the accident and the one thing I understand is, if you have a strong sense of time and strong hunger you are wise to assume everything is the reversed of what it appears, because you will be less prone to believing delusions that way. So, civilization meets these natives" and determine they need to be "saved" or "helped" and essentially killed them off, when in reality the only abominations that needed to be killed off was the "civilized ones". That reality perhaps throws a wrench in everything, perhaps. So I will put it like this. Buddha, Moses, Jesus, Mohammed did the best they could based on the fact they were trying to reach the cerebrally dead. I do not love any of those beings because they did not cut the mustard. They tried the best they could but obviously they fell short of the mark because the whole world is still killing each other over grains of sand. I am pleased with their efforts but I will not mess up like they did. Don't you ever assume they are in my league. I am certainly leaving these last few comments in my book as a fear conditioning tool. I will now discuss something relative.

71

I don't pander or reason with illusions, so save your judgments of my words for the illusions you are owned by. Are you going to slander me in the public eye or hang me on a cross? Is that best plan your mind can up with? You are going to need an infinitely bigger boat than the sinking one you are in. I am pleased no one even reads book's that have misspellings in them anymore. Certainly one who has no mastery over the language rules and laws, is retarded, and has nothing of value to say, and nothing of value worth listening too ever, into infinity. After all if a person cannot spell and use grammar "properly" they are certainly stupid and retarded and an idiot and delusional and a waste of life and on top of that if they use cuss words they are far worse. They perhaps are the devil himself if they use cuss words in their books. They cannot possibly have any intelligent comments to make. Everybody who is anybody understands that, only a total fool would NOT. Only an idiot would FEAR NOT words.- 11:10:56 PM

"In much wisdom is much grief; and he that increaseth knowledge increaseth sorrow." Ecclesiastes 1:18

This is complex. Knowledge is in relation to the tree of knowledge which is in relation to the script and math aspects which increase the left brain and increase the emotions and thus the sorrow.

First off remind yourself men invented language and Moses simply said women invented language or ate off the tree so the men would not slaughter him so swiftly.

Gen 3:6 "And when the woman saw that the tree was good for food, and that it was pleasant to the eyes, and a tree to be desired to make one wise, she took of the fruit thereof, and did eat, and gave also unto her husband with her; and he did eat."

These old texts are the only things that keep me from spitting blood into my books. The points in the comment in relation to the "knowledge" comment is "desired to make one wise". If one gets the script and math they are assumed to be wise, so that knowledge appears to be "good for food" or " good fruit" or "pleasant to the eyes" or "it looked like a good idea at the time" or "it looks good on the surface".

Gen 3:17 "And unto Adam he said, Because thou hast hearkened unto the voice of thy wife, and hast eaten of the tree, of which I commanded thee, saying, Thou shalt not eat of it: cursed is the ground for thy sake; in sorrow shalt thou eat of it all the days of thy life;"

This "sorrow" is in relation to the "sorrow" mentioned in Esslesiastes. It is simply a characteristic of the script /left brain, the emotions are turned up way too much, one is essentially an emotional wreck. They cry over the dead and sometimes they kill their self because they lost a loved one. That's abnormal. And that is just the tip of the iceberg. They kill other people over a grain of dirt, because the left brain wants to control things and if it can't control things, it kills them. A parent says "I provide you food and clothing and a roof over your head, so you do what I say or I will throw you to the curb and you will die." That's called a control freak and one who is extremely mentally ill because of the scribe conditioning. You do as I say or you will pay, that's an abomination of mankind's mindset and will never be anything but an abomination to mankind. Quote me on that I beg you.

Gen 3:14 " And the LORD God said unto the serpent, Because thou hast done this, thou art cursed above all cattle, and above every beast of the field; upon thy belly shalt thou go, and dust shalt thou eat all the days of thy life:"

This is simply saying because of that scribe and math knowledge you conditioned the intelligent aspect of your mind away or silenced it so you are dumber than a beast in the field and the belly comment suggest you are in the belly of the beast, and the dust comment suggests, everything you think and say has the wisdom of dust and dust is valueless. So essentially this delicious apple made us as a species dumber than a rock. Do you perceive we are not dumber than a rock in general? So essentially we are cursed as a species in relation to a cow, mentally speaking because of the scribe aspect. That means I will save a cow from a river before I will save you from a river, and I will be wise for doing so. That means because of this scribe aspect, in relation to your mental ability, a cow is a genius compared to you and a cows value is far beyond your value, because this script aspect has levied a curse upon your mind. Moses was quite sinister. I take great pride in my unfailing ability to ruin my thick pamphlets effortlessly.

I cast no stones on this matter.

Gen 3:13 "And the LORD God said unto the woman, What is this that thou hast done? And the woman said, The serpent beguiled me, and I did eat."

This comment is where the comment "The devil made me do it" came from. Of course this comment also gives one much to ponder. On one hand the scribe invention could simply be an honest mistake , something that appeared like a good invention but turned sour mentally speaking. On the other hand, if this supernatural snake aspect is real, and it was able to trick humans into making this invention then this snake aspect in relation to supernatural is one millimeter less powerful than god and that means human beings are screwed because they cannot fight against something that powerful. So you see now I am back up on the fence and now you understand why I am never going to be intelligent enough to speak about supernatural aspects. I simply make ponderings because if some sort of supernatural power can ruin the entire human race with a disguise of wisdom and knowledge such as scribe and math then we are screwed because we cannot defend against that kind of power. So I am on the infinite fence into infinity about supernatural powers. I do not want to even know. I want to be ignorant about such matters. I don't mind if you insult me as long as you understand you are unable to.

Gen 3:11 "And he said, Who told thee that thou wast naked? Hast thou eaten of the tree, whereof I commanded thee that thou shouldest not eat?"

This is perhaps the mind blowing comment of the universe ", Who told thee that thou wast naked?". God asked who told you , you should be ashamed of nudity and you should be shy, and you should be afraid, and you should have guilt, and you should have embarrassment. It is sarcasm. Who told you, you could feel shame and guilt and shyness? God is saying I didn't tell you, you should feel shame when you see nudity and you should feel guilt about what you are, and what you think, so who told you, you should feel shame and guilt and shyness and bitterness and embarrassment? Basically if you are a rule freak and are ashamed of nudity and cuss words and have these moralistic delusions in your pinprick brain it is because you are so far under the influence of the snake you should never speak again because your neurosis is beyond my ability to understand and that is a very deep neurosis. We as human did this to ourselves with our invention of scribe and math and that is not saying math and scribe is bad, it is saying one has to know the antidote after they teach people these aspects, or they ruin the people mentally. If you have any problems with that understanding please be mindful I do not reason with what I own.

7/13/2009 12:33:48 AM - Oh great it's a brand new day and now I can disregard everything I have said in the past and start all over. I will start off this day with this comment. I am good you are bad. Now that I have ruined today's writing I can get on with writing. I get this impression everybody already knows all of these things I write about and so I am just engaged in infinite vanity, but that is clearly impossible. I am just very humble and I take for granted how much I woke up. I am biased. Certainly no human being alive understands these concepts or they would have told everyone by now, and society would not be abusing the children as they do, and then suggesting they are wise. If any human being understood all of this and they did not write infinite books attempting to tell others, and even give the books away due to the fact of how important this information is in relation to how they things are, even if it costs them their life, they would be the most self centered being in the universe, and I am mindful there simply is no one who understands all of this because If I was mindful there was, I certainly would not have this stone hanging around my neck. So since my fifth book became live today that means I am obligated to make a pdf file out of the original text and upload it to a pirate site and allow people to download it for free and now you know I am insane, because I don't even have any money and I have nothing, and I give my words away so I am cursed and it harms me. This is why you never get to talk to me, and I will never talk to you. Okay back to reality.

One sentence at a time. My favorite lines I hear when speaking to the lefter's is "That is not what I said" and "Where did you hear that?" Where did I hear that? I can write infinite books alone answering that question. It is as if they cannot even think for their self they need to go back and reference a book about what someone else said in order to verify what they should think because their heightened awareness is totally gone. They cannot even form a thought unless it has 1000 text books of long gone dead people agreeing with what is said. Essentially they cannot even think anymore they are simply regurgitating other long dead peoples comments over and over and never coming up with anything original. There whole life is centered around what is written in a book and anything that is not mentioned in their book of choice cannot possibly be true and the stranger still is, they cannot understand what is said in their book of choice. They read the books and assume they understand the books when in reality they do not have a clue what the books say. I find the humor is so thick with that understanding it is as if this cannot really be reality. The scribe aspect has made people so dumb mentally speaking, I am uncertain if they are even able to legitimately claim they are human beings any longer. Moses suggested they are lower than a cow I am quite certain that is perhaps the most compassionate statement in the history of mankind, to suggest the ones on the left are simply just dumber than a cow. Perhaps the compassion of Moses was far greater than mine will ever be considering I will never have such a thing as compassion or mercy, ever, into infinity. Vengeance is the only word I still believe in.

So now that I have uploaded volume 5 to the pirate site, a person came along and assumed some person stole volume 5 and decided to give it to others, so they downloaded it and now they have this secret treasure and its free and so they will be obligated to read it. Did they steal my volume 5? No they didn't, I gave it freely. Do they perceive they stole my volume 5? Yes they perceive they got away with something. That is why they will read it. Perhaps they assume it takes effort to write these books. Perhaps they assume a normal person requires many months or labor to pump out a book with such knowledge. Perhaps they assume the books I write take any effort at all. Perhaps they assume a conscious human being has so much brain power there is nothing in life that is anything more than effortless. That is why a well baited hook catches many fish to eat. I perhaps have no stress because I am not concerned about what a person with the mental complexity of a cow says about me. Moses said that not me, I am not that compassionate. Some people's wisdom is deafening. Never expect to win and you will always be pleased.", thou art cursed above all cattle" it is perhaps job security to attempt to communicate with an animal this in fact below a cow in mental ability because it was brainwashed by the adults as a child. I simply have job security because a cow is extremely dumb right off the bat but "cursed above a cow" denotes dumber than a cow. They are dumber than a cow mentally and factually speaking. If you like facts, scribe and math have a side effect called "you become dumber than a cow". That is a fact. Your mind is altered down so much and your heightened awareness is altered down so much, Moses said, you are in fact dumber than a cow and I prefer to suggest brain dead mole cricket is perhaps closer to the truth. So I write books to remind you, Moses called you dumber than a cow and I call you a brain dead mole cricket and then I publish it and let the whole world read it, and then I write another book and do the same thing over and over into infinity, and you have to apply your rules of tolerance or you are evil. Perhaps you have come to an understanding. One publisher told me they don't publish hate writings. The humor in that is thick. They also said we don't publish books that have bad grammar which means they are racist against people in the extreme right because that is a trade mark of beings in the extreme right because they have kicked the scribe curse and lose all the brain conditioned aspect of scribe as in past and present and future tense sentences. So they are racist and hateful and biased and no person in the dam world understands that but me. So do not ever tell me your insanity about democracy and about compassion and about understanding and about tolerance because your mind is dumber than a cows.

2:14:38 AM – Apparently my eyes turn black with rage at around 3Am and if you do not know why by this point, you should perhaps give up on everything. I hear the sunshine skyway bridge is a wonderful thing to experience as long as you hit the rocks. If you hit the water from 190 feet up, you might drown. I am mindful to never reason with the cows because their milk is poisoned and their words are foolishness.

Luk 15:6 "And when he cometh home, he calleth together his friends and neighbours, saying unto them, Rejoice with me; for I have found my sheep which was lost."

So he called his friends, ones who were also in the extreme right brain, and he let them know he found a sheep and converted it back to right brain out of the scribe aspect, and so he made the lost, found and the blind able to see. So Jesus called you a sheep, Moses called you a curse above a cow and I am uncertain which is dumber, so I stick with brain dead mole cricket. I am already aware I cannot reach you because I cannot tell a blind man they are blind because they perceive blindness is normal. So I just write to myself in my stupid retarded books and I play my video game and act like the cows and sheep and brain dead mole crickets are just a joke the afterlife is playing on me.

Luk 12:48 ".... For unto whomsoever much is given, of him shall be much required"

This is infinite humor. This is saying whoever wakes up from the scribe neurosis be prepared to write infinite books until the cows, sheep and brain dead mole crickets either hang you on cross, poison you with lamb chops, or poison mushrooms or hemlock or send you away to die alone on a mountain. If you wake up prepare to die because you are in an insane asylum, that's what nizchez or whatever name is, says. So all these people were trying to let us know we accidentally mentally harmed our self with scribe and math and they were trying to wake us up, and the ones on the left slaughtered them and then we walk around assuming it certainly was not us who did it. But what is funny is these ones on the extreme right , there physical sense of pain is greatly altered, so in some ways pain hurts more but in some ways it hurts less. A cut for example stops hurting right after the cut is made. The pain is not long lasting because the physical aspects are essentially numb. And when it comes down to it, they were trapped in hell, in relation to everyone around them was asleep or unconscious or in neurosis, so they perhaps did not mind dying just to get the hell away from "them". Perhaps a cow, a sheep or a brain dead mole cricket would not be able to grasp that, perhaps. To clarify if you have a strong sense of time and strong hunger you are either a cow, a sheep or a brain dead mole cricket, whichever is dumber. But to put it in perspective you can at least spell words and make grammatically correct sentences and use past and future tense words properly but you lose brain function, heightened awareness and telepathy.

Sheridan V (19) committed suicide by taking a deadly cocktail of antidepressants-Mydeathspace.com

This could have been me because I did not take the scribe and math indoctrination to well, so do not ever assume I am going to be compassionate or I am going to be merciful because you keep pumping out your insanity into children day after day and then you say you are wise and righteous in your determinations. You go to your god for mercy because you aint getting none from me in this lifetime, or the next. I do not know who this young girl is but I certainly know who the whores who killed her are. I am taking down the whole house of cards and if you don't like that, you prepare yourself for death because death is infinitely closer to you right now, than you could ever imagine.

Back to reality.- 5:33:22 AM

9:24:44 AM - The education forces us all into left brain and the laws make sure we pay for it. The education forces us into left brain and the drugs remind us to regret it. We start school with an open mind and graduate with a closed mind, and society seldom minds and is full of never minds. Thinking comes naturally, making sure one does not think too much requires effective scare tactics. It is easier to put your faith in god than to put your faith in your mental abilities. Fear is a symptom of mental confusion and fearlessness is the ability to admit it. Fear turns a powerful mind into a never mind. Being afraid to say certain words is being afraid to think. Testing limits is better than accepting them; ignoring limits is better than needing them. Freedom is scary and slavery is safety.

Mic 1:11 "Pass ye away, thou inhabitant of Saphir, having thy shame naked:"

"Thy shame naked" is simply a symptom of the scribe and math conditioning. Fear of words, fear of nudity , fear of saying what is on your mind, need to control others, inability to tolerate what others are doing. The bottom line, you may have to spend the rest of your life trying to undo this brain damage the scribe condition has done to you so you need to focus on that log in your mind, so you do not have time to run around telling others what they should or should not do because I assure you once you accept the fact the script aspect has ruined your mind, you are going to be fighting a mental battle for the kingdom (right aspect/subconscious) that is going to require every ounce of fortitude in your body. That is an indication of how much damage the side effects of the scribe conditioning has caused you. So I will throw this out there before I continue in my thick pamphlet. Messiah is simply a human being that in one way or another woke up from the script neurosis and tries to wake up others or tries to "save mankind" from the script neurosis that has blocked 90% of that human beings mind or closed it or damaged it. The reason Moses threw the ten commandments down on the rocks is to demonstrate there is no labels and there is no rules because the right aspect of the mind is all about freedom. Throwing those commandments into the rocks and breaking them was a nice way of saying, stop being afraid of breaking rules, stop being afraid to do things, stop being afraid of all the rules on that tablet. All of those commandments are simply humble suggestions but are not rules because rules are strictly left brain and a symptom one is in neurosis. Are you ashamed of nudity or cuss words or saying certain combinations of words? Moses had these rules and then he threw them and smashed them and destroyed them because rules are left brain and a symptom of one who is under the influence of the snake. These wise beings were not about rules they were here to destroy rules because rules are not of one on the right aspect, and rules hinder the mind not open up the mind.

I am still afraid to say words and I assure you I am on the fast track in relation to progression or to waking up and I am still ashamed to say words, that means if you start to unlock subconscious it may take your whole life to get back to "the garden of Eden" because people around you are going to say "You shouldn't say that word" or "you shouldn't do that thing." And they are going to put guilt trips on your because they are under the influence on the limits and the isolation. So the whole premise that religion is about laws you should not break is a lie. Religion is about freedom and no limits and that is why they slaughtered these beings because society itself is all about keeping the sheep in line and these beings were saying, no rules and limits only freedom. They bucked the establishment and the establishment cannot control ones who are free so these wise beings were deemed dangerous. Moses took the law and threw it on the rocks to demonstrate it is bad and should be ignored. I have not yet begun to fight, to write, to have sight.

We are creatures of freedom and wandering and experimenting and gathering understandings and this scribe invention has turned us into narrow minded, short sighted, isolation abominations. This is why Moses took people out of the city, as in out of the law establishment. As in back to freedom but the thing is, the scribe aspect is so powerful or is so mentally complete in its ability to destroy the mind, that he didn't have the tools to figure out how to break the mental isolation the scribe invention instills in people. When a being has no inhibitions and no labels they are conscious but the thing is, a person on the left can subscribe to these labels and limits for long periods of time and one on the right can emulate having labels with their words but mentally they cannot. Many of the words I say are not judgments on an person, but really me trying to get over my fear of words. Jesus said do not judge but he judged like hell. He judged everything and everyone, he called people on the left the darkness, that is judgment, but his mindset, was not cut in stone, in relation to the ten commandments. Nothing is carved in stone which is what freedom is, it means sometimes laws and rules apply but sometimes they are ignored, that means they are not cut in stone as in absolute things to follow. No law or rules is absolute. There is a time to follow rules and a time to break those same rules, because that is what freedom is: Freedom to follow and freedom to not follow. Control freaks do not like that ideal. A control freak wants everyone to always follow their rules so right brain is against rules and so they need to be killed off swiftly. That's what happened to Jesus, Moses, Mohammed, and Buddha, they were threats to the powers that be because the powers that be are under the influence of the script conditioning. Try to apply rules to school of fish in the ocean. You cannot do it because they are free. Try to apply rules to a flock of birds in the sky, you cannot do it because they are free. Animals should not be ashamed of nudity or grunts they produce, but humans are ashamed, have shame and have many unspoken petty rules.

"Right brain is not concerned with things falling into patterns because of prescribed rules. " that is proof our species is abnormal mentally speaking. Something we invented called script damaged our minds as a side effect and now we have shame and fear and guilt and embarrassment. One on the left will say this is very dangerous and we need rules and laws to function, but they will also admit at times rules and laws should be broken under certain circumstances. They will say murder is bad but it is okay to murder people in times of war. This is why laws are not valid because they are in the eye of the beholder. You just consider how many people in America are in jail because they broke stupid, isolationist, idiotic retard laws. You did some drugs you go to jail and sit in a cage for 5 years or 10 years. People pass a law to lock other people up for doing a drug. Those people who pass laws like that, their mind is so isolated and ruined they have no right to even breathe my air. I do not do drugs but I am not going to tell someone they are bad if they do drugs because that would make me a whore against freedom of choice. I don't give a dam if the entire nation says people who use drugs on their own free will are evil, I will tell that nation they are control freak whores under the influence of the snake. I take your rules and hang you with them. That's my rule. I publish that in my books so for the rest of eternity the universe will know the ones who push the rules are nothing but neurotic control freak abominations to the words human beings.

They are not human beings they stopped being human being about the time they were 10 or 12. That's about when they became scared of the dark and started to be ashamed and shy from the script and usually by about 14 they are pondering suicide and self harm because they mentally understand something is very wrong in the core their being. So to any of these high class religious teachers of these wise beings, if you are going around pushing laws and rules and making people feel ashamed and shame so they will give you money , I spit in your face and declare you are a control freak whore who is simply a false prophet and should be ignored. I will eat you for no reason for using scare tactics and gilt trips on my fellow human beings. I will rip your heart out and eat it in front of you.

Apparently I am fighting the battle within. I have determined I cannot fail because I am mindful I cannot win. If I started subscribing to rules and morals in the light that this entire civilization is in fact in deep neurosis from the script conditioning, I would just give up. Simply put, all bets are off, I do not care who you are, you get in the way of my goals and you meet the maker. Your god is not strong enough to save you if you get in my way.

Forty one people have downloaded volume 5 off the pirate site in one day and that is 41 people who have a chance of waking up, and they may tell others how to wake up, and you may be able to grasp, my methods are far beyond the abilities of the ones on the left to deal with because I suggest freewill and freedom to determine one's own destiny and the ones on the left are all about control and rules and isolation and to top it off they only have 10 percent brain power, so they do not even have a chance in the hell their mind is in. The Mac truck has already hit them but it may take a year or so before they realize it. Freedom is scary but only if you are left brained as a result of being conditioned with the script neurosis and have not properly left go of the fear side effect. Freedom is great if you are not in neurosis. If everyone is working on the log in their eye which means they are trying to wake up or fight the battle within the mind, then there is nothings to be afraid of.

If some wishes ill harm on others, there is still nothing to be afraid of, you deal with it and move on. There is no room for fear in the machine state. Death is an acceptable alternative to living mentally in a slave state of isolation and closed mindedness. Being willing to die to achieve mental freedom suggests one is dying to wake up. Some of these spying and watching others techniques are quite primitive because the ones on the right use this heightened awareness or telepathic aspect and so one might suggest they move in mysterious ways. I can type a sentence and it will be a clue to ones on the right about how to contact me but ones on the left will never figure it out no matter how many computers they have, so it is like a secret society that is not secret but it is just on another level of awareness. It is simply an unseen reality that is happening right under the noses of the ones on the left. My only conclusion so far since the accident is the mind once at full power is very powerful beyond the realms of what the norms understand the mind to be. That is as far as I can go so far because it is not on a tangible level. I can suggest things that are happening and one on the left will suggest that is not what that comment from that person means because they are not using the heightened awareness because the script neurosis is inhibiting their mental ability to understand that is what that comment is suggesting. They hear that comment but do not understand that comment would be the proper way to look at it. Facing fear is relative to understanding fear is an illusion caused by the script neurosis side effect caused by written language. I will now discuss something relevant.- 6:22:11 PM

7:03:18 PM – I have a right to life, liberty and the pursuit of happiness. I have determined to be happy I must bring down the house of cards. I must attempt to write books to wake up my fellow human beings from the script neurosis. This in turn will greatly alter the powers that be. That denotes I am a threat to the powers that be. That denotes I am a threat to ones who desire to control and keep the herd in line. That denotes there is a vast conflict of interest in relation to my pursuit of happiness and ones who wish to control, pursuit of happiness. I submit I am willing to engage in a blood bath and total revolution to achieve my pursuit of happiness. I submit I am willing to go the full measure to achieve happiness. I submit I am willing to die to attempt to wake up my fellow human beings from the script neurosis. I submit I have already let go of life so it will be no great loss. I submit the ones who wish to control others and make others feel guilt and shame should swiftly consider plans against me, because I am certainly beyond considering plans against them. There will be either the left or the right standing on the battlefield when the battle is over. I will not reason or negotiate with what I determine is my pursuit of happiness so this indicates the metal will certainly be meeting the meat. If I required an army I would have one. My lot has been cast and will not be uncast. The earth is my witness and you are it's supplicant. Thy will be done. I submit you will submit. I will now discuss something of value.- 7:12:46 PM

7:39:37 PM - Fear keeps your cage door locked. This is in direct relation to nothing to fear but fear. That is in direct relation to Fear not. Not denotes nothing. So Fear nothing. That is confusing to ones on the left because they attempt to use 10% complexity to understand it and they only convince their self it is dangerous and then they get scared and then they panic and then they deny it is true. Without fear common sense does not go out the window it actually increases. If I had weak common sense I would resort to physical violence instead I am resorting to verbal violence. If verbal communication does not work then I may resort to physical means. I am an experimenter. That denotes one who forgets the rules and only seeks to become better at what their goal is. The problem with that is relativity. I may write 10000 books before I resort to physical means, another person may write 1 book till they resort to physical means. The difference is impatience. I may be willing to discuss a situation for the rest of my life before I determine physical means is required. That is patience. That is the problem with relativity. A person with a strong sense of time and strong fear may pass a law that locks up his own countrymen at the drop of a hat relative to one who has no sense of time and heightened awareness with the ability to think with deep complex thought patterns.

7/14/2009 12:27:42 AM – Brand new day. Past is past. I have pondered myself into a pondering. We are lemur monkeys. We invented a tool called planned language and planned math which is very heavy on rules. This made us in general all go into extreme left brain. This made us very prone to physical violence , physical cravings ,physical focus in contrast to cerebral focus. So the ones who woke up early on were prone to make this an "Us against them" situation. This is what created the wars. It is impossible to be" us against them" when we are all there is. We created the language and math and so we brought it all upon ourselves. We in turn created the" us against them" situations and we brought that all upon ourselves. We are our own worst enemy so the only way to counter that is to convince everyone we are all the same thing, lemur monkeys in varying stages of neurosis caused by the script and math inventions. The proper argument would be to suggest the anti-venom to the scribe and math neurosis is to be free and avoid assuming you are wrong, and avoid assuming you are capable of doing anything that could be considered grounds for shame or guilt because a lemur monkey can only be what it is. The next argument would be, conditioning away from fear would be a valid avenue to peruse in order to counter the strong emotions and other side effects the scribe neurosis caused. If one is afraid of a word say that word. If one is afraid of objects face those objects. Attempt to avoid things that may cause you physical harm but outside of that all bets are off. Fear of pornography is a strong symptom one is still under the influence of the scribe and math neurosis. Fear of cuss words is a strong symptom one is still under the influence of scribe and math neurosis. One is free to attempt to counter the left aspect conditioning and is also free to avoid countering the left aspect. An animal is not capable of doing bad or good deeds but is capable of assisting itself to achieve what it perceives is happiness by focusing on the log or the mental conditioning it desires. It is impossible to be against a lemur monkey when one is a lemur monkey. This scribe aspect has changed our minds so we have in turn become very violent lemur monkeys. That is all this is about. It is not a permanent condition but it does require one to be mindful it is real, and for one to be mindful of the anti-venom as it were.

"Education is the ability to listen to almost anything without losing your temper or your self-confidence." Robert Frost (1874-1963)

This comment denotes nothing if off limits. We are lemur monkey so we are easily fooled by aspects that are simply not happening. We as a species are in fact exactly like all the other animals except we developed some tools that in turn altered our minds to a degree we became naturally inclined to violence against each other. Our nature is not violence but the scribe and math condition has indirectly made us prone to violence. We are prone to violence against others and most harmful is we are prone to violence against ourselves because of this conditioning. We as a species using the creativity of the right aspect of the mind simply invented a tool that made us prone to violence and in order to counter that we simply need to be mindful that in order to achieve the right complex aspect of the mind that is more cerebral one simply conditions away from fear. This is not a group effort because everyone has this "log" in their mind in general, because everyone has been conditioned into scribe and math. As the fear decreases the right aspect of the mind increases. As the cerebral aspect of the mind increases, the violent aspect of left mind decreases. As the telepathy and clear thinking increases the judgment and intolerance to ambiguity decreases. As the emotions decrease the machine state increases. Your goodness is relative to what you understand is bad. One being suggested the battle is within, it is indeed one hell of a battle and perhaps one worth fighting. The whole conditioning process is difficult to approach from a group effort stand point perhaps, simply because everyone is at a different level. Some minor approaches are to use words such as cuss words to see how people react. This is a mindset of experimentation. So one in fact assumes the role of a researcher and thus is in a state of mind they are "working on their own log". What is someone you know or a peer going to say if you say a cuss word? No matter what you say if they insult your or degrade you simply say the magic word, Perhaps. No matter what anyone says to you if you want to silence their attempts to get a rise out of you simply respond with perhaps. Am I the devil? Perhaps. Am I a prophet? Perhaps. Am I a lemur monkey ? Perhaps certainly perhaps. I detect this right aspect of the mind is very powerful and can easily convince one of many things in relation to supernatural aspects. I do not detect supernatural aspects but I certainly can suggest in extreme right brain or what is known as Nirvana, it is very easy to point to supernatural aspects. This vision from feeling is as far into supernatural as one can get.

I can read other people through "telepathy", from talking to them on the phone, listening to people on television. That could easily be labeled as supernatural but what I understand it the right brain or subconscious aspect of the mind is so powerful it is a machine and can sort through an entire lifetime of understandings in short order and reach the final conclusion. This may take a lifetime to do with left brain because it is sequential based and has the time stamp aspect and so things get very bogged down. So everyone is the same because everyone has the right aspect of the mind but some have it unlocked a bit further than others, but everyone can unlock it fully with some simple cost free conditioning methods. Sooner or later I have to go to a cemetery at night all alone to experiment and see if I detect ghosts, but I am already aware, I can watch very scary movies in the dark all alone and all I see are actors in makeup. I can even read them and tell which ones are having trouble acting and which ones are "good actors". Not by looking at their deeds or the outside but by reading them with the feeling through vision. I watched a world war one documentary and I could read the people in that and they are dead. So this whole concept of a person's "spirit" being caught on film is in fact well founded and in fact easily detected but one has to have extreme right brain, so it again is relative to the observer. You will see it and feel it and understand it once you are on the right side or aspect of the mind, that is a fact, it is a trait, just like left aspect one tends to be very emotional and get sad easily and

has attachments and seeks physical satisfaction, right aspect seek cerebral satisfaction. There is no good or bad because they are anti or contrary to each other. One cannot compare apples to oranges, and that was extremely out of context.

This anger waxing is in reality a symptom of the mind letting go of emotions that tend to be very strong on the left aspect. When the conditioning starts working patience is a virtue because what is patience but time based. When you have slight sense of time or nearly no sense of time, how do you determine patience? That is what I noticed early on after the accident. My patience was very thin because my sense of time was going and I couldn't tell. When one achieves extreme right brain one year is a lifetime and more. There is no more "time flies" or "that year went fast". That is what the fountain of youth aspect is all about. I am mindful ones on the left aspect perceive seven books in seven months or so is very fast but relative to me in no sense of time, seven books in seven months is slow. I could do much better and write much faster but I in fact try to write slower because the books would get to big. That is not supernatural, that is the contrast between the processing power of the right hemisphere when it is dominate and the processing power of the left hemisphere when it is dominate.

I understand the trick is to not get complacent in the conditioning. I understand doing dangerous things physically is not better than doing things that are not physically dangerous for conditioning away from fear. Standing in your bathroom looking in the mirror all alone at night is for some very scary, yet also very physically safe. It is hard for me to tell what would scare another person at this stage but everyone has phobias. If one is scared of spiders they can hold a spider that is not poisonous or if one is afraid of snakes they can hold a snake that is not poisonous and maybe let it bite on them a bit, so to speak. There are infinite possibilities that do not require you to risk you health. Buddha nearly starved to death from fasting which is how he had his accident and this is why he said "Health is important." Because he became aware one does not have to go to such harmful extremes to counter the script neurosis. This is something I came across and it is a good example of the mental relativity of fear.

"Ghosts at Bhangarh: The Extent of Fear

The Government of India was to set a military centre to patrol the place all over the night to solve the puzzle of ghosts but could not dare. None of the military personnel were willing to participate in the operation. Even the ASI office is a kilometer away from the place and has a board that says: "Staying in the Area after Sunset is Strictly Prohibited." This indicates that something is very wrong, to the extent that even the paramilitary forces are not venturing into the area after dark."

This is describing a haunted place in India. The description makes it sound like there are ghosts and demons flying around everywhere. But in comments on the article some people, I am mindful they are in a degree of right brain look at it as an experimental place.

"Hi,

I am A. S.. I am 25 years old. I strongly believe that there no evil or ghost exist in this world. I don't believe in it. tihs is only a discovery of superstitious people. According to me it is just a frame of mind of people. Once a person start believing in anything he/she start thinking from that point of view & there there mind start to connect all those thing from that particular thing.

I can stay in that area for a nihgt & can proove that there is nothing like ghost.and proove it as a myth.A. S."

First thing is to notice his spelling errors. He has no problem with leaving words misspelled at it were but also, he is looking at this "haunted" location as simply a mental conditioning aspect to condition away from fear. In relation to "Fear Not" and "nothing to fear but fear itself." Maybe in a haunted location you will find ghosts, but maybe you will not find ghosts, and maybe you will find your mind is playing tricks on you. It is not reasonable for a person on the left who has fear to go to a haunted location alone, on the other hand a person on the right who has little fear would look at it like going to the park or making sure they have no fear by going there. So the moment these people mention the place is haunted the ones on the left want to go there in large groups because they want to be scared, they like to be sacred because being sacred in fact makes one feel alive in contrast to how they feel in general on the left aspect of the brain. An adrenalin rush makes one mentally "high". But that is also how one feels when they are dominate right brain or in Nirvana. Only people on the left can get drunk or high in relation to the euphoric feeling, because people on the extreme right are high all the time, they are euphoric and that is what heightened awareness is, a euphoric feeling. But one gets use to it, so this euphoric feeling is relatively a normal feeling after one adjusts. I still get the sensation that I revert back to sense of time and this clarity is all gone, that is because I am adjusting to it, it is a new world as far as mindset. The first two months I was certain I must have a brain tumor because it was such a huge mental change but like all things, one adjusts to it so one has to expect a huge mental change and not panic and assume the worst. Some beings suggest it is like raising from death to life. That is simply a contrast statement suggesting on the left the awareness is not as high and on the right the awareness is very high.- 2:12:34 AM

It is in fact very logical to understand that language and grammar have many rules, rules on how to spell a word, rules on how to form a sentence, and rules on how to arrange words. Rules are right in line with the aspect of the left brain and as a result not in line with the aspect of the right brain. So a child is born extreme right brain and has imaginary friends and also says things wise beyond their years, is not shy or ashamed to speak their mind. Then they go to school to learn to write and start getting these rules conditioned into their mind and eventually go left brain and as a result become shy, embarrassed and afraid and have many strong emotions. So it is nearly impossible for an adult to tell, because they were conditioned at such a young age they were not alive long enough to notice the contrast. Children tend to be taught very early so by the time they are 15 or so, they have no recollection of how they use to be as a child because by that time the neurosis has kicked in from the script and math conditioning. So the only way a person can wake up or totally fall out of the neurosis to a degree they can explain it all to others is "Those who do not try to save their self will find their self".

That's a hard core wake up method. It is perhaps very rare to do that because it is unintentional or it is an accident.

"No man knows the hour or day (of an accident) but the father (of that accident.)" Oct 31st 2008 1:38PM. Relative to me I understand exactly what that means but I am uncertain if you know what that means.- 2:22:02 AM - I am not an authority I am an accident. Education is no substitute for consciousness.

5:31:01 AM – In summation, is there a supernatural aspect? Perhaps. Are we just lemur monkeys that greatly altered our minds unknowingly with the invention called script and math? Perhaps.

6:46:33 PM –
"By desiring little, a poor man makes himself rich."
Democritus
This comment is very far out of context. Extreme right brain alters short term memory as it increases long term memory. So desire is altered as well. A person on the left can work their self into a frenzy to get something they desire and because it is in their short term memory the longer they go without it the more they crave it, on the contrary on the right ones short term memory is so altered. If one thinks of something they want, within a minute or two they will forget about it. This is perhaps why I have very little stress. I understand my books on

the realm of "norms" are the worst things ever published but I cannot remember what exactly is in them and I cannot feel a sense of dissatisfaction or satisfaction, so no highs and no lows, so no desire and no stress. It could be simply looked at like a person with a strong sense of time that has a strong sense of desires, because the short term memory and the sense of time allows them to perceive absence of things they desire strongly. This comment perhaps suggests one who is not materialistic tends to be cerebrally focused. So in this quote "rich man" would denote a person who is rich in the cerebral world, right brained, as opposed to rich in the physical world, left brain. This is not about morals as in do not like physical things, it is more a trait of being in extreme right brain, so it is more a characteristic or symptom.

This is why many of these beings who spoke in parables were taken to be saying literal things, like the parable of Adam and Eve, by the ones on the left simply because the ones on the left think in physical translations when the ones on the right, have to use parables to explain cerebral ideas.

A good example of this is this comment.

Act 11:16 "Then remembered I the word of the Lord, how that he said, John indeed baptized with water; but ye shall be baptized with the Holy Ghost."

This is a classic example of right brain inability to use sequence based language properly. They tend to sound like Yoda." "Then remembered I the word of the Lord" The left brain person who is all about sequencing would think "Then I remembered the word of the Lord" is proper, so you see the author was on the right aspect and his words and comments prove it because the sequencing in his comments are out of sequence. "Then remembered I the word of the Lord," he sounds like he is "drunk" or "holy" to the ones on the left, that's why they butchered him.

The "word" denotes the random access words spoken by the ones on the right and the "clarity" or "wisdom" to reach the right brain "fear not" and Baptized denotes one who is converted from left brain to right brain usually by a person who is right brain. One can look at it many ways but for example a Buddhist monk who takes a student and talks him into a state of right brain, no sense of time, Baptized that student. So the concept of baptism is not dunking someone under literal water, but the ones on the left assume that is what it means, because the ones on the right used a parable to explain a cerebral concept. So I talk to someone and suggest they condition away from fear and say "perhaps" a lot, and maybe in time they will become baptized into the right brain aspect in relation to "fear Not", but it is psychological conditioning which denotes , cerebral and not physical. The ones on the left take many things that are said in these texts literal and physical because that is the characteristic of the left brain. There is no intrinsic value to dunking someone under the water in relation to making them go to the "right aspect" unless one holds them under until they nearly drowned and then that person gets over their fear of death, but that is perhaps not what this is about, but now I wrote that, perhaps that is what they were doing.

You are not going to negate the left brain scribe neurosis simply by dunking your head underwater. The neurosis is so strong you perceive you are not in neurosis. It takes time and it is not a quick transition. After the actual facing fear conditioning is done to the proper degree it may take three months for it to really hit you and then it may take 8 months for you to go all the way to right brain extreme or nirvana or no sense of time, but you can't tell the moment you do this conditioning, it is not instant karma, it is a slow process but once one goes the full measure in conditioning away from fear it is irreversible, so then it is just a matter of time. So the whole premise of many of these "religious" rituals that are physical based or inherited as physical based, are simply proof the ones on the left took a cerebral parable or idea and did not translate it properly because they are on the left and see perhaps every story in these texts as a literal physical suggestion when many are in fact simply parables explaining cerebral concepts using physical descriptions. Many of these physical "rituals" only prove the people who subscribe to them "hear the word but do not understand the word". That is like a key or the "proof is in the pudding". Only a person who goes so far to the right extreme can decipher all of these "religious texts". So it is like a tests or a proof situation, similar to pulling the sword out of the stone. Only one who goes so far to the right , can decipher what all these texts are saying. And what is more complicated is that one that can decipher these texts, is one who reached that extreme right brain, by being "meek" and meek is one who is so depressed they find they are unworthy to even be alive. So many things must align properly to find one who can decipher all of these texts. The Buddhists suggest I got tapped which denotes I am not saying I am so good, I am saying I am a machine and I have no emotions and that is what is required to reach this level of clarity, so it is not possible for me to brag because I cannot feel satisfaction from bragging, if I could I wouldn't have the clarity to write as swiftly as I do. My mind would be cluttered with all of these cravings and desires and the concentration would suffer. So as the desires decrease the concentration increases. One tends to suffer greatly for a little happiness. This happiness ideal is a symptom of left brain, in the right brain machine state absence or nothingness is more accurate. Whatever makes you happy may make others sad. This machine state is the void, void of all of these desires and cravings. This is what is required to reach this extreme concentration.

I am not happy and I am not sad, I am void or nothingness. This is because the short term memory is altered and that is contrary to how the left brain dominate person is, they have strong short term memory. A left bran dominate person can remember something 20 minutes down the road, that is quite a feat for a right brain person in relation to cravings and desires. One can look at a drug addict or any kind of addict and that desire for that drug or item is very strong in their short term memory, so it festers in their mind, they crave it, they desire it and thus it controls them. That does not really happen in right brain extreme. One is processing information so fast, these desires and cravings tend to pass swiftly. Essentially right brain dominate is the reverse world from left brain dominate, total reverse or anti left brain characteristics. One might suggest I am having an extremely long epiphany.

Consider the story of medusa. She turned men to stone when they were so scared of how she looked. So a person faces death which is what medusa's head represented and then they were turned to stone or void, which means they faced fear and went extreme right brain dominate which is void or nothingness or the machine state. This is in direct relation to the Torah story of a woman being turned to salt and that is in direct relation to "the thinker" sculpture. Look at the that sculptor, that man is not happy and is not sad he is in fact void of happiness and sadness. That is the best way to look at the extreme right brain and if you are left brain dominate you are going to be afraid to think about being void of emotions, but the one thing to keep in mind perhaps is the concentration and clarity and the many other aspects that are "unlocked" or "opened up" cancel out the loss of emotional capacity. So it is not about good or evil as much as it is two different worlds one cannot even compare. One cannot compare an apple or a person who bite off the apple to a person who has the orange and that is why they killed these wise beings because these wise beings were alien in every form of the word to the ones on the left. I am rather obligated to write about something. I am so insane I write books and explain to people why happiness is a symptom of script neurosis.

One way to look at it is to think about a shark. This great white shark kills a baby seal. It rips that seal apart and blood is everywhere and that cute little seal is eaten. That shark could not do that if it had emotions. It would be grossed out by all the blood, it would be sad that is killed such a pretty seal. A doctor could not perform surgery if he was emotional to the extent the blood bothered him. So you see lack of emotions is valuable and in the extreme right brain dominate state emotions have to go and that means judgment has to go to achieve the extreme heightened awareness and concentration. "He must increase as I decrease". Anything less than machine state in not going the full measure. One must focus on eliminating all emotions and all fear to reach the extreme level of concentration. This is why "worry about the log in your own eye" is important because you are not going to just achieve right brain extreme, you may have to spend the rest of your life doing it unless you get medieval in your "seeking" of it. I understand the ones who are depressed and suicidal have the best chance of understanding what I am saying because they are more aware than anyone what emotions lead to eventually. One simply has two choices, purge all emotions and reach the machine state or remain an emotional wreck and neither is good or bad because one cannot ever compare the two. These two states are totally contrary to each other. There is nothing you can compare about the two, totally different worlds, psychologically speaking. One either has cravings and desires and longings to be accepted, and longing to be loved, and is in turn a slave to those things, or one is a machine. That is the trade off for the clarity and concentration. That is why I am certain none of these "wise" beings called prophets were pushing this state of mind as something you have to do to be good or saved. You are not in a machine state and just saying that to you scares you, and you come to conclusions based on that fear, and you try to use logic to explain how that is dangerous because you can't understand it until you are in the machine state, just like I cannot feel what it was like to have satisfaction. I cannot feel what it is like to have euphoria from drinking beer. I can drink beer but I cannot get high. Seven months or eight months is an eternity when you have no sense of time. One month is an eternity and I get no satisfaction when I publish a book. I have no sense of accomplishment. I just start the next book that same day I submit the last book. There is no need to relax or have a vacation because the mental processing never stops. This also means there is no stress and there is no up's or down's. I can't get depressed because I can't get happy. If you are on the left and have strong emotions you will already determine this is way too dangerous and then you understand why none of these religious teachers ever communicated it properly and only turned a world full of left brain neurotics into butchers of each other over supernatural god ideals. It does not matter how many degree's you have in these religions or how many speeches or how much you have read of these religions if you have a strong sense of time and strong hunger, you cannot translate the codes in the texts, they are simply to full of complexity.

You are simply lost in your world of delusions. You perhaps will never reach the machine state to its maximum unless you get seriously hardcore about the fear conditioning and that means, "fear not". Your mental conditioning strategy comes before everything and everyone because you have to live with yourself, and you do not have to live for others. You have to live with your mind first and foremost above everything else in the universe into infinity. Perhaps it sounds selfish but only if you have emotions, it is in fact not selfish, it is true.

I wrote this song when I was deeply depressed about four years ago. Perhaps you can detect I no longer wanted emotions.

http://www.youtube.com/watch?v=zrLYVAOmIhM

Your love is equal to your ability to hate. You hate the things you don't love so your love is hate to a lesser degree. One who becomes sad when it rains cannot see the clouds over head.

"Researchers from the school of psychology at Britain's Keele University have found swearing can make you feel better as it can have a "pain-lessening effect," according to a study published in the journal NeuroReport."

7/15/2009 3:26:08 AM - This comment about cussing is in direct relation to breaking rules or doing things one has been told are bad or evil and in turn they get a rush out of it. What is really happening is the right hemisphere of the mind is slowly encouraged when one does something they perceive is bad or evil. Cussing is one thing, stealing is one thing, killing is one thing , facing certain death, like being a dare devil is one thing. There is no absolute evil or bad thing there is in fact only perceptions of what one is told is a bad or evil things, so when they do those things they "break the rules" and that encourages right brain, which is against rules or is for freedom, and thus the pain mentally and physically is reduced because right brain is cerebral and as that increases the physical aspects decrease. My sense of taste is slight, sense of smell is slight, in general my body feels numb because my cerebral aspect or concentration and heightened awareness is so strong, all of these things must be turned down. That does not mean I cannot feel pain, but in general, I do not feel daily aches and pains or what is known a fatigue.

" We're nuts. They will just take us back to the feed farm."

One Flew Over the Cuckoo's Nest

If you think I am insane, what chance do you have of being considered sane? The reality you are facing is whatever you think you are, I am not. You have a strong sense of time, I do not. You have a strong sense of hunger, I do not. You have a strong sense of attachments and emotions, I do not. So if I am bad then you are good, and if I am good you are bad. I am dumb because I cannot use commas properly then you are good because you can use commas properly. If I can write seven books in seven months then you can write 14 books in seven months because I have mental issues so you certainly can do much more than I can. You certainly have much more mental function that I do. I cannot even spell words properly or form sentences properly or use the rules of grammar properly. I am retarded in contrast to your great wisdom and great mastery of language. So certainly you understand far more than I do, because if the accepted norms of education does not make you understand more than I do, then education itself is meaningless. If I understand things you do not understand and I have no mastery over planned language to any profound degree then that means you are in fact hindered by the fact you have a mastery over planned language. You can form sentences properly based on the norms of the left brain acceptability's but that is only relative to what a left brain person's world. You are sane and normal if you compare yourself to other left brain people who have taken well the planned language indoctrination, but in contrast to one who is extreme right brain dominate you perhaps are not even in the ball park in relation to ability to have a complex cerebral mindset. Perhaps you are extremely intelligent based on a scale of slight intelligence but you perhaps are not even noticed on the scale of absolute intelligence. Perhaps you should apply and see if there is a world record for a person who can form a sentence properly and see if that will assist you in showing the world your vast intelligence and ability to mimic what someone told you is a sign of intelligence. Perhaps if you rub your education degree against your skull it will enable you to come up with one wise saying in your entire life time. Do you perceive you have the mental ability to come up with one original wise saying in the 80 plus years you are alive, that the world would determine is a wise saying and remember for the rest of civilization? Do you even perceive you can do that? One wise saying? I understand you perhaps cannot do it if you have a strong sense of time. It perhaps is an impossibility. Perhaps you can just send them your education degree and maybe they will accept that as a wise saying. Maybe if you hang your education degree on a wall so that everyone can see it, they will not fault you for your inability to come up with one wise saying, in your life time. Are you getting upset that you wasted your whole life trying to become intelligent with education when in fact it was only making you dumber? I would perhaps be very upset to pay money to become dumber. That perhaps is not very intelligent to pay people money to make sure you become dumber. How much money did you pay people so that you would become dumber?

You should perhaps read this comment on this web page so that you can grasp you have been made dumber by the accepted methods of education by the society you have determined is righteous. You have in fact been mentally raped and mentally destroyed in every definition of destroyed. Perhaps that does not bother you. Perhaps you are pleased that you in fact have been mentally raped by society. Perhaps you are a sadist and enjoy suffering and you enjoy self harm. Perhaps you should seek mental health assistance because they have some wonderful drugs to help you deal with your extreme mental neurosis that is a result of your forced mental rape that society has thrust upon you. I am in fact indifferent to your suffering and it does not bother me to see you suffer. We all have our own hands to play. Life simply is also indifferent to your suffering. Life does not care that you were mentally raped and I do not care that you were mentally raped. Perhaps you are trying to use your raped mind to level a judgment on me when in fact you do not have the mental capacity to level a judgment upon me that is worth the paper it is printed on. Perhaps what I am saying is there are some symptoms you can attempt to apply to how you think that will enable you to diagnose the seriousness of your neurosis.

If you care too much, you may discover the helplessness of the situation. In school they have art class which is creative and right brain orientated and then they have reading, writing and math, and then they have history and then they have accounting and many classes that are essentially memorization classes, short term memory, and so they have, art and music, that is right brain and everything else is left brain, rule based, classes. If there is such thing as an opiate of the masses then accepted education is it. Why don't you go tell an education authority that reading writing and arithmetic is making everyone dumber because they don't have any fear conditioning classes to counter the left brain conditioning. I am doing that on a worldwide scale and I perceive nothing will come of it, and I feel no righteousness because I can't feel satisfaction. I eat for no reason. I personally enjoy logging into mydeathsapce.com and reading the children who hang their self because they cannot handle the strong emotions that are a side effect of the "education". That is the only thing that gives me pleasure. I would run out of things to write about if the children were not killing their self when they are 14 because they cannot handle embarrassment and shyness which are symptoms of the "left brain education". I do not want you ever to get the idea, I am trying to assist or change anything. I get great pleasure out of watching lemur monkeys kill their self with food and with drugs and in wars, when it could easily be avoided with some minor fear conditioning. I would run out of things to write about if these interesting characteristics of the script neurosis was gone. I am pleased with the blood bath you call norms of society. These children who kill their self have logically concluded that is the most secure way to get the hell away from you.

Laura E. (15) allegedly committed suicide at her home

Do you think a 15 year old child simply decides to kill their self because of natural mental problems? Does your pin prick mind assume that children just out the blue kill their

90

self because they have mental issues that are normal and not induced by the script and math neurosis? Do you even have mental function anymore? Are you even capable of understanding the script condition has a side effect called very strong emotions like shame? Right around 15 is when the script starts kicking in and the kids start having emotional problems. You do not know what a blood bath is, but I swear to god you are going to understand what a blood bath is. From that point on they are doomed. So this young girl was trying to hold on to the natural right aspect of the mind and she was thrown so fast into the left aspect she became ashamed and depressed and envious and shy and then she killed herself. You did that to her. I do not give a dam what your pinprick logic concludes. I do not give a dam what your laws say little boy. I do not give a god dam what you think about anything ever, little boy. If you think I am going to have compassion and mercy on your ass, you truly are brain dead as hell.

Lisa V. (19) allegedly committed suicide by overdosing on Cymbalta

You create the mental problems with education and then you create drugs and try to treat it. You do not deserve mercy or compassion but you do deserve infinite gnashing of teeth and I am all about infinite gnashing of teeth, boy. You do not have a big enough boat to land this fish. You bring all your laws, and all your weapons, and all your armies so when I assist you in understanding total obliteration, you will understand who I am, just before you close your eyes for the last time. I am strictly vengeance based. Do not ever assume I am here for peace and love and happiness. I am here to make a red sea. I have one thing you do not have, and that is the ability to bring it all down with my words. You will be at my feet, and you will wash the dust of my enemies off of my feet. "For the right brain, processing happens very quickly " this denotes I will take over everything before you even have a chance to figure out I am taking over everything. So much for democracy and freedom.

"America is a mistake, a giant mistake."

Sigmund Freud

America is a mistake because if someone determines their pursuit of happiness to take over everything and they can do it using their words, it is simply a dictatorship. I have determined to take over everything using my words. I have determined to raise an army to take over and eliminate anything that gets in the way of my pursuit of happiness. You can attempt to burn my books but that will only ensure victory for me sooner. You can attempt to lock me up but that will only bring more popularity to my books. You can attempt to kill me but that will only ensure my books are read further. The word is already out. You are already defeated. The house of cards is coming down. Perhaps you do not have the brain function to realize that. Perhaps you assume I am talking on physical terms. Perhaps you assume I am just kidding. To the victor who unlocks the right aspect to the extreme goes to spoils. It is not important what you think or what you may try to plan to stop my pursuit of happiness because you have already lost. It was not a battle because the Mac truck hit you before you could even fire your weapon. Everything you think about society will not exist, sooner than you think.

Joh 10:10 "The thief cometh not, but for to steal, and to kill, and to destroy: I am come that they might have life, and that they might have it more abundantly."

I am here to let people know they can have the intelligent aspect of the mind. The carpetbaggers who like to keep everyone dumb with their education and math, and keep everyone stupid, are going to hate me, because I am going to use their "righteous" laws of reason to hang them with. I am here to annihilate the control freaks, and the ones who want to keep everyone stupid. I beg the control freaks to attack me first because once I exterminate them the flood gates will be open. The thief's want to kill the mind, and destroy the mind, and keep it on the left. I let everyone know they have a right aspect of the mind than can be easily unlocked, and then they will have brain function and be free and do things at the speed of light in contrast to how they are in the left brain darkness.

Who do you think is going to lose? The thief's better start passing laws to outlaw my books and pass laws that say I cannot put them freely for free on web site for others to download. They better start passing laws against my freedom of speech and freedom of press. They better start burning books swiftly. I will now discuss something important. How big do you think my army is? If I was afraid of you, I certainly would not be telling you my battle plans and then publishing them for the world to see. Back to reality.

I try very hard to keep this left aspect from coming back. I have great fear of these cuss words and that is why I put them in books. There are some very deep seeded fears in my mind in relation to words. I came from a religious background so I have great fear in using words like god dam and many cuss words. So I have this aversion to certain words still. I am mentally afraid still. That is what the neurosis is all about, it instills shame, embarrassment and shyness to say what is on one's mind. I do not publish these words so you will think I am tough, I publish these words because the left aspect of my mind says "If you publish these words you will pay for it and you should be afraid.". I am applying the principle "Fear Not." I publish these words and if I am killed because of it, that is okay, because I have already let go anyway. I have nothing to lose that I have not already lost. I have already made peace with "god" when I did not call for help when I started to convulse, after swallowing all of those pills. I already let go, so what can harm me? The answer is, my mind can harm me if I allow it to persuade me words can harm me. Someone told me certain words are bad to say and it may take me many years to get that "log out of my "minds" eye". So you see I am helping myself with these books because I don't want to publish them. I don't want anyone to read them that's why I give them away and sell them and put them on a worlds stage, because I am not going to be able to help myself if I have any reservations or limits on the table. The world is the stage I use to condition myself away from fear and shame and embarrassment that the script neurosis has enabled in my mind. The log this script neurosis has caused in anyone who has been indoctrinated into it, may take the rest of your life to cancel out. The neurosis is already done so now the treatment aspect is at play. No medicine is going to help you, that is a fact beyond all facts. You have to save yourself from the neurosis. The damage is already done so you can decide to live with the damage or you can attempt to fight the mental battle to negate the damage. It is not a good or bad thing, it is simply a choice. It is not a group effort because the damage to the mind is personal. It varies from person to person. No person can tell how damaged another person is, but each person can tell how damaged they are. You know what words you are afraid to say. You know what music you are afraid to listen to. You know what topic you are afraid to discuss. You know what pictures you are afraid to look at. You know what music you hate and what music you love. You know what chat rooms you hate and what chat rooms you love. You know what religions you hate and what religions you love. You have to kill all of those fears. You know if you are afraid of the dark. You know if you are afraid of ghosts. You know if you are afraid of words. I cannot tell and no one can tell what you are afraid of, only you can work on the "log in your "minds" eye." There is no need to charge or pay someone because it is cut and dry. Whatever you are afraid of in your mind, means the neurosis is strong in your mind. Go to someone who is "sane" and say fuck, and see how they react. Then you will understand how much neurosis they are in. Say the word fuck around your parents and they will take you into the bathroom and wash your mouth out with soap and physically abuse you, and then you will have an idea of how much neurosis they are in. Most people are in such extreme neurosis, they become unhinged with cuss words. You do not even have to get to dangerous words, they become unhinged and have the "inability to tolerate" when you speak even words that are not cuss words. You can just come up with a sentence in relation to nearly anything that you understand they have an aversion to and they will freak out and become emotional wrecks in short order. Essentially their mind is totally locked down and frozen. Shame itself is relative to the observer so you should not have shame at all. One who believes they will be harmed if they say a certain word is so far in neurosis, they may never reach the right aspect no sense of time state of mind, unless they do some serious hardcore conditioning away from fear.

The truth is, they may in fact be too far gone. They are simply so far into the left they are a lost cause or lost sheep. They know the "bad words" and the bad words are in fact in their mind, but they never speak them because they have determined knowing a bad word is not bad, but if you speak a bad word that is bad. That is one who is in full blown neurosis. There is no logic to their determination. A word is a grunt in the mind and if ones speak s it out loud nothing has happened but they translated that word into a verbal sound or grunt. Somehow they determined that means something damaging to their self. That is the problem with planned language. Someone invents words and then labels them good or bad words, and then one is judged by whether they use good or bad words, based on another person's determination about what is a good word or bad word. That means that initial person who decided these are good words or bad words, is god of determining what good words or bad word are. That is impossible to accomplish in any legitimate sense. If I say a Satanist is bad, then I am good. If I say a Satanist's is good, then I am bad. If I just say Satanist, then people assume I am bad. If I say death is good, then I am bad. If I say death is bad, then I am good. If I just say death, then people assume I am bad. This is the neurosis. People are making judgments based on grunts and that is insanity because there is no proof one is good or bad if they make a grunt. You can never prove that a word a person says makes them in fact good or bad in relation to absolute good or bad. Whatever you say, someone will like you and someone will hate you for it, and few will ever be unphased at all. The ones who are unphased at all by whatever you say are in fact not in neurosis. They have the ability to tolerate ambiguity, doubt that words mean anything. Pick out any chat room in the universe and go in there and say something derogatory about that chartroom topic and they will scold you.

I have talked about Christian scriptures in Buddhist chat rooms and they warned me that is not what this chat room is about. I have Islamic comments in Jewish chat rooms and they banned me instantly. I have said physics comments in philosophy chat rooms and I was banned instantly. So these labels make people assume this identity in their head and anything that does not fall under that label they become angry and spiteful. They essentially mentally think in very tight circles. They have no ability to be open minded or see things as a whole, because the script neurosis has made them so left brained, they only see parts and any parts they determine is not like their part, they mentally become angry and upset. They start to hate and they start to throw around words and judgments because it is ambiguous to their perceived "label". "Neurosis is the inability to tolerate ambiguity" which means they cannot grasp everything is relevant. They cannot think outside of the box. They can only think in their little sand box and if anything is outside of their little sand box it must be the devil or evil and wrong. There are no drugs that can cure them from that extreme neurosis that is why the fear conditioning must be very hard core. I rest in the fact people do not read books written by insane people. - 6:34:20 AM

Let's just pretend this comment is true. That means the society as a whole is ruining the mental capacity of the offspring openly and then suggesting they are wise in doing so, and then making sure other countries learn their techniques and encourage these other countries to do the same. I have to mentally pretend this comment is a lie because I might start thinking "they know not what they do." is the greatest description of what is happening to our species that any human being could ever say. There is no other way to say it but to say, they as in the norms of society and acceptable education norms know not what they do to children. A rapist knows what they are doing, a totally insane person does not know what they are doing. A totally insane person will harm children and not even know they are harming children, they will in fact think they are helping children become smarter, when they are in fact ruining children's minds.

Gen 2:9 "And out of the ground made the LORD God to grow…, and the tree of knowledge of good and evil." (good and evil denotes labels) That is a left brain characteristic. Left brain excels in naming and categorizing things.

I will make this very clear. At this exact moment 7/15/2009 7:59:10 AM, the least of your problems in all of the universe is death. Facing your death is the least of your problems at this moment in history. Perhaps you should spend the rest of your life figuring out what that means, because I was just compelled to say it, and I am not compelled to clarify it. One might suggest you will soon wish all you had to deal with are terrorists. You cannot even defeat people, so certainly I am not afraid of you. I will now discuss something ambiguous. Granted that was extremely out of context. I only tell you the secrets that aren't important to me. Granted I am currently trapped in some sort of void. If you will consider being my fan, I will consider being my fan. You should be far less concerned about who I am, and far more concerned about what I am. I am feeling infinitely out of context this fine morning. One might suggest I am going to great lengths to go home. What kind of drugs do you think I am on now?

1Jn 2:18 "Little children, it is the last time: and as ye have heard that antichrist shall come, even now are there many antichrists; whereby we know that it is the last time."

Even now children the adults who are on the left and are anti-right brained will force you to become like they are with their offerings of education. You have no defense against these demons, so you let me take care of them. I will hang them with my sword of ink, and they will know who I am.

1Pe 4:12 "Beloved, think it not strange concerning the fiery trial which is to try you, as though some strange thing happened unto you:"

Once you start to condition away from fear and you go right brain dominate you are going to have this mental battle and you are going to assume "some strange thing happened to you" mentally, but that is because the neurosis is so strong you are going to think you went mad. The reality is you are waking up and starting to use 100 percent of your brain power and so in contrast to using 10% of your brain power it is going to be overwhelming, but you will adjust. Avoid listening to people who say you need drugs so they can fix you. Your mind will work it out. Some people will not make it, they will lose it but that expected because this is life and there are no guarantees, but the truth is, it is better to try and fail than to never try at all. It is better to try and get out of the neurosis than to understand you are in neurosis and remain there, but it is not good or evil, it is simply a personal choice. If you like to get high you condition into the right brain and you will be high and never need drugs again, and so you have to accept you taking drugs is simply a way to achieve right brain dominate mindset for a moment. You simply take drugs to get high so you can feel the right brain sensation for a moment. That is why you do drugs to get high. You want to feel the "power" of the right brain. What that means is people who say drugs abuse is bad, are really in fact saying, trying to achieve the sensation of the right brain is bad. That is how fucked up this whole world is. People do drugs to get high so they can feel how they should feel if they never got the education script conditioning. So people pass laws to lock people up for doing drugs, when in reality the people who do drugs just want to feel the power of the right aspect of the mind. That is how fucked up this world is. Everything is the reverse. Insanity looks like sanity and sanity is insanity. They pass laws and say drugs harm the mind when in factual reality drugs help one reach the right aspect of the mind but the problem is, it is not permanent so one eventually kills their self trying to negate the script neurosis they were forced into by law as a child. That is how fucked up this world is, quote me on that.

Lev 10:9 "Do not drink wine nor strong drink thou, nor thy sons with thee, when ye go into the tabernacle of the congregation, lest ye die: it shall be a statute for ever throughout your generations:"

This is simply saying, you can reach a state of right brain dominate with drugs, but it will kill you because it will not be permanent so you will keep taking the drugs to reach the right aspect, which is exactly why many artists take drugs to be more creative, but it tends to kill them in the end. "lest ye die". You have to do it the hard way, which is face your fears and condition away from them and get them out of your head and that will make it permanent, then you won't need the drugs to get high and many people will comment to you in chat rooms "What kind of drugs are you on?" and you can say "perhaps I am on very good drugs, perhaps". This is also exactly what this comment is saying,

Eph 5:18 "And be not drunk with wine, wherein is excess; but be filled with the Spirit;"

So you see this is not saying, drugs are bad, it is saying, drugs are not permanent right brain dominate but "Fear not" or condition away from fear is permanent right brain dominate. So we are locking up everyone who does drugs on the pretense drugs are bad, when in reality drugs are not bad at all, they are an option to negate the brainwashing of the scribe neurosis, but the truth is, the fear conditioning will make you filled or is permanent. So wanting to get high is good because you want to be on the right complex creative aspect of the mind, but you have to consider that the drugs will not take you all the way and so the scary fear conditioning is for hard core people who seek to get permanently high, so to speak. The drugs are for the lightweights and the fear conditioning is for the hard core seekers. You are not good or bad if you want to stay on the left or want to achieve the right, that is not how it works. Script looked like a good idea and is a good idea, but it has some major side effects. That is all this is about. Some people like math and language and the trade off is they get stuck in the left aspect of the mind and that means they lose some aspects of the right aspect of the mind. So there is really nothing going on that is wrong, there is simply some misunderstandings in relation to the side effects of the script and math education. One might suggest there is far more going on here than meets the eye, but I prefer to keep those secrets to myself.

1Pe 4:3 "For the time past of our life may suffice us to have wrought the will of the Gentiles, when we walked in lasciviousness, lusts, excess of wine, revellings, banquetings, and abominable idolatries:"

All this is really saying is, in the past I was under the influence of the left brain and I had attachments, or lusts and idolatries and I got drunk to achieve right brain and now I don't because I conditioned away from fear as in "fear not" and now I am drunk all the time and I lost much of those left brain side effects like, eating too much, and lusting over physical things and attachments to physical things because I am very cerebral now. If one doesn't have a strong sense of hunger, one tends not to over eat, and the fact many Americans do over eat proves that they are way too far into the left. Essentially all of societies problems are a symptom of that dam "apple" of knowledge called reading, writing, and math. I am up for counter arguments but you don't have one.

So I am trapped in this pondering that either a human being is intentionally making people take this education to keep them dumb so they are easier to control, or this reading and writing aspect looks very good and it just is not logical that it could do anything wrong or have bad mental side effects. The bottom line is the script invention looks very sweet but it actually destroys your mind if you don't counter it with fear conditioning. If everyone was on the right side, people would not tend to over eat and that would save lots of medical costs to treat people who are obese. People would not be stressed out so that would save lots of money on treating hypertension. People would not be so prone to abuse drugs because they would be high as all get out, mentally and the drugs would not even work on them. I drank while I was like this and I drank a lot at one sitting and all I achieved is to reduce my motor skills but I got no mental sensation and no euphoria. Drugs simply do not get you high when you are on the extreme right so why even do them? That's right there is no point in doing drugs when you are on the extreme right. If I did something like cocaine I would not write faster I would probably write slower because in contrast to how "strung out" or "wired" I am like this now, cocaine would be a sedative.

Speed would be a sedative. I have no stress so all of the drugs used to relive stress do nothing, so why would I do them? No point at all in doing drugs if they do not do anything. So that is the cure for all known drug abuse. All drug abuse is a symptom people are trying to negate the left brain indoctrination caused by script and math. They simply want to go back to how they were as a child mentally. They like the "light". They are not evil or bad or stupid, they are trying to go back to how they were before they were mentally raped by the 3 R's. We truly are our own worst enemy. For the last 5000 years we have been paying for that one invention. We wasted so much time and life because of that one invention. And what is perhaps tragic is beings tried to tell us this and they never could pull it off. One might suggest Heimdall is going to pull it off.- 9:46:18 AM

To have a person with a strong sense of time working on creative aspects or inventing things is a total joke. Right brain is associated with creativity, so a person with a strong sense of time and strong hunger and strong emotions is unable to invent anything in comparison to one without strong sense of time and strong hunger. Edison, Einstein, Tesla were certainly to a degree right brain but I understand they were not to the extreme. If they were to the extreme they would be writing these books and explaining what all the religious texts meant and they didn't because they couldn't. We have all these people in the military trying to "think out of the box" but they are all about rules and regulations and so they are extreme left brained and they are in fact not capable of thinking out of the box ever. That is how fucked up this world is."The right brain has been associated with the realm of creativity."

Why don't you try with all of your might to disprove anything I say. You can say I am crazy . You can say I am insane. You can say you won't even respond with a reply, but the truth is, you cannot respond with a reply. You are not even in the ballpark. I just assume you're the one who voted to make a law that said I had to go to school so you are pretty far from being considered my friend. Imagine if I started trying. Perhaps you think writing all this crap is hard on me mentally. I recall I suggested I am simply fiddling on the roof and watching the mice scurry about. I don't play your rules anymore because they almost made me kill myself so you don't even get to talk anymore, to me. You do not even get to look at me. That is the reality you are facing. You are simply an illusion until further notice. - 10:04:03 AM

Perhaps someone wishes to counter argue my counter arguments. You want to be humble and meek. You go apologize to all the people in jail you ruined with your education. The drugs addicts, the sex offenders, the murders, the haters, the molesters, the rapists, the greedy, the lustful, the envious. You go apologize to all of them because you ruined their minds with your forced education and if you cannot do that, never ever speak of being meek and humble.

"Children are God's spies." Elizabeth Bowen (1899-1973)

This means children are naturally on the right aspect or right brained, in relation to "I sit at the right hand side" and "suffer the children", and your education ruins them. I am going to write so many books you are going to drown in my books and society is going to ban freedom of speech and freedom of press because of it. I am going to kill you with my words and you are going to beg that there never be freedom of speech or freedom of press and you will hate the founders who said we should have freedom of speech and freedom of press. That is my pursuit of happiness and I beg you to get in my way. You do not have the brain function to grasp how many I have in my army. I am just the bait. One might suggest I am expendable, so imagine who the generals are in my army. I am the least in my army. I am the loose cannon in my army. My army cannot control me, I have way to big of a mouth and I tell way too many secrets, so even my army is worried about me. My own army wishes I would shut up. I am an outcast in my own army. That gives you a good idea of what chance you have, and the correct answer is: Perhaps I have zero chance. I will now discuss something pertinent.- 10:22:30 AM

10:23:05 AM – What is very funny is my strategy in my writing is to scare the fearful away and that will only leave the seekers who read my words. This is in relation to "separate the wheat from the chaff". If you have problems with what I write, you go run and climb back into your little hole, because I do not have time for weak minded fearful beings even though I have infinite time. Maybe you will have better luck next time around. Do you really think I woke up to the fact you are raping children mentally and I am going to let that slide? Do you think I am going to have tolerance? Do you think I am going to have mercy? If you think I am not going to annihilate everything in my path, you truly are insane, psychologically speaking, so to speak, what have you, and then there were none. Armageddon is an insult to the war that comes with me. One in a Buddhist chat room once said about me "He is an angry one isn't he." One might suggest that is an infinite misunderstanding that needs infinite clarification. To clarify that comment I would have to write a book. Maybe one day I will write a book. These are simply thick pamphlets or poorly disguised diaries. I am just toying with the idea of writing a book. These are all just experiments to determine if I want to even bother writing a book. I will remind you when I start writing books. I am way too high to figure out if I am the blessed one or the cursed one so I will leave that up to the world to decide. I personally do not give a rat's ass about such labels one might suggest, at this time, psychologically speaking, so to speak, what have you, and then there were none. My mindset is simply, because I am so far into the right everything I say seems normal to me and in turn seems insane to the ones on the left. The ones on the left are not insane, what they do appears normal to them, so relative to their observation they are sane and they perceive I am insane. Relative to ones on the left, Einstein seemed "out there" or "wise" but he was not wise or out there, relative to him, he was normal or sane. Einstein was simply on the right to perhaps an extreme degree. Look at how creative his ideas were, that is a symptom of right brain. He could think out of the box. Freud is known to have done a lot of cocaine but he also said "Sometimes a cigar is just a cigar." He perhaps did not get high on the cocaine because he was on the right side of the mind. He was high all the time. I simply cannot reach you because you are too far to the left, or, I am too far to the right. I am on the opposite shore. I say tomato and you hear potato. I can have faith some who are leaning to the right can grasp some things I say, but at the end of the day, even they assume I must be totally insane. I have talked with ones in nirvana and we can communicate to a degree but it seems when I start really communicating they dismiss what I say. That is a generalization of course, but it is like this accident I had threw me so far to the right, people's inability to tolerate ambiguity catches up to them. So I write with the understanding people who read my books maybe 200 years from now will understand what I am saying. I cannot communicate with people who are alive now because I am too far to the right. I am too far out there. Granted it was not my doing it was an accident. The last thing I remember is I was convulsing on the couch and a red beam of heat went over my body and I thought "I needed to call 911." And then I thought "No, this is what you want" and then I went to sleep, woke up in the morning, and I felt better. So now you can go look that up in your little books and figure out what that is and then you can call me and make a diagnosis and everything will be better. All I need is a good diagnosis. One might suggest I need an infinitely good diagnosis. I am not sure why I said red beam of heat but I associate heat with red. I did not see the beam but I felt it. I know exactly what it was, but you don't get to know those kinds of secrets. You just get the piddle diddle secrets, so to speak, psychologically speaking, what have you.

The true humor about western religions is none of them speak about no sense of time so that proves they are not "on the right hand side of the father(brain)" so they are not even in the ballpark in relation to understanding the texts they 'preach" they have been killing people over for the last 2500 years or so. The humor in that is truly infinite. It does not matter what they preach, if they are not preaching condition away from fear in relation to "fear not" and are not pushing for no sense of time and slight hunger as a sign post in ones mental progress, they are what is known as false prophets beyond a shadow of a doubt in absolute reality. One might suggest I give an American spin on religion. The gospel according to an American. The Americans figured all the religions out. We are the new holy land in relation to "holes in my head" or people saying "what drugs are you on?" often to me. You guys over in the middle east have been killing each other for 2500 years over your misunderstandings and some retard American figured it all out in seven months. So the little grains of sand you have been killing your offspring over for thousands of years, do not mean anything. All the dead people that are the fruits of your misunderstandings died for nothing, because they listened to your delusions and false understandings of the teachers you suggest you understand. Obviously you do not understand a thing about the teachings you so swiftly kill your offspring for over a grain of sand. All of the rocks and dirt you kill for do not mean shit. Nothing you have assumed in thousands of years is correct. Not even one thing you have talked your offspring to die for is right or correct. You sent them to their deaths for absolutely nothing. Now you have to live with that. Why don't you have your religious teachers contact me so I can teach him properly so he will no longer have his offspring dying over a dam piece of dirt. No charge. If you are just going to continue to slaughter innocent people over a worthless piece of dirt I will go ahead and throw you some free charity teachings. I can't charge you because your soul wouldn't cover the fee. I want to attack Hindu's but their religion goes back 50,000 years and I can only find nothing to attack. They don't have religious texts. I try to find some but they just say look on google for our history and that's the joke. They are history before recorded history. They are what we are before we all got screwed up mentally with the scribe and math. So the world is so backwards and screwed up I cannot possibly fix it so I just mock it. It is beyond my ability to repair. The neurosis is far too strong. Clinically speaking there are far too many crazy people to heal. Mohammed tried to cut off all the crazy peoples head s but that didn't work because crazy people I think are able to grow back their heads. One might suggest Mohammed had a very progressive strategy and I understand Jesus would have used that strategy also but the lefters didn't give him much of a chance to form an army. He got three years before they butchered him. I am quite certain the disciples did not want to die but they were dealing with insane people they are not mentally thinking clearly because of the neurosis. They were quite brave to attempt to wake up people who are crazy, in person. I sit in my little isolation chamber with machine guns sticking out of every window and they are setup up to shoot on sight. I am a little more proactive like Mohammed because I just assume the crazies are coming for me. It is not people on the left are crazy they just use such a small portion of the mental faculties they are as Moses suggested "cursed above cows". I am not sure even what that means because there are perhaps some rather wise cows in the world. I have not personally met a wise cow, but "cursed above cattle" is rather harsh. I try to stay well grounded and suggest brain dead mole cricket but I am biased and perhaps cursed above a cow is more accurate. Perhaps you can figure out for yourself whether you wish the title cursed above a cow, brain dead mole cricket, darkness, infidel, adversary, viper, sheep or "sane". All of these titles are acceptable. One might suggest I find no fault with these determinations. Cursed above a cow is worse than infidel so Mohammed was actually quite merciful. I understand Moses was the big fish. He was the main man in the western religions. He is the Buddha of the age for the west for that time period. The Buddhists understand that but you perhaps never will. Perhaps you cannot even grasp the Buddhists agree with Moses, Jesus and Mohammed at least the Buddhist who would never admit they are Buddhists, which are the "real" Buddhists. You need to wake up because you are in the dark about so many things. It may take your lifetime to get up to speed. The west is so fucked up the Buddhist won't tell us they agree with our "wise" teachers because we would call them the devil. That's how fucked up we are mentally speaking. I am a loose cannon because I am not on anyone's side because I do not want to rob myself of a chance to attack someone. I will do some wise quotes because I keep ruining my thick pamphlet diaries when I talk.

slackOR at 2009-07-15 09:13 CET:
Is this VOLUME 5...or VOLUME 6...or other?
What's VOLUME 1 (or 2).
These are great mind bending books, I must say..but perhaps who am I? Keep up the good work and perhaps I can continue reading this infinite series of infinite books, adinfinitum... perhaps.
peace...perhaps.."

See this is a comment from a guy who likes my books. I do not remember what is in Volume 5 but I uploaded it to the pirate site and he is reading them. I can't tell if anyone can reach this extreme right brain like I did without doing it the "hard way" but I am certain it can be reached to a degree using far less "invasive" techniques than I used. He certainly is saying perhaps a lot. He is getting a little crazy or "holy". That is what frees up the mind from the frozen left aspect. Why isn't life funny? You are going to die and you cannot do anything about it, so that's pretty funny. No need to be stressed out because you are meeting the maker and no matter how much you don't want to, it is factually beyond the realm of certainty. Why wouldn't I give my books away freely. It does not take any effort to write them, and I am going to write them anyway, so there is no reason to horde them. I am not intelligent enough to determine who will "get the message in my books" and who will not, so I just give them to everyone I can. Everyone essentially thinks I am on drugs and insane and that is pretty accurate but extremely out of context. One monk suggested I have the laughing bug which means people on the left laugh at what I say and that really pisses me off.

You can look at my situation like this. I had an accident and woke up to some major crimes being committed against people, and I am still in the writing stage, and when I have given up on the writing strategy, one might suggest I raise an army and start leveling civilization. That is what I understand is on my plate. I would not underestimate what I say. One might suggest subconscious is rather haughty and rather good at predicting the future.

I happen to own a blue heeler dog named Jake and they are known to be good sheep herder dogs and I will use him if I have to. He can herd sheep and that is all you need to know. I am trying to figure out what is possessing me to publish this book. This book is a nightmare. I will give you this book and you publish it. I do not want to publish anything in this book, it's all evilness, granted that is extremely out of context. I need far less sedation than the few who have faith in me. My secret weapon is that I can look at women's eyes and feel this eye beam thing. I cannot tell what it is. It's an eye beam thing. I am afraid to ask the ladies what that eye beam thing is because they may assume I am onto them. I prefer to call ladies infinite wrath potentials because their wrath is potentially infinite and that of course is relative to my observations. If you mix in the infinite wrath potential with the eye beam thing, you have infinite eye beam wrath potential thing and I am not even sure if that is a word.

"Wisdom, compassion, and courage are the three universally recognized moral qualities of men."
Confucius

Intelligence is the moral quality of women. Einstein ruined all of this stuff because it is all relative to the observer. There is no absolute wisdom, compassion or courage there is only perceptions of these things.

Then you have archeologists who ruined the moral quality aspect because what is a moral to a lemur monkey. I have yet to hear anyone dispute the fact they discovered we are in fact lemur monkeys. People can say no we are human beings but in reality, no we are not human beings we are lemur monkeys that lost our hair but that is about it and ruined our minds with an invention called script. That is it. There is no more complexity to the situation than that. I am waiting for someone to tell the archeologists that it is not a lemur monkey that we are related to. Perhaps you guys are building your case to dispute a fossil. How well are your delusions of grandeur holding up in the face of reality and fact? My defense in all of my books is "I am a lemur monkey what the hell do you expect from me." I can live with the fact they just told the entire universe we are just lemur monkeys but I will not start saying infinite wrath potentials are lemur monkeys because I still have an ounce of common sense in my head. These archeologists are beyond my power because they called women lemur monkeys when they said we are all lemur monkeys. One might suggest they will certainly be sleeping on the couch for about the next infinity. Perhaps that is their opening pickup line when they go one a date 'Hi darling do you know you are a lemur monkey?" No wonder they go far out into the desert and dig holes in the ground.

6:37:05 PM – I tried to write a fiction book but I kept telling the truth.

"China's Health Ministry has ordered a hospital to stop using electric shock therapy to cure youths of Internet addiction, saying there was no scientific evidence it worked."

If there was no scientific evidence it worked, then they were just experimenting.

A being said "The kingdom is within" that denotes cerebral.

Gen 1:1 In the beginning God(Unnamable, nature, fate, evolution, something,(1) don't preach supernatural or you are a sorcerer) created the heaven(Cerebral, right aspect of the mind, "the light", the infinity aspect of the mind, the heaven and not physical based aspect of the mind) and the earth(the left hemisphere which is , time based, and physical based, and less complex and thus the "dark" aspect of the mind). - 7/16/2009 12:08:29 AM

Earth denotes physical aspects which is left brain

Heaven denotes cerebral aspects which is right brain

Act 13:6 (1)"And when they had gone through the isle unto Paphos, they found a certain sorcerer(someone that makes money by making supernatural claims), a false prophet,…, whose name was Barjesus: "

Have faith I will never be intelligent enough to speak as an authority on the supernatural.

Gen 1:2 And the earth(left brain was not dominate in man) was without form, and void(void denotes nothingness or nirvana, so man was initially right brain dominate or in a state of void or nothingness; machine state); and darkness(left brain) was upon the face of the deep(right brain or the complex aspect or the "deep waters). And the Spirit of God(right aspect of mind) moved upon the face(denotes the crescent moon, meaning the right aspect and the left aspect make up the brain, the dark aspect(left) and the deep aspect(right)) of the waters.

So up to this point it goes like this. Humans have a right and left aspect of the mind. Left aspect is darkness in contrast to the "deep" right aspect.

Gen 1:3 And God said, Let there be light(right aspect of the mind): and there was light(right aspect or hemisphere).

Gen 1:4 And God saw the light(right hemisphere "deep aspect"), that it was good: and God divided the light from the darkness(left aspect).Divided denotes there is a equal portion to the brain left and right hemisphere.

6:50:04 PM – Its quite funny that people suggest this is some conspiracy when in fact people have been trying the best they can for 2500 years and the ones on the left just cannot seem to get it into their mind it is in fact reality. Certainly this is all just a dream. Human beings cannot be this blind. For one to be so blind and deny this script neurosis after 2500 years of people attempting to suggest it is true, one would have to go to great lengths to describe what kind of mental state that person must be in to still doubt the script neurosis. I am uncertain if darkness, adversary, cursed above a cow, "sane" viper, lost sheep, blind, the dead really even explains it properly. Certainly I have died and gone to hell and I am just talking to a wall because for humans in general to suggest they cannot grasp these really obvious and right in your face explanations of the situation this script has put their mind in, we are certainly doomed as a species because "infidel" would be a great compliment. Brain dead would be a great compliment. That is what I woke up to. That is the reality I woke up to. So clearly in relation to our species to me is a huge joke. For a person with a strong sense of time and hunger to even suggest the word intelligence is a huge joke beyond all jokes. That is the reality I woke up to accidentally. I am not going to knock myself out because I am in fact in all reality, attempting to talk to the mentally dead, in general. That is the reality I woke up to. I cannot come up with a word to explain what this script neurosis has done to people in general. I do not give a rat's ass if you suggest I am racists because you in general do not know what racist even is. In general the ones on the left do not know what anything is, in general. They simply are not capable of know what anything is, in general. Some of these wise beings suggest compassion and mercy in dealing with the "sane" but that is foolishness. That is why they blew it, because they were foolish. They attempted to be a helping hand because they were still in neurosis. They did not fully understand what they were dealing with. The assumed a few carefully formed sentences would solve the problem because they underestimated what this script has in fact done to the minds of the "sane". The script has turned off the mind of the "sane". In general they have no mind they are simply mindless specters. The 'sane" perceive crying is normal when it is abnormal. Tears are in fact a function to wash the eyes and clear the eyes of dirt, but the "sane" assume crying is normal. The "sane" assume when they cry that is a normal function of an animal but it in fact is definitive proof they have so many emotions as a result of script neurosis, they turn a bodily function into a flood of tears from their tear ducts and assume that is normal. I am simply unable to reach a being in such deep neurosis their entire foundation of what is normal behavior is in general, is simply symptoms of the neurosis. The ones who give out medicine are in deep neurosis. The ones who take the medicine are in deep neurosis so there is no chance to even reach any of them. They may get lucky and have a stroke or get cancer and maybe that will wake them up but in reality that won't even do it to the extreme. Those are simply people who partially wake up. They do not go the full measure. They get trapped at some stage along the way. The "sane" ones run around and assume they are well balanced mentally. They say retard things, like " One needs to have half of each aspect of the mind to be well balanced." The "sane" perceive they are in the middle. They perceive they have right aspect and left aspect working and a normal person has the two in harmony. It certainly is all just a joke. The "sane" with a strong sense of time and hunger in fact do not have any of the right aspect of the mind working, they only have the left aspect of the mind working and they are all the way to the left. The "sane" have to do major drugs to come up with anything creative. The "sane" kill their self with drugs just to feel the right aspect of mind because it is totally silenced beyond the definition of silenced. There is no right aspect of the mind working at all. It is in fact dead. They have only one half of their mind dominate and that is the left and the right is totally none functioning and reduced to simply a subconscious role. They have to do so many drugs to feel what the right aspect of the mind is like, they perceive they are high, but in reality it is just a symptom of how little brain function they have when they are stone cold sober in their "left aspect" neurosis. So morals or "doing it the right way" in relation to communicating with them is foolishness because I am dammed if I do and dammed if I don't. I am simply unable to reach ones who are so mentally "ill". I can communicate my sentences and make them all pretty and proper in their eyes, and then they will determine I am paranoid. I can cuss and yell and insult them into infinity and they will assume I am "ill". I can have patience and fail or I can have impatience and fail. That is the only choice I have , failure to communicate. There is no hope for our species because we ruined ourselves with the script invention. We are essentially as a species waiting to walk off a cliff and we cannot see the cliff because we are blind. That is all that is happening. We are simply waiting for Gadot.

The 'sane' have simply been in neurosis for as far back as they can remember and so they perceive they are normal. In fact they have not been normal since they were about eight or nine maybe ten years old. They do not even remember what normal is. The "sane" spend their whole life trying to come up with one wise saying or with one invention or with one creative thought and even when they perceive they do, they do not. They come up with a creative idea based on the norms of a society that is not capable of creative ideas because they killed the right creative aspect of the mind. Inventing a weapon that can kill people more effectively is not a god dam creative idea. Doing so many drugs one is able to paint a painting or create a song is not a god dam creative idea, it is simply a phantom creative idea as the result of being on the right aspect of the mind for a limited time as the result of drugs. They will attempt to use their meager logic skills and assume I am stupid because I cannot use the language properly because using language is in fact a symptom one is totally in the left hemisphere of the brain mentally. I submit I am very angry in my words but I understand these emotions are still attempting to surface, it is as if they are so ingrained even after eight months, the comment "worry about the log in your eye" is so true. I perceive I am spitting blood in my books yet I am not angry but my words are. They will attempt to perceive I am stupid because they cannot grasp they in fact are stupid, they have no mental function at all in relation to what they should have. I nearly killed myself because I tried to fit in with their insane model of being "normal" and I will never attempt to be like they are because I know what they are. They are the living dead. I will not edit my books so they will like them because they may assume I am like them. I am everything in the universe but like them. I will not pander to what I fucking own. The "sane" will wish I died. I will now discuss something of value. - 7:50:21 PM

You want some wisdom. Is that what you crave. Here is the only wisdom you need to ever understand.

jumper: 09.28.07, 7:22am, female, hit rocks, died, body found same day – jumperpool. com

This female jumped off the skyway bridge and made sure after falling 190 feet she hit the rocks. Now you are wise because you understand the definition of "love on the rocks." The society made this being determine falling 190 feet and landing on rocks was much more inviting than living one more second in this civilization called hell. That is what your script and what our great invention language has done to our species. When you see the hieroglyphics the Egyptians invented you now will understand this is the curse. That is why Moses said "we are cursed above cattle". All of your inventions and discoveries are not going to ever get you out that curse. I am not conscious because I still fear words. I still ponder if I can even go into the most haunted house in the universe alone at night with no chance of escape. I can translate every single comment and religious text known to man, but I am still not conscious. I am still in neurosis. I have no sense of time and no strong hunger and nearly no emotions and I am nearly a pillar of salt, but I am still in neurosis. What chance in hell do you think you have since I am still in neurosis. I am still under the influence of the snake.

Luk 17:21 "Neither shall they say, Lo here! or, lo there! for, behold, the kingdom of God is within you."

I am far closer to the kingdom than you are but I understand I may never be able to negate the effects of this script neurosis. That is how damaged our species is. We destroyed the kingdom which is the right aspect of our minds with language and math inventions. We destroyed it.

This is what we did to ourselves : jumper: 09.28.07, 7:22am, female, hit rocks, died, body found same day

We as a species jumped from the bridge and into the rocks and we keep doing it every time we tell people if they don't have "education" they are stupid. The ones who try to avoid the education are automatically abused just as the slaves in ancient times where abused. The ones educated by the script simply made a rule that anyone that is not educated is stupid, and so people either became educated or they became slaves. This is why Moses said "Let them go". Stop saying they are stupid when in fact they are wise to avoid the "snakes curse". They do not want to be cursed above cows but you make then become cursed above cows because the whole society is biased and racists against anyone who does not "conform" to the education of the snake. Now you understand why I have no mercy and I have no compassion and if you want a god dam blood bath I am all fucking about blood baths.

I pray for a blood bath. I will make a red sea and drown you in it, and I will not blink. I will remind you when I start to try. This is my love song:

http://www.youtube.com/watch?v=MEfmZOhTJvk

"Something like me sealed your fate. There is no need for me to wait." I will now discuss something of value. - 10:25:32 PM

I prefer the wood in case you misunderstood. I prefer the 12 inch nails because one might suggest your nine inch nails didn't kill me enough. And make sure you kill me very slow so that I might feel. If you are going to kill something, you better make dam sure you have the brain function to understand what dead is. The one with the most convincing argument is the only vote that counts. I told you subconscious is haughty. Back to reality. Mental hell is achieved when an insane person is absolutely convinced they are sane. I submit I am absolutely insane. Reasoning with a rabidity requires imagination.

7/17/2009 2:49:43 AM – I am totally doomed. - 2:50:07 AM

3:12:07 AM –

Mar 15:34 "And at the ninth hour Jesus cried with a loud voice, saying, Eloi, Eloi, lama sabachthani? which is, being interpreted, My God, my God, why hast thou forsaken me?"

This is why he said he was forsaken.

"we have been traditionally taught to master the 3 R's: reading, writing and arithmetic -- the domain and strength of the left brain"

He woke up and realized the "apple" had put everyone to sleep and he tried to let everyone know, and they took it all wrong and butchered him. One is unable to win but one can try to lose with grace. He lost with grace. Do you think for one minute I can convince you language has put you to sleep? I cannot convince you of that.

Joh 15:13 "Greater love hath no man than this, that a man lay down his life for his friends."

Who is my friend? The human species is my friend yet they will want to kill me when I try to convince them language has put them to sleep. My God, my God, why hast thou forsaken me? That is what he meant when he said this. My friends are killing me because I tried to wake them up from the slumber caused by the "apple".

I am a lone wolf looking for lost sheep.

"The intentionally uneventful and repetitive plot of Waiting for Godot can be seen as symbolizing the tedium and meaninglessness of human life, which loosely connects the play to one of the themes of existentialist philosophy."

I am more certain about my future than my past.

<Lestat9> Buddha starved for 39 days and a little girl found him and she said he reminded her of a spirit she once met

<Lestat9> so buddha "died" but was found by a little girl just in time

<Lestat9> so he was trapped in limbo

<elmental> i think gahndia got buddha's reccord

<elmental> gandia

<Lestat9> so he looked at the world from outside the world so he understood everything

<Lestat9> hindsight is 20/20

<Lestat9> so he said health is important, because he just wanted to go home

Carbon atoms, which have 6 protons, 6 neutrons and 6 electrons. When one reaches Nirvana by accident they are supposed to seek a teacher so they don't embarrass the clan, like I am doing. I tend to convince people drugs are bad. I am buying everything you are selling. If I knew what I was doing, I wouldn't be doing it. If I knew what you were doing, you wouldn't know it.

"In some causes silence is dangerous."
Saint Ambrose
Lost causes tend to be silent. Keeping silent may increase the danger. Being silent is better than being silenced. Telling the truth often leads to a dangerous silence.-12:33:39 PM

2Ti 1:7 For God hath not given us the spirit of fear(left brain caused by script); but of power, and of love, and of a sound mind(right brain)."

Rev 1:17 "And when I saw him, I fell at his feet as dead(Lost fear of death or conditioned away from fear). And he laid his right hand upon me(went right brain dominate),saying unto me, Fear Not(Lost fear); I am the first and the last(Lost sense of time)"

I would say today has been an on the fence, off the fence kind of day, in an on the fence kind of way.

I believe in the fence I sit on.

7/18/2009 1:32:30 AM

This is a chat in a Christian chat room.

01[00:10] <Lestat9> In the beginning god created the heaven(right aspect of the mind or hemispehre) and earth(left apsect), right is cerebral based left is physical based so they are opposites or anti to each other, jesus said i sit at the right hand side

01[00:10] <Lestat9> To achieve right brain onehas to condition away from fear in relation to fear not

*So I make a statement and then KarenJ starts to incite judgment to get the room on her side.

[00:11] <+KarenJ> HUH?

[00:12] <+KarenJ> Does that make sense to ANYONE?

*So what I said does not make sense to her which proves she is on the left side mentally and it in fact should not make sense to her.

[00:12] <rhondstat> nope

[00:12] <rhondstat> bit hi tech for me anyway :)

[00:13] <+KarenJ> I'm reasonably well educated but that one is nonsense as near as I can tell

*Karen says she is well educated and what I said makes no sense to hcr, so then she determines I must be wrong or insane or evil.

[00:13] <rhondstat> i got lost after midn

[00:14] <+KarenJ> Oh I didn't get lost. It has no meaning.

*So then she says, I didn't get lost what Lestat9 said has no meaning or is totally out there or wrong

01[00:14] <Lestat9> If you reflect back upon our own educational training, we have been traditionally taught to master the 3 R's: reading, writing and arithmetic -- the domain and strength of the left brain.

01[00:14] <Lestat9> This is the tree of knowledge, it make everyone left brained and physical based and so we fell from the grace of right brain

01[00:15] <Lestat9> so jesus said suffer teh children becasue everyone was making children learn this math and script and making them go lcft brain

[00:15] <+KarenJ> ummmmm that is NOT what the Bible says

*She says that is not what the bible says, so what I am saying is beyond her mental ability to grasp or it is too deep or complex. As if the bible times they had a good grasp on the brain aspects.

01[00:15] <Lestat9> so then he said, they know not what they do

[00:15] <+KarenJ> When he said that it was NOT about children

[00:15] <rhondstat> Lestat9 you got this way wrong

*I have it way wrong, so now they are god himself because they "KNOW"

01[00:16] <Lestat9> No man know the hour or day (of an accident) but teh father of the (accident). Oct 31 2008 1:38 PM

[00:16] <rhondstat> you are translating god to man?

[00:17] <+KarenJ> Again you are taking things out of context and twisting meanings

108

*This is accurate I am hearing the words and understanding them , one on the left takes everything at face value.

[00:17] <+KarenJ> Lestat9 you are twisting Scripture. There is great danger in this.

*Great danger denotes , fear, now she is afraid for me and afraid what I say may harm others, and she is afraid and scared, so she is starting to assume authority role and determine I am evil and should be expelled from the room to protect everyone.

01[00:18] <Lestat9> You are accurate karen, if one has a strong sens of time and a strong hunger they are on the left, so they ehar teh words and do not undersatnd, only one in teh extreem right can undersatnd the words in teh texts

01[00:18] <Lestat9> in reation to

[00:18] <rhondstat> kick his twisted butt lol

*here is the first suggestion. SO I say something and they do not get it so there is already voices saying "Hang his ass on a cross." That is called inability to tolerate ambiguity. If it is different kill it. That is left brain because if it cannot control something it kills it, left brain is all about control. You do as I say or you are evil and bad and I will take of you, in this case ban you from the room.

 01[00:18] <Lestat9> On the contrary, the right brain seems to flourish dealing with complexity, ambiguity and paradox.

[00:18] <+eagle`s> Lestat9 so often people who are highly educated can'tr see the wood for the trees

01[00:18] <Lestat9> contrary means anti- left

[00:18] <+TaraJo> anti-left ?

[00:18] <+TaraJo> wha?

01[00:18] <Lestat9> so jesus was on teh righthand side so anyone with a strong sense of tiem is anti-christ

01[00:19] <Lestat9> The kingdom is within

[00:19] <+eagle`s> they can't see what is being said because he can only see the technicalities his mind assocaites with the words

01[00:19] <Lestat9> denotes the mind left and right hemisphere

[00:19] <+KarenJ> TaraJo don't worry about him. He is talking gibberish

*This is very common, because I speak in random access thoughts ones on the left assume I am rambling. So I am not like they are so I am evil or bad, or stupid, when in reality they cannot grasp I am very far from stupid.

01[00:19] <Lestat9> the bibel has many complexity, ambiguity and paradox. so its not seqnetial, its random access, left brain is seqnetial

[00:19] <rhondstat> ah hem, hes not going to change,

[00:19] <+TaraJo> ah, might be why i don't understand it

[00:19] <+TaraJo> heh

[00:19] <+KarenJ> I would strongly suspect he is a college student taking his first philosophy class.

*I detect so much hate in this comment she made like she is god of all creation arrogance, I guess she missed the lemur monkey story

01[00:20] <Lestat9> The left brain is associated with verbal, logical, and analytical thinking. It excels in naming and categorizing things

[00:20] <+KarenJ> They tend to revel in using big words and odd concepts

01[00:20] <Lestat9> Cateogizriinf thinsg emans judhments

[00:20] <+eagle`s> Lestat9 scripture doesn't say anything about cerebral hemispheres, so we aren't really interested. How about you forget all that stuff and just concentrate on what the word says?

*If I was in person these people would stone me to death. Imagien what the disciples and jesus and Msoes and Mohammed had to go through. They did this in person.

[00:20] <+TaraJo> let's do brain surgery, and find out

[00:20] <+TaraJo> LOL

01[00:20] <Lestat9> Well 2500 years ago they didnt know much about teh brain, so I find no fault with their efforts they did the best they cdould

01[00:21] <Lestat9> I will not screw it up like they did

[00:21] <+KarenJ> TaraJo I wonder what would happen if we severed Lestat's left and right hemisphere

*The hate in Karen is so strong I can tell. Everything she says Is hateful to what I have said. She is attacking me in every word and making herself look so smart, but in reality I understand she is an illusion so I just keep typing and she keeps getting more and more hateful. Its pure hate. She cannot even say perhaps you are right.

[00:21] <+eagle`s> and the bible has no paradpoxes of that nature. It is when we start to believe what the Bible says we realise it isn't contradictory my friend

*Now I skip ahead to the end

[00:32] <+KarenJ> You are coming across as self centered and egotistical in the extreme.

01[00:32] <Lestat9> yes your judgemnets are perhaps relative to yoru state of mind

[00:33] <+KarenJ> If you want to stay here and chat like a normal person you will drop the attitude

*Karen simply says be like we are or act normal and act right. I am acting normal in relation to a person in extreme right brain, but she assumes I am not acting normal so she is determining I am evil or bad because I am not like her. That is what a racist is. If its not like her it is evil and bad.

[00:33] <+KarenJ> OK Go take a time out. Good night

[00:33] <+KarenJ> up

03[00:33] * isaiah40 sets mode: +o KarenJ

*this is where Isaiah gives Karen power or Ops, so now she can show everyone how powerful she is. Note I do not comment after this because I understand she has already determined to "hang me on a cross"

03[00:33] * Stengah (~apple@203.109.162.207) has joined #christian

03[00:34] * KarenJ sets mode: +b *!*lestatnin@c-76-108-80-221.hsd1.fl.comcast.net

03[00:34] * You were kicked by KarenJ (Would you like fries with that?)

*So you see why they butchered Jesus, they being the ones on the left. If I was in a town talking to KarenJ 2000 years ago, she would hang me on a cross and all her little friends would laugh and determine Karen was just and righteous for doing so because clearly I am evil and bad because I am not like they are, only because I had an accident and went extreme right brain dominate and have random access thought patterns as opposed to sequential thought patterns.

Session Close: Sat Jul 18 00:34:11 2009

Now you understand why I will never talk to you and I will never acknowledge you are anything ever into infinity but an illusion. This is not reality at all, this is a very convincing illusion. There is only me and if I start thinking there is anything more than illusions I will destroy myself mentally because this cannot be real.

I am pleased KarenJ acted natural so the entire universe will forever see the name KarenJ and understand what KarenJ represents.- 2:16:58 AM

3:57:15 AM – I just won something worth 22 dollars in the video game and someone asked me to sell it to them and I decided I won it as a test to see if I could give it away. And I did give it away to them and I am stupid and I am idiot and I curse this accident and I curse this universe . You go to hell. I am doomed. I am so stupid. I am doomed and I am cursed, and you will never understand that. - 4:02:15 AM

4:05:45 AM – I understand everything is an illusion and the illusions are simply here to test me to see if I have self control. I can see the illusions as angels or as demons, but how I see the illusions is my choice. I do not see my words and books as devils, I see them as angels even though many may suggest they are devils, that is their choice, not my choice. - 4:06:34 AM

4:12:37 AM – The worst thing that can ever happen to me is I will start to deny myself and my thoughts and then I will destroy myself . - 4:13:32 AM

This is a conversation I had with a friend who was in the channel when the KarenJ experiment happened and after I got banned he was still in there and he commented

[00:45] <whomasect> "[22:36] KarenJ: dogmatic people at least seem to know what they believe and this guy couldn't talk in plain English."

[00:45] <whomasect> female is Maya

[00:45] <whomasect> she is anti-truth , at every step

01[00:45] <Lestat9> yes she would hang me on a cross

[00:45] <whomasect> whatever SHE says, is anti-truth , and luring away

[00:46] <whomasect> when maya gets ANGRY we know we are making progress ok ?

01[00:46] <Lestat9> yes

[00:46] <whomasect> ok, that makes sense

[00:46] <whomasect> (on the brain sides)

01[00:46] <Lestat9> strategic words

01[00:46] <Lestat9> she is thinking and pondering

[00:46] <whomasect> i guess it is better that the sides "vibrate" back and forth faster, or more conveniently

01[00:46] <Lestat9> so she is upset but she is also talking about me so she is bothered

[00:46] <whomasect> maya is in your home

[00:47] <whomasect> if she doesn't get angry, if you work to please her and make your life comfortable, you are being NERFED

So you see I am not biased. I am not racist. I use to be on the left. I use to be like KarenJ I hated anyone who was not like me or anything that did not fit into my own tiny isolated point of view, which denotes I was very narrow minded and that is what Left brain is all about.

A narrow minded point of view that is unrelenting and unable to say the word "perhaps". Things like "Perhaps the language I was educated with did reduce my heightened awareness ." "Perhaps it is no ones fault because planned language looks like a very tasty apple to everyone that's why they taught it to me." A being should be able to say perhaps about anything no matter what is. I can say that and in fact publish it in my books. Perhaps I have everything wrong and I am totally wrong about everything I say in every single book I write, perhaps. That is mentally healthy because it keeps your mind pondering. It keeps it guessing and that keeps it functioning so it does not stagnate. I am not an authority I am an accident and I am so far to the right perhaps, I cannot put myself back to where I was on the left in every respect. I use to be very afraid after watching certain horror movies. Afraid of the dark and afraid of ghosts that may be in the dark, but now I have none of that at all, I Fear not. I cannot tell exactly what scares you. Some people are scared by a bad haircut. You think about how hateful and racial this comment is, racial in respect to being against a person because they have different thought waves in their mind. That is perhaps the harshest form a racism because a person cannot help what they think.

KarenJ: dogmatic people at least seem to know what they believe and this guy couldn't talk in plain English."

She said I could not talk in plain English. So she says I am stupid and retarded when in reality I am simply so far to the right I lost my sequencing ability to form sentences and so my sentences come out in strange arrangements in contrast to ones of the left, so I appear "drunk".

Act 2:15 "For these are not drunken, as ye suppose, seeing it is but the third hour of the day."

So these left brainers said to the apostles, you are drunk or high because of the way you talk, and they said we are not drunk as you suppose, look it is 3pm.

So KarenJ said "and this guy couldn't talk in plain English." So she said I sound like I am drunk and then she has the balls to sit in a Christian chat room and suggest she is of love. So there is this opposite thing between left and right brain, and it's a total disconnect. I would spend my entire life trying to communicate with some of these left brain people in an honest attempt and still they would say You are stupid and drunk and I would say , no, you are stupid and drunk and the problem is, they are physically based and so they end up doing harmful things and right brainers are cerebrally based in general and so they take the punishment. But that is a generalization, I am not a lamb, in fact I am a lion cerebrally and I eat the lost sheep, left brainers, and turn them into cerebral lions. I am faced with a total opposite disconnect so I cannot afford the luxury of rules and laws and morals because I cannot win even if I cheat.

I have to just talk to myself in my stupid diaries and I hope people insult them and say I am the stupidest person in the universe to publish such poor books and then I will write about them like I have KarenJ to let everyone know what the score is. She is either hateful and biased and mean or I am. You judge. I understand which is which but I forgive her because she is under the influence of the snake and she knows not what she does. I do not hold a grudge because I have been kicked out of so many chat rooms and insulted by so many people since this accident for just saying what is on my mind but its comes out in sentences in strange arrangements, that I would destroy myself in rage and anger , so I just have a mindset they are simply illusions because the opposite disconnect is very hard to overcome. What I understand is, no matter what they say consciously, when I type in a chat room that goes into their subconscious or right brain, and it is there, so I always win. I just ignore what they say in response because they can't take it out of their mind. What I say may not wake them up or make them go right brain but they will never forget it. It may sit in their head for the next 5 years, but eventually it will come to their conscious aspect again and they will think it over. So you cans see why Jesus, Moses,, Mohammed ,Buddha and Socrates and Joan of Arc and many others were killed. They appeared "crazy", "Holy as in holes in their head", "insane" in relation to the ones on the left and visa versa. What I see they say is stupidity and what I say they see is stupidity. I will translate a sentence form the bible and they will say, "You are stupid because that is not what that is saying" because they see parts and not the whole. I get the "spirit" of the sentence and they do not. It is a fact of the two opposite aspects of the mind. Left see's parts and makes judgment calls on parts, and right see's the whole and makes judgment calls on the whole picture. So I can look at this KarenJ and say she is mean and evil, but then I can look at the whole species and say, well they are fine. Now a person on the left will look at the species and say "this type of religion is evil." And they will go through their whole life thinking this certain religion is evil because, they cannot see the whole picture, they see one little tiny pinprick of the picture. I do not see anyone as evil, I see people in various stages of neurosis caused by planned language called the "apple of knowledge". So I see I cannot find fault with a person who was forced into this neurosis by society as a child because perhaps society did not notice that is what they were doing. I cannot even find fault with the guy who invented planned language 5000 plus years ago because he used his right brain creativity to invent it, and it looked like a good thing. I cannot find where the fault is.

Gen 3:6 "And when the ... saw that the tree(language and math) was good for food(knowledge), and that it was pleasant to the eyes(looked like a good idea at the time), and a tree to be desired to make one wise(if you learn language you will be rich and get a good job), she took of the fruit(learned language/script)thereof, and did eat, and gave also unto her husband(taught both males and females) with her; and he did eat."

So it is not even a question that it is a good invention. It is a good thing. It is a wise thing. That is a fact about language and math. The side effects when one does not condition away from fear is the problem. It hinders the mind. That is a fact. So I am not suggesting language and math are evil, I am suggesting they are good things but one

should consider the side effects may be harmful to their overall mental aspect. I am on the fence about supernatural at this stage since the accident - 7/18/2009 6:31:11 AM.

If you find fault with that, you should perhaps contact someone who has determined you are more than just an illusion. I have spoken with some interesting people as of late and they suggest certain supernatural aspects but, I ponder if they are not testing me. I have no fear of death and no fear and thus no fear of a supernatural punishment. I have already taken death to its final conclusion and I discovered there is nothing to fear at all. So I take my time and think things through so I do sound like a sorcerer and start charging people money on the premise I KNOW about supernatural things. I ponder supernatural things and I am convinced I am translating these ancient texts properly. I am aware I am too far to the right and I cannot reach anyone on the left in general. I have clues I may be able to but then when I talk further they say I am crazy or drunk or on drugs. So I am not able to reach them to the full measure only in slight conversations like two ships passing. I can see them and they can see me, but there is no connection. - 6:36:35 AM

What one does not see is often what one should seek to see. If you want to idolize something, idolize that huge log in your eye, I have mine in plain sight.

2:59:03 PM – I am finding it strange to adjust to this amount of sleep situation. It seems like I go to lay down and my mind is pondering and I close my eyes and about 30 minutes later I am ready to go again for a while. So it is almost like a catnap is not a catnap, as in I lose consciousness, but I just simply close my eyes and then I am regenerated. So I get a bit tried and lay down and closed my eyes and within a few minutes I am not tired.

"Heimdall, as guardian, is described as being able to hear grass growing and single leaves falling, able to see to the end of the world, and so alert that he requires no sleep at all."

So in extreme right brain or heightened awareness grass grow denotes heightened awareness, single leaves falling denotes hearing and is tuned down so low one can tell slight changes is sound, I understand this is why I can mix my songs so well, because I can tell what is slightly to high or to low, it sticks out like a sore thumb, like my poorly written thick pamphlets. Perhaps "see the end of the world" is in relation to the fact I can tell why the world "drowned" in the flood, as in language or script or planned language made everyone go left brain dominate and silenced right brain, as a side effect of learning the language. Then "requires no sleep at all", I am not at the stage of no sleep at all, but I am sleeping far less than I did even three months ago. I am certain this Heimdall is not a god at all, it is simply a person who goes extreme right brain after waking from the "script neurosis". There was language at least 5000 years ago and maybe further back, so certainly the this Scandinavian mythology taken from Northern Germanic pre-Christian religion was well within the time frame of planned language. So this "god" suggestion is perhaps relative to the observer.

"On the contrary, the right brain seems to flourish dealing with complexity, ambiguity and paradox."

So, right brain flourishes that means the cerebral activity is intense in contrast to the left brain in complexity and the antonym of complexity is simplicity or simplemindedness. So a person with left brain dominate as a result of the planned language neurosis in contrast to this "Heimdall" person would be simplistic in their thoughts and assume this "Heimdall" person was some sort of "god" in relation to thoughts and even activities. I am certainly not a god or possessed by a god but I am doing things I never did before as a result of my mental faculties have gone from simplistic to complex. One might look at it like I am on about 20 cups of coffee and I never come down and I never get tired and when I sleep I only need a few hours sleep at this stage, and to top it off, I am not nervous or stressed at all. I publish these nightmare books in contrast to an observer on the left aspect of the mind, and I am aware they might not get it, and I might say things they cannot grasp, but I am not afraid, ashamed or shy, so I am not stressed. I cannot get stressed because my short term memory doesn't allow me to focus on things for very long, this is because the cerebral activity is so great, it has to cancel out this "festering" in short term memories. I have not slept in over 20 hours and I notice I get a bit sloppy. I feel maybe like a drunk person does, but I tend to mellow out as far as my anger and rage. I tend to become docile in my words, but when I wake up from sleep I am maximum clarity and I tend to get upset about what I write about quickly. So it is as if my mind turns off my emotions all together when I have been awake so long to reserve the energy for the concentration. I just keep telling myself I am not writing a book to tell anyone anything. I am writing a diary to keep track of what is going through my mind. That is what this series of books is. I am not preaching I am giving my take on things since I had an accident. The reality I understand is, I am not like a person mentally fixed. I am still in the mental progression I detected for the moment the accident happened the "ah ha" sensation. I understand I am climbing this mountain and at times I feel I am at the top but then I find I am only at a rest on the way to the top. I have always felt this sensation that there is no top. Peeling the onion to reveal the onion. - 3:30:57 PM

Anger is the gift for understanding too much and using self control to allow it to be.

12:11:48 AM – I did another experiment tonight.

01[23:53] <Lestat9> and left brain is totally opposite to right brain, in extreme right brain one see's everything as a whole and loses sense of time, thus the comments like I am the alpha and omega or infinity

01[23:53] <Lestat9> so left brain is anti right brain, so anyone with a strong sense of time adn strong hunger is abti-christ as in christ was on the right hand side

[23:54] <+TaraJo> oh hell

[23:54] <+TaraJo> this again?

*Notice how people rember me from the day before but I am in a different Christian chat room because I was banned from the other one.

[23:54] <+GamerTony> <3 /ignore

*This GaMer person is letting everyone know he would ignore me, yet he didn't ignore me, so he is looking to influence others and let them know what he thinks about what I say

01[23:54] <Lestat9> Perhaps the darkest vipers venom acts swiftly

[23:54] <+KarenJ> up

*This is KarenJ the "overseer" and up mens he gets ops so she can ban me again from another channel she is "master" of

03[23:54] * isaiah40 sets mode: +o KarenJ

03[23:54] * KarenJ sets mode: +b *!*lestatnin@*.fl.comcast.net

03[23:54] * You were kicked by KarenJ (Blacklisted- false doctrine lectures)

*So now I have been banned from two of her channels and this time is because she determined I am a false teacher. I do not detect what I say is false or I would not say it, yet she determines I must be false so she bans me. I do not cuss. I just monologue words into the channel and I get banned. If I was in a town speaking in person I would get killed or abused or harmed by this KarenJ person. The left brain is so narrow minded, anything that is not in it realm of understanding must be evil or bad.

Session Close: Sat Jul 18 23:54:57 2009

I messaged her and spoke with her and she replied.

[00:02] <KarenJ> Lestat I perceive you are mentally ill and need help very badly.

This is classic. I need mental help very badly because I woke up in a lunatic asylum. If I said cuss words, even though words are nothing, that is one thing. But to just type words and explain how I see things and then to get called mentally ill, shows one this disconnect between left brain people and right brain people. I would never ban someone for speaking in a chat room I would converse with them and consider their point. There is no need to ban someone or call someone mentally ill simply because relativity suggests everyone has their own perception of things. If I had emotions that would be a pretty harsh comment to say I am mentally ill, but I simply look at that comment and detect hate and bias, but I do not detect it is against me, I just get the spirit of hate from it.

[23:54] <Lestat9> Perhaps the darknest vipers vemon acts swiftly
I tried the word perhaps and I see they do not even acknowledge it.
The darkest viper's venom acts swiftly.
The darkest viper's venom acts swiftly.
The darkest viper's venom acts swiftly.
The darkest viper's venom acts swiftly.
The darkest viper's venom acts swiftly.
The darkest viper's venom acts swiftly.
I deal in hate.
Ideal in hate.
I do not hesitate I seal fate. I will go play my video game and ponder why I have infinite compassion and mercy. –
12:59:04 AM

Love is a better liar than hate.

7/19/2009 5:06:40 AM –

I cannot go back any further in history than i have, so perhaps i have "peeled the onion to reveal the onion"

"Haste is of the Devil."
St. Jerome

This is a complex statement. Haste denotes quick to judge. Haste also is relative to the observer. To one on the left with less than complex cerebral activity, writing a book in a month is haste, relative to me in the extreme right, writing a book in a month is sloth. So Haste in this comment is suggesting judgment because one in extreme right can judge but they tend to take it back so they do not rest on their laurels.

I can make a good case that one's on the left are the devil, but I also understand I use to be on the left and many are because of the planned language that was forced on them when they were a child. So then I cannot judge them because I understand they are doing the best they can based on their mental state. One cannot judge someone who was mentally abused as a child. I cannot go back 5000 years and find the idiot who invented language and if I could, I could not say language and math is bad, it is simply is an invention that's looks very tasty but has some nasty side effects, as in 5000 years of killing each other over dirt and rocks, side effects. Five Thousand years of people becoming depressed and hating and killing their self, because the emotions are far too strong, side effects. So relative to what I understand at this moment about this world and what is going on, since the accident, I assure you I am infinitely patient.

This is another experiment I tried in a different chat room
* Now talking in #philosophy
<Lestat9> Socrates said no philospoher fears death.
<Lestat9> anotehr philospoher said, " i defeated death" as in his fear of death, and he also said, Fear NOT
<Lestat9> If you reflect back upon our own educational training, we have been traditionally taught to master the 3 R's: reading, writing and arithmetic -- the domain and strength of the left brain.
<Lestat9> A side effect of the 3 R's is strong fear, so it kills the right aspect of the brain, and makes ones life very difficult
<Lestat9> So the only remedy to counter the 3 r's is to say things you dont want to say and when yo get hard core sit in the dark after a scary movie to kill this fear side effect
<Lestat9> if you fear words no matter what they are you are under the control of the "tree of knowledge" or left brained fear based
No one responded because its 5:31:34 AM EST, but that is better than getting banned perhaps

"Keep doing some kind of work, that the devil may always find you employed."
St. Jerome

117

This is way out of context. Work denotes cerebral work. If you are on the left brain cerebral work is not going to be happening relative to the cerebral work on the right brain. He is trying to say one who does not have lots of cerebral actions in relation to "the kingdom(mind)" is the devil. It is far too easy to be biased. I can be biased against every single person on the planet right now and I would be justified. That's way to easy. It actually takes self control to think about it and understand, the planned language is inviting, it is "knowledge:" it is "wisdom" and if you want a good paying job, you better get lots that conditioning. That's reasonable. But the truth is also, the side effect is, you lose the complex right brain or it is nearly silenced if you don't condition away from fear. That is a cold hard fact above all facts. That fact hurts. So people are forced into the education, and then society blames them for becoming addicted, and greedy, slothful and envious and depressed mentally speaking. So then I could suggest society is a mental child abuser, but that is not logical because society see's education as "wise".

Gen 3:6 And when they ….saw that the tree was good for food(knowledge),…. and a tree to be desired to make one wise(WISE), she took of the fruit thereof, and did eat,'

I simply have no one I can blame yet so much misery has happen because of this invention. This invention nearly cost me my life and that is enough for me to understand about its bad side effects. It is one thing to take drugs and slowly kill yourself, it is another thing to be forced by law into the left brain as a child and have it ruin your mind for the rest of your life, based on the premise, you do not get the "education" you will be reduced to slave labor jobs and it will be your own fault. That is the harshest racism in the universe, to tell a child they are a failure if they do not get the left brain conditioning, which is the less complex aspect of the mind. You can have money by being indoctrinated into the script neurosis and all it will cost you is the complex aspect of your mind. "Give me liberty or give me death." Simply put, I will take the complex right aspect of the mind and if I cannot have that you go ahead and kill me because death is nothing compared to being stuck in the simplistic left aspect of the mind forced onto me by the law of the land. The great humor is this. I woke up and am on the right now, and nothing can make me go back to the left, but I will certainly suggest things that may help others go to the right, and no being in the universe can burn my books or there is going to be a blood bath. So you see I have already won. I keep writing and saying things but there is nothing left to say. I will keep writing and saying essentially in spirit the same things over and over into infinity. I do not expect this generation to "get it". Perhaps five thousand years from now someone will find one of my books and "get it". I do not even expect that. I simply write for no reason. So the comment by Jerome would be better understood if it said. "Keeping busy is relative to which hemisphere of the mind is dominate."- 6:03:44 AM

In life one needs understanding so they can realize when they misunderstood. I would never give up but I may give out.

9:39:54 AM – The philosophy channel is very open minded. I can tell I am getting better at presenting my case but that is only perhaps an illusion. I mowed the lawn and the ants bit me above expectations.

Ants – http://www.youtube.com/watch?v=R3wULTBAHfU

9:55:44 AM – The concept of prayer or meditation is relative to one in extreme right brain. I could suggest that at times the cerebral processing is so fast I feel like my heart is going to burst. I feel like I am going to overload, but that is just an illusion. The right is so powerful that in contrast to the left brain processing power it is god, it is infinity, it is light. I cannot tell you how powerful it is because it is unnamable. No human being could make a machine that could determine how power or how fast the processing is in a person with extreme right brain dominate as a result of conditioning away all fear. You could not contrast it with the processing power of the left brain. Dark and light is accurate. Night and day is accurate. So the only solution to this sense of "overload" is to close your eyes and sit for a moment. Mohammed suggested five times a day which indicates how extreme the processing is. Some suggest always say in a state of prayer. That also indicates how extreme the processing is. It is as if the processing takes over everything. I submit I am not use to it. So I have moments of panic and I play the video game because I just kind of stare at the monsters and push the mouse button and this calms the processing down to a degree. This is not abnormal for the right brain dominate person. Some monks sit in meditation often. I am more of a talker. Talking or writing is my meditation and calms me down but there are moments the processing is over whelming for a moment. I do not get scared of the "overload" because I understand it is a result of the accident I mentally "went to heaven (right brain) in a chariot(swiftly)". You go sit in a cemetery at night far away from lights all by yourself for many hours and you certainly "will go to heaven in a chariot". That's hardcore, but you can do it slowly also and I am not saying you have to do it, I am saying you have freedom of choice and right brain is there for the taking and it is not good or bad it is simply an option. Perhaps, if we had 6 billion Einstein's no one would read my infinite, poorly written, thick pamphlets I suggest are diaries. - 10:11:03 AM

Looking at Medusa turned a person to stone, Moses looked at a woman and turned her to salt. This is in relation to conditioning away from fear or facing fear makes one right brain dominate and purges emotions, so makes one stone as in no emotions or silenced emotions.

<Lestat9> In the case of Moses salt denotes longevity, in right brain without stress it is healthy on the body thus the story of people living well past 120 years like Methuselah

<Lestat9> one does not really live past 120 years, but relative to their perception of no time, they live very long

<Lestat9> in relation to the fountain of youth

<Lestat9> so the holy grail is simply right brain and FEAR NOT is how one gets to it, and the holy grail has miraculous powers, or heightened awareness such as "telepathy" and extreme concentration

<Lestat9> many on the left take the stories and translate them into physical means, but the stories are relative to cerebral aspects

<Lestat9> The man upstairs is perhaps right brain, it is infinite, and no sense of time, in relation to alpha and omega, with no sense of time one see's everything as one thing.

Time gives off the illusion of growth.

"A foolish Consistency is the hobgoblin of little minds" Ralph Waldo Emerson
Rules give off the illusion of security but often they can put one mentally in a cell.
It's not the big rules that are the problem it is the minor rules that kill freedom of thought.

When an adult scolds a child for saying certain words they are telling that child their thoughts are bad or evil, and they are also abusing that child mentally because they are making that child feel evil for thinking such words. I am not saying mentally abusing a child is good or bad, I am saying it is mental child abuse because, right component of the brain is not concerned with things falling into patterns because of prescribed rules. So an adult who says to a child "Do not say that word" is in fact conditioning that child mentally into the left brain because they are threatening that child with "harm" for speaking there mind. The right brain is simply anti rules. It is not about morals is does not mean a person in extreme right brain goes around killing people and stealing from people, that is a physical control aspect that is generally left brain, Right brain is creativity and open mindedness, one cannot be as creative and open minded if they have this stone of rules around their neck. "You can't say that or you are bad." That is in fact left brain brainwashing. It's not about not being able to yell fire in a movie theatre. The entire society in general has so many words one cannot say or they are deemed evil or bad or stupid, the list goes on and on, then society wonders why there are not more inventions. Why are there not any inventive people in contrast to the fact there arenearly seven billion people on the planet? Because there are so many rules that are unspoken it kills the right brain totally."Don't say a cuss word or you are evil and I will beat you and wash your mouth out with soap." Why don't you just shoot the child because you are simply dooming them into left brain, and their mind is going to be just like your mind, 10%. Ten percent proves I have infinite compassion because it's not ten percent it is closer to .000001%. The more rules the less brain function or the further one goes into left brain. That is the reality. The difference is night and day and death and life. There are few laws against mentally abusing someone. You are better off killing themthan dooming them to left brain without giving them an option to remain in right brain. One is better off dead than facing mental and cerebral death forced by the hand of one who is cerebrally dead. I am not saying left is bad or good, I am saying you are mentally abusing children when you do not counter the scribe neurosis. I do not give a god dam if you abuse children, if you can live with yourself, that is all that matters. But do not go around and think that is not what you are doing because then I would have to assume you know not what you do. And once I assume you know not what you do, I will assume you are unable to make proper judgments, and then you may be relieved of your ability to intake oxygen, swiftly.

There simply has to be a class in school that is called "speak your mind" class. And during that class the kids in that class can say anything they want, cuss words and all, about anything with the understanding they will not be punished. If you cannot do that, you are going to understand the definition of my red sea, boy. I do not have compassion. I do not have class. I do not have morals. I do not have rules. I do not have laws. That's is what you are facing now. That is reality. So you better think very carefully what I am capable of. You fear Armageddon yet I seek it. I will now play my video game before I implode. I do not love death, I am death. That needs clarifications. "Adjust or abolish" and I prefer abolish.- 12:08:55 PM

12:21:14 PM - I try very hard to be emotional and angry and bitter but that is my minds or my left aspects way of trying to stay in power or stay relevant because it is aware it is dying. The left aspect of my mind is dead but it still has phantom occurrences. As a being I am not use to this extreme mental progression. I did not plan it. It was an accident and there is nothing I can do to stop it. So I am vain in my attempts to act like I have emotions. I can't maintain anger or hate because I talk myself out of it. I always come back to one thing. People are doing the best they can based on their understanding. I understand the Allies and the Taliban are doing the best they can based on their understanding, or they would not be doing it.

"The American soldier who went missing June 30 from his base in eastern Afghanistan and was later confirmed to have been captured, said in a video posted by the Taliban that he's "scared I won't be able to go home.""

He is aware he is dead. Will he die, maybe not, probably. But he is mindful of his death. You cannot expect the Taliban to have mercy when the allies butcher them just as quickly. Both the allies and the Taliban perceive they are righteous and relatively speaking they both are righteous. All I see is human beings killing each other. I do not see right or wrong I just see human beings who have talked their self into killing other human beings. I can make a good case the Taliban are in fact right brain dominate to a degree. I can make a case the Allies are there simply to assert control and gain monetary advantage in that country. I can make a case the Taliban are not allowing people to make their own choice. I can make a case the Allies are attempting to make sure people are allowed to make their own choice. But having said that, I still see human being who have talked their self into killing other human beings so I understand neither are in extreme right brain but perhaps some are in extreme left brain. This whole concept about fruits simply means if you go the full measure or fully extreme right brain dominate, you are going to be in a cerebral battle and you are going to be far less concerned about other people's battles and far more concerned about your own mental battle. You are going to be focused on your log mentally. You are essentially going to forget about thephysical insanity because you are going to be drowning in the cerebral pondering. If one likes drugs, when you go right brain dominate you are going to understand the definition of "high". I personally lost my desire to get high because I am far too high now. I want to come down a bit at times but I cannot. I perceive I get use to it but that is an illusion. I just keep going higher and higher and higher. I have said from my many years ago or relatively speaking 4 months ago, I end the day by saying I cannot go any higher and I wake up and I just go higher, and I do that day after day, and I say, it cannot get any better , I cannot get any higher, but I am always wrong. If one does not believe right brain dominate will cure them of any addiction on the planet, they clearly unestimate how powerful the right brain when dominate is. In relation to the power of right brain when dominate, all I can say is unnamable. I would like to describe it with words but I cannot, I can only try with the understanding, I am vain in my attempts. When I wrote the first word of volume one, I am in fact exactly where I was here in volume seven. I have not even begun to explain it. That is an indication of how complex it is to explain. It is as if this right brain persona is not me at all, and one might think they are possessed, but it is simply the right brain when dominate is a powerhouse beyond the definition of powerhouse. I am not possessed I simply had an accident and fell into the void. Satisfaction is relative to what one perceives is unsatisfying. Relativity suggests there are 6 billion points of view or observers and they are all right even though they may have contradictory observations. Assuming everyone else is crazy helps one cope with this reality. Being in the void denotes the complexity more than the absence of cerebral sensation. If one is mindfully conscious they are absolutely wicked they will forever strive to show some goodness.

A girl who is submissive still tells the guy what she is not willing to do, so she is dominate.

Here is one in Nirvana or right brain or one who has no fear who I spoke with in a psychology chat room.

<Favicon> well i know alot of people who would sit alone in a cemetery

<Favicon> :)

<Lestat9> I know many who would not say a cuss word becasue they fear they would be evil if they did

<Favicon> that depends on the beliefs that one has

<Lestat9> yes but it is more complex than beliefs becasue a child is torn into the left by force beofr ethey have beliefs

<Lestat9> If you reflect back upon our own educational training, we have been traditionally taught to master the 3 R's: reading, writing and arithmetic -- the domain and strength of the left brain.

<Lestat9> So the comment suffer the children, means before a child is old enough to have belifs they are conditioned into teh fear left brain state of mind, so all their belifs are conditioned

<Lestat9> so they have no true belifs but only belifs based on fear

<Lestat9> Buddha sugegsted contact, what would a person belifs be if they had no contact with the three R's and what would it be if they did

<Lestat9> society nips it in the budd

<Lestat9> but the three r's look good and are good but they have a bad side effect liek sahme and shyness and ambarssment and fear

<Lestat9> so it all goe sback to when man invented planned langauge and staretd saying, if you dont have langauge you get a bad job and are a slave

<Lestat9> so that dorwned the species

<Lestat9> drowned

<Lestat9> in relation to noahs ark

<Favicon> yes

- 1:16:57 PM

Notice how he agrees with what I said. If I said this in a traditional religious room that would get me banned as a false teacher. This is what relativity is. Relative to right brain people or ones in extreme right brain I am understandable relative to some in left brain, I am evil and a monster. And the "spooky" thing about that is both perceive they are correct at the exact same time and in fact are correct relative to their observation.

11:47:40 PM – "Galilean invariance or Galilean relativity is a principle of relativity which states that the fundamental laws of physics are the same in all inertial frames. In physics, the concept of absolute time and absolute space are hypothetical concepts closely tied to the thought of Isaac Newton:"

The "spooky" thing about relativity is there is no such thing as absolute space. One cannot find two places that are exactly the same to make consistent observations. What is true on earth is not true outside the solar system. What is true outside the solar system is not true outside the galaxy. "absolute space are hypothetical concepts" this denotes people are measuring things and claiming it is reality but it is not absolute reality because those measurements cannot be reproduced in any kind of universal way. That is the physical known universe. Then you take it to a psychological universe of a person and it gets even worse, so to speak. Some people drink a gallon of hard liquor a week and find that normal and some people cannot drink a beer a week. Some people can smoke a joint three times a day and some people cannot smoke a joint three times in their life time. Some people have no problem making a porno film and some people would have a heart attack at those prospects. Some people would beat their child for failing school and some people would beat their self for having a child that cannot conform to their expectations of "success". Success in a tribal third world setting is finding enough grub worms to eat for that day and success in a first world country is selling a health pill that in reality does nothing, to enough people to be able to buy a mansion with 20 rooms, even though there will only be two people living in that mansion. So success is in reality nothing absolute. There is perhaps some sort of absolute space or absolute time or absolute goodness or absolute evil, but once an observer is thrown in to that mix, it cannot be measured. So, then these absolutes can only be hypothetical, which means make believe or fairy tales or fictional. A student cannot be a failure as in fail a class in an absolute term , when they are given a failing mark, that is simply a grade relative to the teachers determination they are a failure. A student can be given a spelling test and they may misspell words on that test, but the simple fact they know what the words are means they understand the words. A teacher can verbally say "Spell the word building." The student knows what a building is in their mind so they are not stupid if they cannot spell it properly. There is some thought or idea of what a building is in their mind, but their mind is a hypothetical. Other words, not every person has the same idea when word building is mentioned. When someone says building to person A, person A thinks of a two story building and then person B thinks of a skyscraper that has one hundred stories. Both are thinking the idea building but both have a different idea of building in their mind. Sometimes it is even more vague than that. It is not even in as much detail as the size of the building just some flash of a building. The mind does not work on words it works on cerebral representations and that means every single person has different cerebral representations for everything. Person A may be very creative and thus have extreme right brain active and Person B may have extreme left brain and in turn not be so creative. So person B may "idolize" the inventions of person A but in absolute terms person A is not more creative than person B, it is just person A is not like person B due to which aspect of the brain is dominate. This creates "followers". Person B wishes they were as creative as person A but person B is as creative as person A they just have that right brain creativity silenced because of the "education" they received. The brain does not work like, one is blessed with creativity and one is not. That is impossible because the brain has a right hemisphere and it is all about creativity. So then this absolute creativity comes into play. The more rules and laws one perceives they must follow the less creative they are. That is not suggesting they are not capable of creativity, it only means they are subscribing to all these laws that are mainly based on fear tactics, like, do not cuss or you are evil and bad and will be punished, and these laws and rules are encouraging left brain and left brain is anti or opposite of right brain which is creative. So closed minded or narrow minded is not an absolute ideal, it is simply one who looks at a situation and has so many laws and rules they cannot break, so to speak, they cannot come up with a solution properly because they put their self mentally into a corner. So a person who is extreme right brain will look at painting a picture and determine any form of paint is good to use and any form of canvas is good to use and any form of subject matter is good to usc and so they have this huge selection of things they can paint, and one on the left brain will start applying all these rules, they may say," I won't use black paint it is evil, and I won't paint a nude women that is evil." And before you know it they will have no ideas to paint. Same with inventors. If an inventor has too many rules in their thoughts they will not be able to invent anything of great value because they do not consider every angle. Edison said he had to try 1000 light bulbs that didn't work. So he was very open minded about trying anything to make his light bulb. An inventor does not know what is going to work but they have an idea of what they want to accomplish and that requires many trial and error experiments. The problem with that is, what is one willing to try. If Edison only tried 100 light bulb experiments we perhaps wouldn't have light bulbs. What if it took Edison 100000 experiments to find that light bulb that worked. So this is in relation to a person who is left brained is more prone to impatience in respects to trying something a limited amount of times and then giving up. On the contrary a person on the right may not ever give up. This can be applied in many aspects of reality. Consider the Vietcong, they lost up to two million men and women in that war with the US, but that doesn't matter at all, because they never gave up. Contrast that with the Taliban, they certainly got slaughtered by the Russians and are certainly getting slaughtered by the Allies, but that does not matter at all, because they never give up the "ghost", so to speak. So this alone shows me , the Vietcong and the Taliban are very right brain, or at least their leaders are. And the fact the countries that were defeated by the Vietcong being France and the US, are very left brain dominate or at least the leaders are. Now to go a bit deeper, Hitler tried to take over the world. That is in fact not really possible but that is a very right brain attitude. Napoleon tried to take over the world, and he really liked Washington and Washington decided to take on the most powerful military force of that time, the British. I am not suggesting these people were in extreme right brain or in Nirvana or no sense of time, but they were close. Washington was defeated in many battle and had many things going against him but he never gave up. That is right brain thinking. A person on the left brain would have an attitude more along the lines of, "We lost our 10th battle in a row so its time to give up." One will never ever, into infinity, hear the Vietcong say give up or the Taliban say, give up. They will simply adapt and lower their standards for what victory is. Edison, tried the 800th light bulb and decided "I now understand the 800th light bulb attempt did not work, so that s a victory." To ones on the left it seems like these people are unreasonable because for example the Taliban will lose 50 men in an attack and only wound one ally, and then claim, "It was a great victory." That is exactly what Washington did. He was getting slaughtered by the British but somehow he would go back to camp and explain how they found a weakness so that losing battle was in fact an experiment that made the effort of the war easier. "We lost 100 men and didn't kill the enemy but we understand we lost 100 men, so we increased our understanding, so we are winning this war." That perhaps sounds crazy to one on the left because one on the left has all these rules and "morals" and expectations about what victory is. There is no such thing as absolute victory, there is simply people who give up and people who never give up. This comment ," They never know when to quit." That is perhaps looked at as an insult, but that in fact is a mental strategy that can never be defeated. That is a mental state where a person cannot be defeated no matter what. In a battle on any field, if your mind set is to never give up no matter what, you are undefeatable and that is strictly right brain. This can be dangerous and this can be an advantage. So patience is perhaps best defined as one who never gives up. One who suggests I will give up on the infinite try this is in relation to the comment "Go down swinging." or no limits. Rules and morals are fine and dandy but when you cross the line and have many meaningless or anal retentive rules you just go into such extreme left brain that you defeat yourself in everything you do.

Jesus was certainly aware he stood no chance but he went down swinging. Same with the Disciples and same with Mohammed and Moses. Moses could have given up trying to make the "left brainers" who had turned everyone who was not conditioned in the script, into slaves.

"The Ancient Egyptian scribe, or sesh[1], was a person educated in the arts of writing (using both hieroglyphics and hieratic scripts, and from the second half of the first millennium BCE also the demotic script) and dena (arithmatics).[2][3] He was generally male,[4] belonged socially to what we would refer to as a middle class elite, and was employed in the bureaucratic administration of the pharaonic state, of its army, and of the temples."

What this is saying is simply the "society" is based on the three R's and so the ones in positions of power are well educated into the three R's and in turn they are very control based mentally. Right brain is not concerned with control because that is a symptom of rules. It can be as simple as "Don't say this cuss word or you will not get dinner tonight." That is a fear tactic and a control tactic. That is strictly left brain. So society itself is understood to be a "control" mechanism but that only because society in relation to the "leaders" are traditionally well educated into the three R's and are prone to use fear tactics because they crave control. This is deeper still because for example Hitler had this "We are special" mindset. This is perhaps an illusion because, he was saying our people are special, but in relation to him, he was most special. He was the dominate leader so the ones under him were not special in relation to him, in his mind. This is like a messiah complex. But in reality that is a trait of right brain. I understand he had the mindset to take everything over, just like many other well known "conquers" in history. Khan, Napoleon, Alexander and in the case of Alexander, it is clear to me, he certainly was right brain dominate to a degree because he was very creative in his tactics and his strategy. He could improvise very swiftly or adapt. One in left brain does not like change in general or unexpected events. I recall when I was in my extreme depression my car broke down on the highway and I determined its best to kill myself. Now contrast that with a person who loses their job and then kills their self. A person who get divorced or dumped and kills their self. A person who gets embarrassed in a social situation and kills their self. That is left brain because they give up easily and thus they have no patience, and thus the comment "patience is a virtue" but in left brain patience is not exactly possible because it is not a trait of left brain. Right brain is all about infinity meaning never give up ever and so the opposite of that is left brain and that means give up easily. So this whole planned language invention has essentially turn our species from a never give up mindset to an impatient mindset in contrast.

Perhaps the bigger question is, what is safety, one who gives up easily or one who never gives up. One who gives up easily is perhaps dangerous because they are in a unexpected situation and they panic and make rash decisions and one who is in a never give up mindset tends not to "put all their eggs in one basket", or everything does not rest on the next move. To apply this to a real life situation. After 9/11 the majority of people in America voted to give away freedoms because they perceived it would make them safer. They did something very rash and very permanent very swiftly. They got laid off work and went home and put a gun to their head. That is totally contrary to right brain dominate people. A right brain person would look at 9/11 as a symptom of a problem and thus a challenge to ponder and try to find meaning from and then after the pondering the experiments would start, and it would not start by making more rules and taking away options. It would be a challenge to solve but not a situation to panic and sell their soul as it were. We all know now, 9/11 was a symptom of the US not giving certain people a fair shake. That's all 9/11 was about. These Taliban do not want to take over the world, the people in Pakistan keep them under control. This is why they branch out to Afghanistan because Afghanistan is an easy target in contrast to Pakistan. America seems to forget who she is. America is the most radical country in the world and that the world has ever known. America with its freedom is more radical than the Taliban. The Taliban has many rules and regulations and so do all the other countries. America is based on anarchy or freedom. That's a nightmare to a control freak. That is exactly why the first Americans came to America, to get away from all the control freaks. That is simply why America was formed. People saw the world and said we want to go do what we want without all these control freaks telling us what to do. The control freaks are the left brain educated people, because the left brain is all about control, because the right brain is anti control. This is exactly why Socrates was told by the government to drink the hemlock. They said, you are corrupting the minds of the youth. What is our country going to be like if they do not grow up with the understanding they better fall in line to the understood regulations of the power elite. Moses took all the commandments and threw them down on the rocks and smashed them. Washington looked at the control the British had over Americans and said, we are going to revolt. Jesus went into the money changer location and said you are all controlling people with your money and fear tactics and I am throwing all this money on the ground to suggest you are simply control freaks. You are keeping these people under your grip with your monetary structure. Jesus was saying "let my people go" Just as Moses said "let my people go" in relation to ones on the right hand side. Washington was saying "Let my people go." This is what everything rests on.

The ones on the left make up rules that say "If you are not educated you are stupid," and then the ones who are educated get the power positions because the ones on the right are all about freedom and do not wish to control others. So the ones on the left or ones who took well to the script education, are prone to control tactics and so they tend to make "slaves", they essentially thrive on slavery because that is their mindset. They are afraid of loss of control because they perceive that is dangerous. They do not even want people to say cuss words or they deem them evil and uneducated. That is the biggest Messiah complex control freak mindset in the universe. We will punish you if you say a cuss word and we will suggest you are evil and stupid if you say a cuss word. That kind of mindset is only possible on the left brain and in reality that is deep neurosis. To make a generalization about a person because they say a cuss word is in the realms of deep insanity. In a true vacuum if a person says any word it cannot affect them in any physiological way but it can affect them in a mental way.

"Researchers from the school of psychology at Britain's Keele University have found swearing can make you feel better as it can have a "pain-lessening effect," according to a study published in the journal NeuroReport."

One might suggest a person is conditioned to believe a cuss word is evil so mentally they are going left brained because that is a rule. So then a person hits their finger with a hammer and there is pain so a person yell out a cuss word and the pain is reduced. What is really happening mentally is when one breaks these rules, they go more right brain and right brain is very cerebral and so it reduces physical sensations. This is in relation to the Bible comment

"As he increases I decrease". As this person cusses they mentally perceive they are breaking rules and so they go right brain for a moment and the cerebral aspect increases and thus the physical aspect decreases so the pain decreases. I am essentially physically numb. My whole physical sensitivity is numb. My sense of taste works as I put food in my mouth but the after taste is totally gone. So I feel pain but no after "taste" of the pain so to speak. The cerebral is so strong it just turns the physical stuff off. So this person is in pain and cusses and it reduced the pain because they go slightly right brain by breaking that "rule" of do not cuss. So the inference of this is simply, the more rules you have and subscribe to the more physical pain you will experience. Things like fatigue and daily aches and pains. Little tiny aspects of physical pain are simply there because these people have so many rules they would never dare break in their head. So essentially they bring it all on their self and the deeper aspect is, they were forced into the extreme left brain, rule based mindset as a child by education that is "required" by society to make one feel they are worthy, and then the society does nothing to condition away the bad side effects of this education with fear conditioning or conditioning away from fear. So then people experience physical pain and rush off to find some drugs that will reduce it when if they were extreme right brain from fear conditioning it would perhaps not even be noticed. It is through and through. It is all related to this script neurosis. We invented language and ruined our minds and then we could not grasp these wise being were saying "Fear Not" in relation to that is the antidote for the language neurosis or extreme left brain. To me it is almost as if that cannot be possible. That would be the most unlikely reality in all of mankind, yet I am convince beyond all reality that is exactly what has happened. There is no possible fictional story that could be as strange as this real story. People look around the world and say "we are naturally physically based mentally but that is not true at all, we are in reality naturally cerebrally based but we invented something that altered our minds and it was subtle and over 5000 years it is starting to show. Look at the Incas. They invented numbers and then they disappeared and everyone thinks they ran out of water. They even started to use planned language because they have some codex that still remain,but the reason they collapsed is because they got a flu called demotic script and dena (arithmatics). It is not this demotic and dena are evil, it is all about knowing how to counter act the unwanted mental side effects of learning them. I am starting to feel normal like this. My mind is starting to get use to this new mental state. So this whole perception that I am something special is in error because even with all of these changes to my perception, my mind adjusts to it eventually and it feels normal. I am just a people. I accidentally countered the left brain induced "demotic and dena" education by accidentally conditioning my mind away from fear, by not trying to save myself when I perceived I was dying and in turn I found myself real self, right brain. That is what I say has happened so no matter what anyone says contrary to that, they are mistaken. But what is strange is I do not perceive I am warmed up yet or up to full power. I am just getting started. That is what I can feel. Like every book I write is worse than the next one or my previous books are very bad in contrast to this one because I am getting warmed up with each passing day. But having said that, it was one hell of a mental battle and now the battle seems to be a bit more manageable or predictable. One way to look at it is, I have all this information I have read or seen through my whole life in my mind, and my mind keeps putting pieces together and coming to new understandings. That is not an indication of how smart I am or special I am, that is an indication of how powerful the right brain is. The comment "all glory to god" is perhaps really saying "all glory to this right brain aspect" because it is so powerful

I often feel like it is not me, it is something beyond me. So that makes one very supernatural orientated when they think about that, but they have to grasp, the mind is very powerful and everyone knows the "subconscious" is very powerful. How powerful? Unnamable powerful. No way to describe it fully.

"At times, right brain thinking is difficult to put into words because of its complexity, its ability to process information quickly and its non-verbal nature."

It's cerebral which means infinity because the ideas are not words but they can at times be put into words but there are not enough words in the universe to fully describe these ideas or thoughts. One being said "The kingdom is within.", but that is complex because one on the left brain will take that as a literal and absolute. Here is a comment about the kingdom that is not referring to the right brain or right hand aspect.

Rev 16:10 "And the fifth angel poured out his vial upon the seat of the beast; and his kingdom was full of darkness; and they gnawed their tongues for pain,"

Gen 3:14 ….. Because thou hast done this, thou art cursed above all cattle, and above every beast of the field; upon thy belly shalt thou go, and dust shalt thou eat all the days of thy life:"

These two comments are very a good way to show how these wise beings attempted to explain a cerebral idea in words. They had to use parables because one cannot explain the ideas to others without making a story about it or a contrast. The "beast" that's a contrast comment in relation to Left brain people under the influence of the script. That reality is denoted in this comment.

1Jn 2:18 "Little children, it is the last time: and as ye have heard that antichrist shall come, even now are there many antichrist; whereby we know that it is the last time."

"even now there are many antichrists". An antichrist is one on the left hand side and left hand side is encouraged by the script.

"we have been traditionally taught to master the 3 R's: reading, writing and arithmetic -- the domain and strength of the left brain."

Antichrist is not something evil, it is a contrast comment. It could have said, even now there are people in left brain and that is contrary to me, who are in right brain or on the right hand side. These wise being were not about rules.

"Right brain is not concerned with things falling into patterns because of prescribed rules."

It is kind of what open minded is all about, no rules in trying to understand situations and trying to solve conflicts. When a country says we do not even talk to them, they are closed minded as one can ever be. When a country says "We do not talk with people like them", all I hear is, "We do not even have the brain function to communicate properly with other people." If a person cannot communicate with other people no matter what this situation is, they sure as hell should not be in a control position because they are a hindrance to everyone they control. I do not want a closed minded brain dead person assuming they are in control of me, because I will turn around and convince them I control them. I do not need people to vote me into power, I will just assume it with my words. That's what Washington did. He went on the battle field in front of his army and they all put their swords in a submissive position and he assumed control. Apparently I feel off that train, high on cocaine.

So, "and his kingdom was full of darkness; and they gnawed their tongues for pain" this is simply saying people on the left as a result of the script we mentally in darkness in contrast to people on the right who had great mental processing power and the comment "gnawed their tongues for pain" means they could not communicate properly. They tend to want to go to war and killed each other because they cannot mentally come to verbal communication levels to avoid a war.

The Taliban own the border region of Pakistan and Afghanistan anyway, so make them an offer, say we will give you a portion of that border area and you can live there and if people want to subscribe to your religious beliefs they can go there freely and you can do whatever you want in that region. It may not work, but what it will do is give a

person an opportunity to experiment further with communication. Eventually after so many counter offers and counter arguments we may find we are communicating with the Taliban and then we may stop killing each other. Imagine that prospect, we may just talk with them and then we don't have to kill our offspring or their offspring, because the offspring in reality do not give a dam about the adults they just want to live their life and be free. The offspring do not care about the delusions of the adults because they just arrived in life. The adults tend to force the offspring into their narrow minded bidding and then put fear tactics in the off springs mind to make the offspring conform. That is what this is saying

"Little children, it is the last time: and as ye have heard that antichrist shall come"

The ones under the influence of the script are going to convince you to die for their "righteous" causes. That is why Jesus said "Suffer the children to come unto me." He said, The adults under the script left brain neurosis are the most cold hearted bastards so you children come to me and I will try to protect you even though those cold hearted bastard are going to nail my hands into boards and leave me to die in the sun. And they said the same things to Socrates and said, You are corrupting the youth so you drink this hemlock and you sit and watch as you slowly die as each part of your body becomes numbs and start to die. I will certainly level the fucking universe so the ones one the left should certainly kill me before I get warmed up. Granted I got a little side tracked. Apparently I am still allowing illusions to affect me. I will try to splice these comments together to show what is being said.

"Because thou hast done this(Demotic and Dena), thou art cursed above all cattle(left brain indoctrinated), and his kingdom was full of darkness(left brain dominate and many emotions); and they gnawed their tongues for pain(cannot think clearly) , even now are there many antichrist(left brainers)."

So I took three comment's from three different books and spliced them together and that is an indication of why the comments in these ancient texts are not physical orientated as much as ideas of contrast to explain cerebral aspects. So really these ancient texts are riddles and only a person in extreme right brain can decipher them because they arecodes that only a person with random access mindset can decipher properly. That is why Jesus said, "They hear the word but do not understand the word." Who are they? "even now are there many antichrist(left brainers).", the ones who were taught script and math that were not conditioned away from fear. This is why it is so complex, because I may in fact be experiencing spiritual aspects but I do not perceive they are spiritual aspects, others around me may perceive there is some strange spirit about mc, but I do not. This again is relative to the observer. People may hear my words and see my fruits and suggested I am "wise" but from my point of view I perceive I am still warming up and very unstable in relation to, I am not use to this state of mind totally yet, or it's a learning experience to me still. So I have to be careful and over compensate and tell myself mentally this is heightened awareness and simply altered perceptions, because no matter what I say, I am still in this "mental progression" and if this situation is related to spirituality I am certainly going to find that out eventually, so there is no point in speculating. I cannot stop the

progression, I am getting pulled into the deep water so to speak and there is nothing I can do about it. I lost my fear of death accidentally and that is irreversible mentally speaking. It's permanent. I cannot trick my mind out of it. That's the pecking order. I can speak to people on the left and maybe show them how to go to the right but they cannot show me how to get back to the left. My mind is locked in this progression into the right, because I conquered my fear of death accidentally so I in fact conquered death in relation to my fear of it. Socrates suggest no true philosopher fears death, which is simply saying , no person can be extreme right brain and still have fear because fear is a side effect of the left brain script indoctrination.

Socrates suggested a comment "I know that I know nothing." Nothing denotes nothingness and nothingness denotes nirvana or extreme right brain. No sense of time, no sense of emotional capacity, No sense of strong hunger, No sense of strong physical aspects such as desires and cravings. Of course nothingness is simply suggesting limbo and purgatory in other faiths. It is simply an attempt to describe the mindset of one in extreme right brain. I could say I understand extreme right brain nothingness. So his comment seems to be a suggestion of humility or being meek but he is only saying I understand this "philosopher" mindset which is extreme right brain. Right brain extreme is just the opposite world of left brain mindset. I recall I suggested before to achieve such heightened awareness and concentration the mind turns off many things so it can focus all of it power into one point, so one is mentally in a state of now, and this an indication of how much power is being used. It's like laser beam it takes all the scattered thoughts and turns many off and creates this pin point laser beam of concentration and awareness but it is not taxing on the mind, it is simply a different mental state of being. I do not detect my mind is taxed at all. I am literally just writing and writing and spilling out ideas trying to keep up with all the ideas my mind is pouring out. If I hired transcriptionist I would make them have carpel tunnel symptom in about a week. So it may seem I write a lot but I assure you, I do not write as much as I want to write. I used the video game to keep my books within the limits of what can be published. I have a 700 page limit according to the publisher and so I learned after the second volume which was 500 plus pages that I have to write slower because the world of publishing cannot keep up with my ability to write swiftly. If I spent one year writing and tried to publish it, it would be too large of a book because it would be well over a million words. That is not an indication of how special I am, that is a symptom of the mental processing power the right brain has when dominate to an extreme. The very word writers block is very foreign to me now. If it takes me more than 1 hour to make up as song and produce it down to the finished product including lyrics I am surprised. This is simply because "The right brain has been associated with the realm of creativity."

I am not so much an inventor as I am a talker, but a person who likes to invent or come up with cures or things along that line, if they went right brain dominate to an extreme, they would perhaps cure every disease in short order and invent things that would improve all of mankind on a monthly basis. That may seem supernatural, but the truth is, the right brain is "too powerful". It can turn an impossible task into a joke task consistently. If one can grasp that is truth even slightly they may be able to understand these wise beings we associate with religion were honestly looking out for our best interests as a species. They were simply saying, life is not as hard as you think it is, you are simply mentally altered by the script and math you were taught as a child and if you "fear not" you will see life is very easy in contrast to how life is on the left aspect of brain. I understand this is exactly what they were all saying. Not some of them, Moses, Buddha, Jesus and Mohammed were all saying that exact same thing, they were looking out for our species. They were righteous in their efforts is my point. They did the best they could based on the situation they were in and based on the vocabulary they had to work with. So all these people who insult one or more of these beings should attempt to have humility and start telling people they misunderstood these beings message, because if you perceive any of these beings were stupid or foolish, you in fact are stupid and foolish. I before the accident perceived Jesus and Moses were wise and Mohammed and Buddha were foolish, but now I understand I misunderstood. I submit I misunderstood many things in relation to the history of the world, so I have gained knowledge because I am aware I misunderstood. So one might suggest I took a few chunks out of this infinite log in my minds' eye and that in fact is what it is all about. One chip off the block at a time with the understanding you may never chip the block away, so be diligent in your chipping. The mindset is along the lines of, try to prove what you think is correct wrong. Try to test your beliefs. That avoids one resting mentally on their laurels. I find eventually some beliefs come to rest or come to be accepted but that's is bad news in one respect, because you can't get any more ponderings from them. But that is okay also, because there are infinite things to ponder. It's a brand new day. I notice I am having trouble using the word is or are, I tend to use is and then I get an error on the spell checker and then I use are. So my mind is not able to use these time sense words properly anymore. So these books would be much worse in relation to accepted grammar, if I didn't have this spell checker reminding me what is acceptable. As far as commas I am purely guessing.- 7/20/2009 3:17:34 AM.

I must be mindful I am fighting the battle using a ploughshare and not a sword. I perhaps need to adjust my strategy. Achieving an understanding good or bad is a win in any book.

J D (17) allegedly shot himself in the head
"On april 23 2009 j. d. went home from school and at approximately 1:45 he shot himself in the head."

I swear to you I do not write fast enough. I can never write fast enough. Everything I do and say is in vain. I want this world to understand the definition of mental gnashing of teeth like I do. I want this world to be in a position that no drug invented is going to ease the mental suffering they will experience in extreme right brain when one understands what is going on in this world. I want the world to understand the definition of cerebral gnashing of teeth so the world will understand one thing. I suggest I cannot do that, simply to humor myself. If I could blink I would blink. If I could sleep I would sleep. If you could see, I could drown. I have no desire to clarify these comments, so never ask me about them. - 5:03:32 AM

I am simply a lone wolf probing the herd for lost sheep.
Left Brain =Mental ignorance = silenced awareness = spiritual joy = mental bliss.

Right Brain = Mental clarity= heightened awareness = mental gnashing of teeth = waxing anger.

Gen 49:6 "O my soul(mind), come not thou into their secret(script and math education); unto their assembly, mine honour(right brain), be not thou united(mentally imbalance): for in their anger(strong ability to hold a grudge) they slew a man(so they tend to kill other people), and in their selfwill (strong ego's caused by left brain) they digged down a wall.(they are ruined mentally). = " thou art cursed above all cattle"

Gen 49:7 Cursed be their anger(strong emotions and ability to hold a grudge), for it was fierce(emotional wrecks) ; and their wrath(grudges), for it was cruel(they kill each other over land and grains of sand and over money): I will divide them in Jacob, and scatter them in Israel.(scatter them denotes they are mentally all over the place , they are controlled by their emotions and their emotions control them and make them do things that are not logical, because they know not what they do.)

Some who have determined their degree's have made them educated and wise will suggest the mind has to have harmony and both right and left aspects in equal portions. That is simply not possible. One has two choices and due to laws, the society chooses for a person. You are either educated with script and extreme left brain or you wake up somehow and go extreme right brain or are in various stages to reaching extreme right brain of left brain. One can pass through the middle state of a little both, but one is either becoming more left brain, more physical focused and less cerebral focused or not.

Eph 4:13 "Till we all come in the unity of the faith(we all have minds), and of the knowledge of the Son of God(right brain dominate to an extreme), unto a perfect man(is how human beings were or are before the script and math), unto the measure(full measure either left brain or right brain) of the stature of the fullness(fullness denotes the feeling of emotions one on the left experiences is gone because they are in the "void" or nothingness of right brain) of Christ:"

Translated: Human being have minds and the knowledge of script and math has turned us from "perfect" as in right brain into "emptiness" of left brain. It is this simple. If you have strong hunger and strong emotions and strong sense of time, you are extreme left brain and so you will try to fill this empty sensation you have in your mind, with physical things and you will try to achieve some relaxation with drugs or food or money or control of things, because you are mentally aware, something is wrong. That is what the empty feeling is everyone tries to fill, they are aware something is just not right and they are correct but they cannot figure out exactly what it is. Maybe they need more money or drugs or food or control , maybe that will fill that empty feeling. But it never will so they will simply become more and more left brained until they are on their death beds and they mindfully are aware their time is short and they will to a degree wake up, and then it will be too late and they will say as the Queen said "All of my kingdom for a moment more."

You are going to figure that out when it's too late to enjoy it or when you can still enjoy it. There is no point in me preaching to anyone but myself because I am fully aware everyone is going to figure it out eventually but many will only figure it when they only have a few moments left to live. The only people are who starting to wake up or go right brain dominate without the fear conditioning hardcore aspects are the elderly. They get old enough the script and math conditioning starts to wear off and they start talking to their self, and they are not ashamed to talk to their self in front of other people. And then the "sane" say they are crazy as a bat because they talk to their self, because the "sane" cannot grasp, they in fact in full blown neurosis and they are watching a human being that is trying to negate the effects of the script neurosis and going back to how "perfect man" or right brain man, is supposed to be.

Old people who talk to their self are in fact working their way to the right. They are starting to wake up naturally because the script conditioning is starting to lose its grip, because they are mindful of death because of their age. So this is all an indication of a person who's see's something and determines it is bad, when in reality it is good. These elderly are enjoying the ponderings. They are not really talking about anything in particular they are mentally exercising. I am just like an old person who talks to their self. I will go into a two hour monologue over a simple question. It is not about answering the question quickly, it is about covering all the bases and looking at it from all aspects and the answer is not as important as the mental exercise. A yes or no answer is quite narrow minded. There are no yes or no answers if one has mental clarity. There are simply various stages of agreement and disagreement filled in with lengthy commentary. A mental rock can say "I disagree" but one with mental clarity can expound on that, and usually end up making a case where they find they actually agree. A person who says I am wrong after I go into a lengthy monologue is clearly no threat to me. It is simple to say "I do not even recognize this argument so I will not respond." Then I understand that person is so far into left brain, they perceive they are wise when I understand they are blind mentally. It does not matter who you are, if you want to have a conversation with me, you better bring your smoking jacket.

What is a right answer and a wrong answer? Don't you really mean, a right answer is a suggested correct answer by a person who perceives they are able to determine what right answers are. Perhaps you are just regurgitating answers that others suggest and then you claim they are the right answers when in reality you are just a mouth piece for the person who suggested they are right answers. You are not running around telling me the world is flat anymore because someone told you it is round. Now you spit out what someone else told you. So perhaps you should consider using your mind a little bit because you are starting to sound a lot like a sounding board or someone's little monkey. Maybe your just a little monkey boy. See there are concepts that one on the left simply cannot grasp properly. I certainly could not grasp concepts properly when I was on the left. This is because certain concepts are very complex and right brain deals with complexity and that means left brain is stuck with simplemindedness. That is not suggesting left brain is dumb, that is only suggesting in the realm of complexity, left brain is not even in the ballpark. That is not an opinion, that is an absolute fact. So for me to reach people on the left they literally have to take some sort of recreational drugs to let them go a little bit to the right brain. I am going further into the right or I "went to heaven in a chariot" so I cannot take drugs and go back to the left because drugs do not get me high, because I am high. I define the word high, that is how far into the right brain I am. I recall I discussed this experiment but I have to keep talking about because people on the left perhaps cannot grasp it.

Here is the experiment. A scientist see's a particle. A camera takes a picture and it comes out as a wave. So the scientists have determined it is not a particle or a wave but something else. What it is, is relativity. Granted it may take a thousand years for them to figure that out but they are not seeing a particle or a wave and they never have andthey never will. The problem is, in a true vacuum one is in the experiment and everything is relative to observation, a camera is an observer, a human is also. One has to get outside the true vacuum to be an unbiased observer. Only one who leaves the True Vacuum can look back at the true vacuum and understand it all. I would never suggest I am outside the true vacuum and looking back at it and that is why I am able to understand everything clearly because ones might suggest that is not a humble or meek attitude. All I want is their medals I don't care about reality. If I could just have one of their gold medals around my neck I might feel I am important. But then I might want 2 gold medals, and then I might want all the gold medals. And then I might harm people physically for gold medals to put around my neck so I might feel important, because everyone knows if you don't have a gold medal you are not important on the scale of importance. Everyone knows if you cannot pass the grade you are not important. I am willing to wager infinite gold medals this person was not an A student and was perhaps starting to feel like an outcast as a result.

"On april 23 2009 j. d. went home from school and at approximately 1:45 he shot himself in the head."

I am willing to bet your soul on everything is say. Can you top that? Perhaps you should ponder that for a moment.- 6:48:06 AM

7:05:18 AM – I am not going to blow it like the others did. You can bet all your gold on that.

10:05:33 AM – I have pondered. There is a book in the Torah called Numbers. I read the first chapter and I detect something is amiss. Adam and Eve ate of the tree of knowledge which is demotic and mathematics or Dena, and all the rules in these "knowledge" aspects encouraged the left brain. So then there is a book that is Dena or number or is based on number as tool to count people. That alone goes against infinity, because counting denotes limits , alpha and omega denotes infinity. So the story does not sync up because it is saying "Do not eat off the tree of Dena and demotic" and then there is a book all about Dena and encouraging Dena. So this book of number is rather interesting because it may be an inside joke as it were. It may be a sign post of some sort, In relation to a person who can translate this "code" would hit on this book and understand it is a sore thumb in contrast to the other books.

There is a great misunderstanding. I will get back to the book Numbers eventually. I am not pleased. I tried to speak highly of the philosophy channel and some were pleased with my comments.

<n|nja> you are something of a God-send btw.
<n|nja> i was going to keep it a secret.
<n|nja> but there.
<n|nja> i said it.
<Lestat9> Thank You
<n|nja> i won't go into the details or explain it.
<n|nja> cya...
<Lestat9> Take care

I detect this being was pleased with my take on the Adam and Eve story. But then I speak further and an OP or one in control in said channel says this to me.

<vsihs> lestat stop it now please
<vsihs> you've delivered several versions of these musings over last few days

<vsihs> some of it's quite interesting, too

<vsihs> but you can't just deliver monologues in here - it's a chan for discussion

I detect he is attempting to control me. "Stop it now please" as if the word please means I should allow other to control me. "but you can't just deliver monologues in here - it's a chan for discussion"

Now contrast that opinion from this guys opinion. "<n|nja> you are something of a God-send btw."

The difference is, the one guy has Ops and perceived power and the other guy is just a casual chatter who happened to like what I said. "Absolute power corrupts absolutely." So this guy is trying to show me who is in control and if I do not bow to him he will ban me. That is a fear tactic. Please do as I say, or I will kill you. You are talking too much in a chat room for discussion. This chat room for discussion is for slow discussion not fast discussion. You are going too fast in your discussion and please stop it or I will ban you because I am god himself and you will bend to my perception or die. I did not message him. I was speaking to others, yet he had to "save the channel" from my fast talking. He just right up there with the savior of all that is good. There is a misunderstanding. People on the left assume I have morals and class. Morals and class get turned off in trade for concentration and brain function. You should never try to become right brain dominate to an extreme if you want to hold onto all these luxuries like judgment and sentimentality. You factually will lose all of that emotional baggage. You will lose shame, embarrassment.

"And they were both naked, the man and his wife, and were not ashamed."

(Genesis 2:25)

Perhaps you need to go to school and understand what "and were not ashamed." means. That means you lose all emotional baggage. So you don't want be on the "right hand side". You don't want to be emotionless because simply put

Joh 3:30 "He must increase, but I must decrease."

Everything is in vain if you do not understand what this says. Your emotions are what are called your ego. Your ego must decrease so that the right can increase. So forget about being right brained. You are going to lose yourself so you better save yourself.

Luk 17:33 "Whosoever shall seek to save his life shall lose it; and whosoever shall lose his life shall preserve it."

Those who seek to save their (ego,emotions,self) shall lose it, and whoever shall lose their (self,emotions,ego) shall preserve it. So what is it? IT is the void, nirvana, right brain, extreme concentration, heightened awareness, brain function. So there is a misunderstanding. I am not writing these books because I had an accident. I am not foolish

enough to presume I could ever convince someone to give up their ego, their emotions, their attachments, their longing to have fun, and have material things and joy and pleasure. That's not my goal. I write for me alone. I am trapped here. Do not come here, you cannot handle my pool and I eat for no reason. You stay on the left because that's safe. This place is not safe. This place is freedom and loss of morals and class and rules. I do not believe the definition of words. You don't want that. When someone says fuck you, you want to tell them they are evil and bad. When someone talks too much you want to tell them they are evil and bad. That's what you want so never come over to my pool because I am a big fish and I eat little fish for no reason. I have purged all emotions so I have no shame and no embarrassment at all. I lost my life(ego, emotions, self) and I preserved IT. I am not talking to you or preaching to you because you might start thinking I am concerned about what you think about me. I might say something to you and then you will say "You are evil or you are good or you are humble or you are sinister." You are unable to understand what I am ever.

Luk 17:36 " Two men shall be in the field; the one shall be taken(to right brain), and the other left(left brain)."

Field = brain. Two = left brain and right brain. Condition away from fear your ="fear not" and lose the traits of left brain" seven deadly sins" or they are silenced to such a degree you lose your ego. You know ego, the thing that makes you embarrassed and feel shame and feel the need to control people with fear tactics and makes you think you understand anything ever. You keep your little ego because you aint going to have one if you mess with these teachings, you are only going to have the void. Just admit you love your attachments and you love your ego and you fun and your desires and cravings, and stop reading my private diaries. I am not here to make you feel better I am here to make you feel nothing, void. You abuse to many children, you cannot be trust around children in any capacity. That is a nice way of saying you go back to the void where you came from. Maybe I am evil now or am I good now? Am I good or evil? Maybe you cannot even imagine with the simplemindedness of the left brain what void is. I write infinite books to assist me with the log in my eye. I am not here to suggest you go into the void. If I wanted to trick you into the void I would. I would do it easily but that would denote I care. I do not care about what you do, I care about assisting myself with the infinite log in my eye. You told me I am a loser because I couldn't spell, I assure you I do not care what you do, what you think, what you say. I know what you are. Does that bother you that I know what you are? Are you curious about what I know you are? I am not going to tell you what I KNOW you are. I am fiddler on the roof watching the mice scurry. That must mean I am evil, I mean good, I mean sinister.

<vsihs> some of it's quite interesting, too

<vsihs> but you can't just deliver monologues in here - it's a chan for discussion

I will make sure I let this being know I am adding their comments to my book. That must mean I am evil. The other guys said this

<n|nja> you are something of a God-send btw.

And that pisses me off even more because then when I tell him I do not care about anyone's log but my own, he will say I am evil. I cannot win against this kind of "complex logic". I am a God-send until I cuss. I am a God-send until I do something that breaks their rules of acceptability and then they kill me. I have enough imagination to be able too tell what would happen if I started to talk to you. That is why you are an illusion. You cannot deal with complexity and ambiguity and paradox. That is beyond your mental capacity. I have really good genes that didn't kick in until I was 40. Don't you dare start to attach to me because I have no morals and no class and you are unable to deal with that and you will try to control me and I will tell you to fuck off and you will say I am evil. The reality is, you cannot handle the void and you cannot handle the truth. I am here by accident. I am doomed. Save yourself. - 11:37:11 AM

11:53:58 AM – I will put to you like this. The reason Buddha, Moses, Jesus, Mohammed, Socrates got butchered is because they had complexity, ambiguity and paradox in their words and the "sane" could not figure them out so they killed them. Complexity denotes no labels."The left brain is associated with verbal, logical, and analytical thinking. It excels in naming and categorizing things," Categorizing things. The ones on the left one day said these wise beings were wise, and the next day they heard them speak and said they were fools, and the next day they were wise, and the next day they were fools, and before you know it one of these "sane" beings said, we have had enough of their talking and actions so let's kill them because we are in neurosis and cannot tolerate ambiguity. I say I am insane because my ego and emotions have been purged as a result of the accident. Your ego would not allow you to publish a book and say you are in fact insane. It would ruin you, as if that matters, as if you were not mentally ruined by about the fifth grade. Moses threw the commandments on the rocks because rules do not apply when one has no labels or shame or guilt or fear. That's right brain to the extreme. That does not mean I kill people and steal from people. You kill people and steal from people and assume you are god himself. That is your domain. My domain is cerebral. I fight my battles with words you have no ability to use words and no cerebral ability at all, so you build weapons and kill people who you do not agree with. That is who you are and not who I am. I do not pander to what I own. Lying is a symptom of shame. If you haven't noticed I do not bear false witness because I have no shame I no longer have morals. To clarify, I do not give a rats ass what you think about what I say. Does that bother you I do not care what

you think about me ever? Your opinion about me means zero to me. Do you think I am afraid of what you say about me when you mentally rape children on a daily basis and do not even have the mind to give them a remedy for the forced education you by law cram down their throats, and then they kill their self and you have the balls to say, "We don't know why he did that, he must have been troubled." The reality is, the only being in this universe that is seriously in trouble at this stage of the universe is you. I know who you are. I detect who you are. I try very hard to suggest these are diaries and I am only talking to myself but I am not, I am talking to you. I am just a liar. So I am a liar that doesn't bear false witness. Quite a paradox one might suggest, so to speak, psychologically speaking, and then there were none. I can't go back in history beyond when history started. I put my books in psychology because I am dealing with rabidity. I know for a fact it is rabidity because I had lots of it before my accident so you don't have to guess if I am dealing with rabidity, I know for a fact. So now I am certain no human will ever again say you are a God-send. You do not know what a god-send is, and you never will. You would be very wise to never suggest I am a god-send. Now you understand a paradox. I write infinite books to explain this truth I perceive and then I explain in those books why you should not want it. I am beyond the stage of wondering if I am translating the ancient texts properly. My mind was in such neurosis it is not adjusting easily to non neurosis. Prepare for mental war if you want mental peace. You need to look up the definition of war and put an infinity sign next to it because you are not going to reachpeace. If you want mental peace you engage in mental war and that mental war is infinite. Here is what peace is, when you just sit in a room and meditate until you die. If you can't handle that, then you get the infinite war. That is what extreme right brain dominate is. You are going to reach this state and have a mindset to have fun or party or gethigh, and you aren't going to be able to mentally have fun or get high. I think I am more upset with people on the right than people on the left. I understand I am frustrated today because I get mixed results with what I say to people. One person gets it and other person half way gets it and one person says I am the devil. And to top it off, I have heightened awareness and understand when I say tomato they hear potato.

Php 1:14 "And many of the brethren in the Lord, waxing confident by my bonds, are much more bold to speak the word without fear."

One might suggest I talk to much or say too much or I am waxing with confidence but the truth is, I cannot tell what is too much and I have no ego so confidence is not possible, but to those on the left they may think I am arrogant or confident and they certainly think I talk too much. So this confident comment is only relative to those on the left whoobserve. If I was on the left I would at least have enough pride to not publish these crappy books. I would at least have enough pride to spell check and make sure the commas are right. So my emotions or ego is totally gone. "Speak without fear" that is what I am doing. I may get killed, sure. I am not making many friends with what I say, perhaps.

1:43:07 PM – If you have actually made it this far in this thick pamphlet then you perhaps are starting to lose your fear of words and you are certainly able to tolerate ambiguity.

7/21/2009 3:27:36 AM – This is what I know for a fact. I had an accident and achieved some sort of heightened awareness. As a result of that I discovered humans being are forcing other human being into education and not telling them they must condition away from the side effect fear or they will end up only being able to use a portion of their full mental faculties. Because of this accident and because I became aware of that and because I do not do anything to stop that, I am in fact the most evil vile being in the universe. I am watching people being harmed and I am not lifting a finger to attempt to help them so I am the devil incarnate. I am spitting in the face of a good Samaritan concept so I am a complete failure and idiot and I have learned nothing from all that I have been taught because I am to afraid to stand up and do something about an injustice I am certain beyond a shadow a doubt is happening. So I am evil incarnate and therefore I will never edit my books and I will never acknowledge anyone, because I am the devil. I will never deny that understanding. I have cast my lot and my lot will not be uncast. - 3:32:58 AM

3:52:08 AM – I am not righteous by standing by an attempting to fix a problem such as this with mere words, I am in fact evil incarnate because violence is the only way to change this injustice I am certain of. So I am the devil himself because I stand by and watch people have their minds ripped from them and I am to afraid to use violence to stop it. So I will be the devil and I will act like the devil and I will try to achieve a mindset of violence so that I might get out of this devil aspect I have assumed by standing by and allowing injustice to occur. I will achieve a mindset of violence and I will smite them. - 3:54:52 AM

To defeat the devil one must show the devil what evil is.
The quick and the dead it's not in your head.
 [00:02] <KarenJ> Lestat I perceive you are mentally ill and need help very badly.
* You were kicked by KarenJ (Blacklisted- false doctrine lectures)
[23:54] <+GamerTony> <3 /ignore
[00:13] <+KarenJ> I'm reasonably well educated but that one is nonsense as near as I can tell
[00:32] <+KarenJ> You are coming across as self centered and egotistical in the extreme.
[23:54] <+TaraJo> oh hell
[23:54] <+TaraJo> this again?
<n|nja> you are something of a God-send btw.
<n|nja> i was going to keep it a secret.
<n|nja> but there.
<n|nja> i said it.
[00:12] <+KarenJ> Does that make sense to ANYONE?
<Favicon> well i know alot of people who would sit alone in a cemetery
<Favicon> :)
<Lestat9> I know many who would not say a cuss word because they fear they would be evil if they did
[00:12] <+KarenJ> Does that make sense to ANYONE?

[23:54] * KarenJ sets mode: +b *!*lestatnin@*.fl.comcast.net
[00:14] <+KarenJ> Oh I didn't get lost. It has no meaning.
[00:12] <+KarenJ> Does that make sense to ANYONE?
<Favicon> well i know alot of people who would sit alone in a cemetery
<Favicon> :)
[23:54] <+GamerTony> <3 /ignore
* You were kicked by KarenJ (Blacklisted- false doctrine lectures)
[23:54] * KarenJ sets mode: +b *!*lestatnin@*.fl.comcast.net
<n|nja> you are something of a God-send btw.
<vsihs> some of it's quite interesting, too
<vsihs> but you can't just deliver monologues in here - it's a chan for discussion
[00:02] <KarenJ> Lestat I perceive you are mentally ill and need help very badly.
* You were kicked by KarenJ (Blacklisted- false doctrine lectures)
[23:54] <+TaraJo> oh hell
[23:54] <+TaraJo> this again?
[00:12] <+KarenJ> Does that make sense to ANYONE?
[00:45] <whomasect> "[22:36] KarenJ: dogmatic people at least seem to know what they believe and this guy couldn't talk in plain English."
[00:12] <+KarenJ> Does that make sense to ANYONE?
[00:45] <whomasect> she is anti-truth , at every step
[00:12] <+KarenJ> Does that make sense to ANYONE?
* You were kicked by KarenJ (Blacklisted- false doctrine lectures)
"[22:36] KarenJ: dogmatic people at least seem to know what they believe and this guy couldn't talk in plain English."
[23:54] <+GamerTony> <3 /ignore
Back to reality. - 5:11:58 AM

Berry Mixed- http://www.youtube.com/watch?v=p3_rsPxGgmM

How do you perceive the author is blowing it:
Swiftly
Slowly
Hardly

"The goal of all life is death. "
Sigmund Freud
I do not want the depressed and suicidal to perceive I am on your side.
The meek (depressed and suicidal = fearless) shall inherit the earth(right brain =achieved through fear conditioning).
Mat 16:25 "For whosoever will save his life(fearful and afraid of words and cemeteries at night) shall lose it(right brain= subconscious= understanding= heightened awareness):and whosoever will lose his life(Fear Not; not afraid of fear conditioning) for my sake(because he said Fear Not) shall find it(right brain, the kingdom within).
I will remind you when I get warmed up.

Exo 32:19 ...," that he saw the calf,.... and Moses anger waxed hot, and he cast the tables out of his hands, and brake them beneath the mount(all is fair in love and war=No morals and no class in love and war)."

<Lestat9> [00:02] <KarenJ> Lestat I perceive you are mentally ill and need help very badly.

<Lestat9> [23:54] <+GamerTony> <3 /ignore

<Lestat9> [00:13] <+KarenJ> I'm reasonably well educated but that one is nonsense as near as I can tell

<Lestat9> "[22:36] KarenJ: dogmatic people at least seem to know what they believe and this guy couldn't talk in plain English."

<Lestat9> [23:54] * KarenJ sets mode: +b *!*lestatnin@*.fl.comcast.net

<Lestat9> * You were kicked by KarenJ (Blacklisted- false doctrine lectures)

<Lestat9> "What progress we are making. In the Middle Ages they would have burned me. Now they are content with burning my books."

<Lestat9> Sigmund Freud

<Lestat9> Luk 23:34 "Then said Jesus, Father, forgive them; for they know not what they do."

<Lestat9> Exo 32:19 .., that he saw) the calf,.... and Moses anger waxed hot, and he cast) the tables out of his hands, and brake them beneath the mount."

<Lestat9> Reasoning with rabidity requires imagination.

-<Lestat9> Rabidity: irrationally extreme in opinion or practice. - 12:56:46 PM

[00:45] <whomasect> "[22:36] KarenJ: dogmatic people at least seem to know what they believe and this guy couldn't talk in plain English."

01[00:45] <Lestat9> well both sides are there, as one turns up one side the other side becomes silenced

[00:45] <whomasect> female is Maya

[00:45] <whomasect> she is anti-truth , at every step

01[00:45] <Lestat9> yes she would hang me on a cross

[00:45] <whomasect> whatever SHE says, is anti-truth , and luring away

[00:46] <whomasect> when maya gets ANGRY we know we are making progress ok ?

1Co 14:23 If therefore the whole church(ones on the right) be come together into one place, and all speak with tongues(*), and there come in those that are unlearned(ones on the left), or unbelievers(ones on the left), will they not say that ye are mad?(*)

*Tongues: To ones on the left ones on the right say things that appear strange. Ones on the right at times cannot form sentence sequence properly and say things that make the ones on the left attack them. <Lestat9> "[22:36] KarenJ: dogmatic people at least seem to know what they believe and this guy couldn't talk in plain English." = Maya =adversary = Darkness = Infidel = "sane" = left hand side

*Mad= [00:13] <+KarenJ> I'm reasonably well educated but that one is nonsense as near as I can tell = [00:02] <KarenJ> Lestat I perceive you are mentally ill and need help very badly. = Maya

[00:46] <whomasect> when Maya gets ANGRY we know we are making progress ok ?
[00:12] <+KarenJ> Does that make sense to ANYONE?
* You were kicked by KarenJ (Blacklisted- false doctrine lectures)

"If you're not ready to die for it(face your fear or condition away from fear), put the word 'freedom'(right brain extreme) out of your vocabulary."
Malcolm X

"Nonviolence is fine as long as it works."
Malcolm X
Exo 32:19 ..," that he saw the calf,…. and Moses anger waxed hot, and [he cast) the tables1 out of his hands, and brake them beneath the mount](all is fair in love and war=No morals and no class in love and war)."] = "This component of the brain is not concerned with things falling into patterns because of prescribed rules(commandments.)"
[he cast) the tables out of his hands, and brake them beneath the mount] = no morals and no class in unseen or cerebral war.
1Sa 17:34 And David said unto Saul, Thy servant kept his father's sheep(ones on the right), and there came a lion(ones on the left), and a bear(one on the left), and took a lamb out of the flock(world=church of ones on the right)(in relation to) Isa 65:25 The wolf(ones on the left) and the lamb shall feed(be in the world together= lions and lambs) together, and the lion shall eat straw like the bullock(left brainers do not stand a chance against the mental abilities of the right) and dust shall be the serpent's meat(ones on the left=under the script neurosis= unable to think clearly= just talk foolishness). [They shall not hurt nor destroy in all my holy mountain, saith the LORD.]= Armageddon = left brainers = number the grains of sand in the sea because everyone is taught the script/language but they cannot wipe out all the ones on the right because the ones on the right are far too clever, cerebrally=[On the contrary, the right brain seems to flourish dealing with complexity, ambiguity and paradox.] = Quick(right brains) and the dead(left brains).
I will remind you if I decide to start to try. - 1:44:36 PM

1:46:24 PM - 1Ti 5:8 But if any provide not for his own(condition fear away so they go right brained) , and specially for those of his own house(assist those around him to condition away from their fear so they go right brained), he hath denied the faith(right brain), and is worse than an infidel(darkness, maya,dead,"sane",anti-christ,the left
brainers).= Once one is right brained they are obligated to assist others under the scribe neurosis to wake up or they are in fact worse than the ones on the left because they are not a good Samaritan or a good shepard.(in relation to [Mat 10:8 Heal the sick(lefter's ones taught the script), cleanse the lepers(ones on the left, cerebrally silenced), raise the dead(ones on the left), cast out(show them how to condition away from fear) devils(adversary, ones on the left, darkness, antichrist) : freely ye have received, freely give.(no rules no morals in the cerbreal battle because for every person you help get to the right brain the society pumps out millions

of (infidels, lefters,darkness, left brainers)because they teach them all the demotic and dena and then don't tell them to condition away from fear to counter the side effects such as fear, strong emotions, shame, shyness, embarssment) = A dead horse loves repeat performances.

2Co 6:15 And what concord hath Christ with Belial((*)one on the left, darkness, silenced awareness cerebrally)? or what part hath he that believeth with an infidel?(*Bəliyyá□al; also named Matanbuchus, Mechembuchus, Meterbuchus in older scripts) is a demon(demotic = planned language[we have been traditionally taught to master the 3 R's: reading, writing and arithmetic -- the domain and strength of the left brain] in the Bible, Christian apocrypha and Jewish apocrypha, and also a term used to characterize the wicked[violent, physical based left brainers] or worthless[cerebrally silenced left brainers]. "

[00:13] <+KarenJ> I'm reasonably well educated but that one is nonsense as near as I can tell

[00:02] <KarenJ> Lestat I perceive you are mentally ill and need help very badly

[00:46] <whomasect> when Maya gets ANGRY we know we are making progress ok ?

KarenJ: dogmatic people at least seem to know what they believe and this guy couldn't talk in plain English."

[00:12] <+KarenJ> Does that make sense to ANYONE?

* You were kicked by KarenJ (Blacklisted- false doctrine lectures)

I will not blow it like the others did. - 2:20:42 PM

#christian unable to join channel (address is banned)

#christian unable to join channel (address is banned)

#christian unable to join channel (address is banned)

I'm the devil.

"this guy couldn't talk in plain English."

You will wish I died.

2Jn 1:7 For many deceivers are entered into the world(taught the demotic and dena and are not told to condition away from fear and thus are left brained), who confess not that Jesus Christ(right brain) is come(is a viable option or possible, subconscious dominate, nirvana, no sense of time) in the flesh(the lefters tend to hang the right brainers on crosses and feed them poison and hemlock) This is a deceiver(female(not literal female just contrast) is Maya) and an antichrist.(left brainers) Never assume I am religious I am strictly on a vengeance mission.

Rev 13:2 And the beast(left brainers) which I saw was like unto a leopard(physically violent), and his feet were as the feet of a bear(claws as in one who uses swords instead of ploughshares(words)), and his mouth as the mouth of a lion(angry and judgmental- <KarenJ> Lestat I perceive you are mentally ill and need help very badly= KarenJ: dogmatic people at least seem to know what they believe and this guy couldn't talk in plain English.") and the dragon gave him his power(the snake, the demotic, the Dena, left brain influenced by script education) and his seat(left brain mindset), and great authority(all about rules and laws in order to control others = Left brain excels in naming

143

and categorizing things(you do as I say or you are bad or evil) = anti-right brain which =right component of the brain is not concerned with things falling into patterns because of prescribed rules(freedom is all about few rules not more rules because rules and laws control people's free will to pursue happiness) ,authority.

"Yes, America is gigantic, but a gigantic mistake."
Sigmund Freud
"The price of inaction is far greater than the cost of making a mistake."
Meister Eckhar
"Any society that would give up a little liberty(ones on the left are afraid and signed away my absolute freedom of speech and privacy and my right to do as I wish as long as I do not directly harm others) to gain a little security(to feel safe because they get scared easily because they are left brained caused by the script neurosis) will deserve neither and lose both(will be slaughtered and watered)."
Benjamin Franklin

Morals only apply after one takes a[blood bath](conditions away from fear and goes right brain dominate).

America is a suicide pact and the ones who do not fear death love it. The sooner you understand I have already cast my lot, the sooner you will understand who I am. That's why you will wish I died. I am not a revelation I am a revolution.

Heb 10:30 "For we know him that hath said, Vengeance belongeth unto me(the ones who wake up from the script neurosis, right brainers), I will recompense(compensate the world for making them left brained with the script), saith the Lord. And again, The Lord(ones on the right, the lords of the house in contrast to the ones on the left in relation to cerebral ability) shall judge his people.(be able to make proper judgments because they are attempting to assist the species to wake up from the script neurosis so they are righteous because they are attempting to help others to have 100% brain function as opposed to 10% they have on the left)

[00:12] <+KarenJ> Does that make sense to ANYONE?
* You were kicked by KarenJ (Blacklisted- false doctrine lectures)
I will not blow it like the others did. - 2:20:42 PM
#christian unable to join channel (address is banned)
Translated: I accidentally discovered how human beings can use 100% of their mind instead of 10% and you get in the way of my efforts, we are going to have a blood bath and I defeated my fear of death and went extreme right brain dominate, so I prefer a blood bath because "absence makes the heart grow fonder", I accidentally went extreme right brain dominate and lost emotions and I write books in hopes I can say something that will make me feel fear again because I forget what fear, pleasure, fun, lust, greed, envy is like, I lost my ego. Some try to have less greed and less fear and less envy and I got hit by a mac truck and lost all of that, so I am trying to have greed and envy and fear. This is the extremes, one either has greed and envy and lust and fear or they do not. Everything in between is what is known as "lukewarm" or in a state of "being and becoming". One is either cold(left brain) or hot (right brain) and many are in various stages of achieving these extremes. Full of emotions/ego or lacking all emotions/ego. One is either quick(cerebrally /right brain dominate) or dead (cerebrally weak/

left brain) and the only difference between the two is right has no fear /emotional capacity and left has fear and emotional capacity. Left is under the influence of the snake /script education and right woke up and has the "kingdom" and many are in various stages of waking up(right brained extreme) or going further into the dark(left brain) and known as lukewarm. So "fear not" means on the right brain extreme who is not capable of fear because in extreme right brain all emotions are purged or emotionless is a trait of extreme right brain or a symptom and it required to achieved heightened awareness and extreme concentration.

Even I have moments of clarity.

[00:02] <KarenJ> Lestat I perceive you are mentally ill and need help very badly

[00:13] <+KarenJ> I'm reasonably well educated but that one is nonsense as near as I can tell

[00:46] <whomasect> when Maya gets ANGRY we know we are making progress ok ?

[00:45] <whomasect> whatever SHE says, is anti-truth , and luring away

* You were kicked by KarenJ (Blacklisted- false doctrine lectures)

#christian unable to join channel (address is banned)

"It is the folly of too many to mistake the echo of a London coffee-house for the voice of the kingdom."

Jonathan Swift

Translated: Ones on the left under the influence of the script neurosis tend to perceive the ones on the right as "drunk" or "crazy" because they do not have the heightened awareness and 100% brain function to understand they are the "kingdom= right brain dominate to an extreme".

Clarification: My books are published so I have already won the battle between the "antichrist"(ones on the left) and the light (ones on the right). The battle is already over. I am simply a fiddler on the roof watching the mice(ones on the left) scurry. I am fiddling or toying with them, because the battle was over before it began. They are not allowed to burn my books and they are not allowed to collect all the books I have given freely. So they are defeated. I will now discuss something relevant.- 3:51:53 PM

If I needed an army I would have one.

You are much more cerebrally powerful than "society" suggests, and I will not tolerate that, so the battle is waged. I encourage ones to test me and my resolve. Back to reality.

[00:02] <KarenJ> Lestat I perceive you are mentally ill and need help very badly

This comment is an indication of the problem with planned language and verbal language in general. When one is in nirvana or extreme right brain they have essentially negated the left brain conditioning and in turn they lose emotional capacity and ego. The problem with that in relation to verbal language is, verbal language is ego and emotional based. I can say "I hate the universe." Then a person on the left will assume I am hateful but in reality it is impossible for me to feel hate or assume a mindset of hate because I have lost my ego or emotional capacity. So anything I type a person with left brain and language heavy mindset will make assumptions about me that are patently wrong. I am without emotion and ego and I am using a verbal language based on ego and emotion. This is exactly why some in nirvana go into silence. A vow of silence. This is because anything they say will be taken as them being arrogant or egotistical by the ones on the left who believe the definition of the words. If I say "I" to often ones on the left will assume I am egotistical and always talk about myself. If I say "thank you" to often the ones on the left will assume I am either humble , gracious or if I say it way to often, "annoying".

The ones on the left are simply so verbal language indoctrinated they fear words and so the words control them. They react and judge others by the words they say because they believe the definition or every word they hear. "Sticks and stones may break my bones but words will never harm me." The ones on the left have no idea what that comment means. They say that saying and then they attack people for saying certain words, so they are totally blind to what they do, totally and unconditionally mentally blind. Without the fear conditioning on top of the planned language education a person is factually mentally dead in contrast to one in extreme right brain. A terrorist is one who manipulates others with fear tactics. Manipulate would be they pass a law that says a person must be educated into planned language and then they manipulate that persons brain. They would not be a terrorist if they then had classes that conditioned one away from fear which is simply a mental anomaly caused by the extreme left brain conditioning planned language and Dena create, but they do not do that, so their goal is to make sure people are fear based mentally. So "they" are in fact terrorists. They manipulate people's minds to keep them using 10% of their mental capacity when they could let them use 100%. So this is what is known as "controlling the herd" by keep the herd dumb. Opiate of the masses.

8:53:22 PM -666 is simply ego or mindset. Six is a perfect number. A person who is left brained tends to think they are something great, that is ego. They are never wrong and they will never admit they are wrong. That is pride and a symptom of ego and strong emotions. When a person on the left is insulted their ego or pride is hurt and then they want revenge and because they are left brained that tends to be some physical attack on someone or something. When in extreme right brain all emotions are purged so ego is also purged. I cannot hate because I cannot love that is good because that means I cannot get depressed when love is lost and so I cannot hold a grudge and want actual physical revenge. I cannot care and therefore I cannot get depressed when I lose what I care about. This is all in relation to "Let the dead bury the dead". This is what coveting is, a left brain person is sentimental and it harms them. In India some take their dead and float them down a river and dolphins come up that river for one reason, to eat those dead, because the relatives can let go. A person does not need to bury the dead, let the dead go back to the earth so one is not tempted to covet the dead. The whole world should not go into a nervous fit when a "popular" person dies. That is mentally unhealthy. People die and when they die give them back to the earth and don't try to covet and control them with a marker because you will only turn them into a idol. One can never control anything they can only try to achieve a mental mindset of letting go of the desire to control.

So Armageddon started on Oct 31st 2008 at 1:38 PM and it ended on 7/21/2009 9:21:25 PM EST

The script neurosis that has devastated the mind of humans for over 5000 years is going to end now. Now mankind will slowly all become Einstein's and we will be far more interested in cerebral concepts such as inventions and creativity to assist each other instead of physical things such as control of grains of sand and rocks and control of others. You may not grasp that, but I understand that. - 9:24:25 PM

I prefer the comment, One, in the land of the free, understood absolute freedom accidentally, explained it to everyone in the world, and everyone in the world became absolutely free, with two words, Fear Not.

[00:02] <KarenJ> Lestat I perceive you are mentally ill and need help very badly

[00:13] <+KarenJ> I'm reasonably well educated but that one is nonsense as near as I can tell

* You were kicked by KarenJ (Blacklisted- false doctrine lectures)

#christian unable to join channel (address is banned)

[00:12] <+KarenJ> Does that make sense to ANYONE?

Rev 15:4 Who shall not fear(those who condition away from fear and achieve right brain dominate) thee, O Lord, and glorify thy name?(and assist other to achieve right brain dominate) for thou only art holy(will be asked what kind of drugs they are on, by the left brainers = [00:02] <KarenJ> Lestat I perceive you are mentally ill and need help very badly) for all nations shall come and worship before thee(because every human being has a right brain and it is just veiled due to the script neurosis or it is like a crescent moon)); for thy(right brain dominate person) judgments are made manifest.(judgments will be proper because they will use 100% of their mind instead of 10%)

Rev 1:17 And when I saw him(achieved right brain dominate), I fell at his feet as dead(because right brain is so powerful and dead denotes conditioned away from fear of death).And he laid his right hand upon me(condition away from fear and achieve right brain), saying unto me, fear not; I am the first and the last(denotes no sense of time, infinity, seeing everything a whole) = "The right brain looks at the whole picture"

1Jn 4:18 There is no fear(condition away from fear) in love(one is in a state of now so they do proper deeds and their fruit is love but its not a controlling type of love like left brain love);but perfect love(right brain love where you see perfection in everything and everyone with the feeling through vision) casteth out fear(condition away from fear): because fear hath torment(is a side effect of the script and dena and it makes one left brain dominate and the strong emotions are a hindrance). He that feareth(that does not condition away from fear and thus is left brained) is not (able to achieve perfect love just controlling love, which is why the "apple" invention, demotic and dena, is an invention that had unintended side effects on the whole species)made perfect in love."

1Pe 2:18 Servants(ones on the left brain still under the influence of the script neurosis), be subject to your masters(ones who conditioned away from fear, and reached right brain) with all fear(meaning listen to the masters because they are only trying to assist you to achieve right brain so you will be a master and can assist others to "wake up" from the script neurosis); not only to the good and gentle(good and gentle are ones on the left who proclaim love but it's not perfect love and proclaim to be gentle but it's not perfect gentle), but also to the froward.

(forward is someone who talks a good game but they are still on the left so they are perverse in relation to they are still on the left or under the influence of the script neurosis)

Heb 13:6 "So that we may boldly say, The Lord(right brain when dominate to the extreme) is my helper, and I will not fear(one is purged of all fear and emotions when in extreme right brain) what man(one on the left under the script neurosis) shall do unto me.(what person on the left would turn down a chance to be an Einstein if they only had to do a little fear conditioning, no man would, so the ones on the extreme right have an easy task because everyone wants to be an Einstein.)

Heb 11:7 By faith(by heightened awareness he understood) Noah, being warned of God(right brain extreme with heightened awareness he could tell the future or tell what was going to happen) of things not seen as yet(the future), moved with fear(saw the script had made everyone left brained and they had strong emotions such as strong fear), prepared an ark to the saving of his house(got his family away from the ones on the left because he knew they were violent and dangerous); by the which he condemned the world(He said , world your script and Dena is ruining everyone's mind), and became heir of the righteousness(became one of the few at that time who could "talk" others back into right brain so he was "righteous" or a "master" because he had this knowledge of how to counter the script neurosis) which is by faith(he understood that fear conditioning was the remedy to the neurosis).

2Ti 1:7 For God(right brain dominate to the extreme) hath not given us the spirit of fear;(is not capable of strong emotion or is absent of emotions like fear) but of power(extreme concentration , feeling through vision and many other things), and of love(perfect love not controlling love like left brain love), and of a sound mind.(100% cerebral function instead of 10%)

Gen 2:2 "And on the seventh(volume) day God(Todd) ended his work which he had made; and he rested on the seventh(volume) day from all his work which he had made."
This is in fact a predication that has come to pass. I am uncertain how they knew this and I presume it was Moses who understood this, but it is perhaps testament to how powerful the right brain is and is in fact unnamable in its power. You perhaps are thinking I am suggesting I am God. I am not suggesting I am God, I in fact will never be intelligent enough to speak about the supernatural. I am suggesting Moses understood how many books or volumes it would take me to "peel the onion to reveal the onion". In fact, the onion is peeled, but I am mindful and I understand I will only rest long enough to start volume eight. I do not feel satisfied so I do not feel dissatisfied, I just start the next volume. Apparently I understand, I have not yet begun to write, to fight, to have sight.

7/23/2009 2:24:33 AM – This book is a total failure so I need to write another one. No more talking just wise quotes.

"A rock pile ceases to be a rock pile the moment a single man contemplates it, bearing within him the image of a cathedral."

Antoine de Saint-Exupery

A rock cannot build a house but it's possible to imagine it did. How you see things determines your imagination level. Judgment has more to do with imagination than morals. It is much easier to talk one's self into something than nothing. Proving something requires equipment, proving nothing requires imagination. Convincing yourself of an absolute truth is much easier than convincing others.

I had a near death experience and went subconscious dominate. In the seven months since that I have discovered if one conditions their self away from fear of words and fear of what they fear they will unlock the complex creative aspect of the mind and go from using 10% of their mind to using 100% of their mind and the telepathy and heightened awareness make nice parting gifts.

"Fiction reveals truths that reality obscures."

Jessamyn West

Some are afraid to tell the truth so they write fiction, some have no fear and tell it like it is.

Forgive me for I know not what I do.
Forgret me for I know not what I do.
Forget me for I know not what I know.
Regret me for I know not what I do.
Regret me for I forgive what I forget.
Forget me for I forgot what I regret.

I still tear so I am still in full blown neurosis.

If people did not say the exact things they said to me in my life, this accident would never have happened, so I cast no stones on that matter.

Regret me for I forget what I forgot to forget.

When you allow the creative aspect of the mind to become silenced you make everything much harder. The ability to work out solutions becomes much harder and much more difficult. With the creative aspect of the mind silenced you only make mountains out of mole hills. With enough creativity any invention is within reach with enough experimentation. So the script silences the creative aspect of the mind and then a very easy simple existence becomes very taxing on the system or the body. Stress is created because on perceives everything is so difficult. Life or existence is not really difficult at all, but the script silences the right creative aspect of the mind and without proper fear conditioning to counter act that education, life becomes overwhelming or one perceives life is over whelming and so they swiftly run out of options and thus become impatient. With the right aspect of the mind dominate there are infinite possibilities or way to approach any problem one can encounter, so one's mind is in a state of experimentation in relation to any problem in life. So the whole concept of failure and winning becomes mute because there is always one more experiment to try. One's mind is in a state that there is always one more sentence or argument to suggest before they start doing rash permanent physical things to their self or others. It simply is not a matter of morals it is only a matter of mindset. One that perceives they have failed may also perceive they have been insulted and it is okay to perceive failure of insult but when it becomes a grudge in the mind and one allows it fester in the mind, it starts to control them. When one is on the right these things tend to be easily forgotten. The mind set of one on the right aspect tends to be "past is past" because the "machine" is calculating and pondering things so swiftly, insults or failures simply become another thing to ponder or another tool to ponder. So all these ideas in the mind like pride, regret and insult and hate no longer have their meaning but are all reduced to this one pool that are things to ponder and come to further understanding from.

Granted I am not talking about slightly right brained, I am talking far to the right that time is totally altered and emotions are nearly silenced and hunger is nearly silenced. This is not a person who is slightly right brained this is a person who is nearly all the way to the right so that left brain becomes subconscious. So when left brain is subconscious emotions are nearly gone, sense of time is nearly gone, sense of physical sensations are nearly gone. One mentally goes from emotional and physical attributes to simply machine state of cerebral creative ponderings. As one increases the other decreases is perhaps the best way to look at it. This is not "make your life a little better" this is a totally different world or mindset on every level". It is perhaps more along the line of letting go of one aspect and grabbing on to the other aspect. - 5:44:54 AM

7:01:10 AM – The problem with locking someone up or putting them behind bars is that punishment is simply a scare tactic. A person who has lots of fear will be afraid to be locked up. A person who has been locked up many times is no longer afraid to be locked up. So the deterrent no longer works. So then it goes even deeper than that. A person who has been locked up understands when they "break the law" the worst thing that will happen is they will go back to prison and they do not mind that because in many cases they get fed and get to have some security in prison, in contrast to how life can be on the outside where their meals and security is questionable. This is why making many "petty" laws for example making drugs illegal is simply creating people who are attached to the prison system.

There logic is, if I get out of prison I go back to making money selling drugs and if I get caught I get to go to a more secure environment where my food is provided. So they are in a win, win situation, but they may not be aware of it consciously. A transient who lives on the street is in a much more difficult situation than a person in prison. A person in prison may not even be able to live like a transient does. So a person in prison is not "evil" or "hardcore" even slightly compared to a transient mentally speaking. A transient has to be able to eat out of garbage cans and has slight hygiene and so they must also have a great tolerance for unknown. A transient is essentially totally absent of the norms of acceptability. Simply put they have no morals and no class. One on the left would assume that is very evil and dangerous because one the left perceives "acceptable norms" are absolute acceptable norms. What is an acceptable norm in the wild , perhaps in a pack of wolves? There simply are no morals in a pack of wolves. Then to go even deeper , a great white shark is a lone wolf. They might mate with another shark and perhaps have offspring but outside of that they are a lone wolf. The only way a lone wolf can be a viable lone wolf is if they mentally lose all attachment type emotions. Many on the left crave to be accepted that is a left brain trait. The groups one on the left will aspire to are totally irrelevant in relation to what those groups represent it is only important that they are accepted by a group. In life there are religious groups, political groups, fringe groups ,gang groups and all of these are simply people on the left looking to be accepted because the left brain craves acceptance. A leader tends to be a lone wolf that these groups put in charge. That is an indication that ones on the left covet or envy. Ones on the left tend to want to be controlled. When one is controlled they feel safe because they "follow the rules" and if they do that they understand they will be "safe". A person in the military understands as long as they kill a few people in battle they will be accepted by the military "group" and so they will kill people to be safe. One in a religious cult will give money because that is "rule" they follow so they will be accepted. When the offering plate is passed around people make sure other people can see them put money in that offering plate. It all comes down to this acceptance craving that left brain instills. Moses, Jesus, Buddha, Mohammed, Einstein, Jung, Edison, Washington, Joan of Arc, Socrates were all path creators and not path followers. This is the nature of right brain. I perceive I am simply explaining things others have been explaining but in reality when I speak in some chat rooms I detect I am saying things that are very new to some. They are perhaps so conditioned to their way of thinking I appear alien with what I suggest to some degree but from my point of view I perceive I am just saying what others have said before, but then I realize my time stamps are gone and I am talking about people who lived thousands of years ago and to ones on the left the time stamps are still there, so they perceive I am someone from the past. I can try to explain the right brain when dominate to an extreme is very powerful but powerful is relative to the observer so that word may not even work. I can suggest the right brain when dominate to an extreme is infinitely powerful then ones on the left may assume religious or supernatural aspects. I could use the word god to explain how power right brain is and then that would start a cult and people would start killing each other. So I understand and am compelled to make sure I do not lead anyone to believe I detect supernatural. That is not a statement of humility that is an honest statement. The reality is, I was so far into the left in contrast to how I am now, it may seem like I got really aware, but the truth is, I am simply adjusting to being conscious. It is not a person's fault I was unconscious it is simply the planned language as a side effect makes a human being in any culture have silenced mental cerebral awareness. That is not sorcery that is psychology. Cause and effect: Planned language is the cause, silenced cerebral activity is the effect, conditioning away from fear is the antidote. It is no more complex than that, but that still will not get me out of writing infinite books because what I perceive is simple and easy to understand is not an absolute in relation to many perhaps. So I must stay on the fence because my observations are very biased. I perceive everyone is perfect and wise and in extreme right brain because no matter what they say or do, I can see wisdom in it. I can't find fault with anything anyone does because they are doing the best they can based on their situation, so my counter to that bias is to attack people verbally, everyone, and that way I can see how they really are. This is my "taste test", some of the people I have become friends with since this accident I have attacked and they brush it off and now we are friends because I am aware they are not able to hold a grudge. That is my only way to determine who is on the right and who is on the left. The ones who hold a grudge and ban me and hate me, are on the left and the ones who ignore my attacks and still speak with me are on the right. That is my only way to tell because I see wisdom in everything everyone says. So that how I adapt, it perhaps seems strange but I see people even in pictures and all I see is perfection then I hear them speak and I say "That is a wise thing to say" and so I am blind and I have to go to great extremes to get back the judgment. The judgment is the left brain so I am so far into right brain I see everything as one thing and in my case it's not evil or sinister its perfection. That's my bias is I see everyone and everything and everything everyone says as wisdom so I have to attack that perception or I will not be able survive psychologically speaking. I would be reduced to sitting alone in a room in silence because there would be nothing left to say. Everything is perfect so there is no need to say anything ever. That's the illusion it is not perfect I am just very biased. Humanity is not going to all go right brained simply because society keeps pumping out offspring every year that are extreme left brained. That's realty. Every time a child graduates from high school that is a 10% mind because they do not condone fear conditioning as a remedy to the education. It is not an opinion it is reality. That's the price that is paid for not understanding the remedy to "knowledge". One is always paid in full for their ignorance but wisdom seldom collects a pay check. I will go play my video game because I get this feeling what I am doing is infinitely vain. - 7:47:06 AM

I am trying to tell these religious beings that they are unable to understand what they read until they go to the right. God said who made you afraid and who made you ashamed? Who destroyed your mind and the answer is we did. We killed our minds and no one wants to understand that. We did it to ourselves. I understand the enemy and he is us. This is our handiwork.

Tina W (41) allegedly committed suicide
Donald C (23) allegedly hanged himself after a fight with his girlfriend
Kayona C (16) allegedly took her own life
Laurie W (35) took her own life by an unknown method
Taylor M (16) took his own life by an unknown method

So our species was this wonderful adaptive thing but we gained just enough wisdom to invent something that turned us in sadists and masochists because we never figured out what "Fear not" meant. Over five thousand plus years of this mindset because we are good tool makers. No human being in the universe could write a fictional book that could touch that reality. The truth is very painful but if one is on the right and the emotions are gone, the truth is simply the truth.

Gen 3:10 And he said, I heard thy voice in the garden, and I was afraid, because I was naked; and I hid myself.

Gen 3:11 And he said, Who told thee that thou wast naked?

Who is the devil and the snake? We are.

Who is evil? We are.

Who is the darkness? We are.

Who did this to us? We did.

Who is the enemy? We are.

Is God the enemy? No we are the enemy of god.

We are 666.

152

Php 1:11 "Being filled with the fruits of righteousness(right brain to an extreme), which are by Jesus Christ(sit at the right hand side), unto the glory and praise of God."

My strategy is to keep ramming the religious ones scriptures down their throat until they wake up. They will hate their religious texts or they will wake up when I am finished, and I am never finished. I have not even started writing books yet. I have not even started saying anything yet. I am just experimenting with things I may say or may not say. I need to get warmed up before I start writing and I am certain I will never be warmed up. I am in reality simply fiddling with the idea of writing.

I have written a new song called forgret. This is a new word and I will define it and then I will explain it.

Forgret : One on the left who suggests they forget a physical or mental assault on them but in reality they only regret the physical or mental assault against them.

A person on the left is hit. They may turn the other cheek and say I forget or forgive but in their mind they do not, it builds up in their mind and it turns into a grudge. A parent has 10 dollars stolen from them by their child. The parent says I will forgive and forget to the child. Then the parent hides their money better next time from the child. They suggest they forget but they do things to show they didn't forget so they really regret. They regret the fact they cannot forget. That is called Forgret.
   Ones who are religious may go on for many years killing others who are not on their religious side to make up for all the ones on their religious side who were killed. Someone who insults you and then you take no action but you go home and that assault festers into a grudge. Forgive those who trespass against us. That is not possible to accomplish in left brain state of mind. I will repeat that is not possible because the short term memory will not allow one to forget it. That may be a good thing because then one is unable to be taken advantage of twice. On the other hand taken advantage of is relative. It all gets very complex. Someone you know might come over and smoke a joint in front of you. You might not smoke pot. So when they leave you are angry they did that. You may not say anything or you may say "That is against the law so you are bad and I will not allow that in my house so get the hell out and never come bad again." I have talked with enough people to understand their best recollection of Freud is that he did a lot of cocaine. So they recall he did a lot of cocaine and so everything he said must be bad or evil or wrong. So he is showing everyone essentially that they are unable to tolerate ambiguity even after he said "Sometimes a cigar(cocaine) is just a cigar." It does not make one stupid or evil or bad. Misspelling a word does not mean one is evil or stupid or bad. Saying a cuss word does not mean one is evil or stupid or bad. They are perhaps ambiguous but that is okay unless one is in full neurosis. If one is in full neurosis they will probably do anything to stop that perceived doubt. They will abuse children, kill people, hate people, insult people, hold grudges, attack people. They are in full neurosis. I just type all this stuff with the understanding I am never going to associate with this society.

Jas 3:17 " But the wisdom that is from above(The man upstairs in your head is right brain and is wise)is first pure(complexity and understanding), then peaceable(docile), gentle(is not prone to killing things for no reason, like children with pills), and easy to be intreated(easy to approach or easy count on, one who will try to harm you no matter what you do to them) , full of mercy(you are still breathing = I am merciful) and good fruits(they are trying to wake up the species from the script neurosis so they are in the right as in righteous because 10% brain function is their enemy), without partiality(means they see everything as a whole and they are slow to judge others if at all, they can see a hooker and understand she is only trying to make a living in a world that is in full neurosis from the script, so they see now fault in her actions)), and without hypocrisy.(this denotes the ones on the right are trying to wake everyone up, they are trying to help everyone go back to 100% brain function that is their goal, so they never stop trying to do that no matter what they say, that is their goal, so they are not hypocrites because they are looking out for the species as a whole.)

Do you want 10% brain function and very strong emotions or do you want 100% brain function?

I do not need a stupid test to prove that reality. That is the only question. If I am unjust to want to assist the species to try to achieve 100% brain function after society kills the 100 percent brain function then just kill me, so I can get the fuck out of here. I will never edit one word in my books because it is all pointless anyway. I am doomed with this stone around my neck no matter what I do. So it is all for nothing but on the other hand, that's good because essentially I cannot reach anyone because they think I am an alien and crazy. So I just act crazy and give them what they want because I understand fully, so in fact do get it. The wheat get it. The ones who get it get the 100% and the rest the chaff get to stay in the fire of 10%. I do not care if they stay in the fire, I do not care if they get out of the fire. That may make people assume I care. I do not care, I just write what comes to mind into infinity. Caring would denote I get a break. I do not detect a break. I do not detect a vacation. I do not detect a rest period. I do not detect fatigue. I cannot win no matter what I do, so there is no point in resting. If you go to the right you will see you cannot win. You will become an observer of ones in neurosis. You may assist a few but in general society itself will pump out so many in neurosis every year because society makes laws and society wields the power and so they can pump out way more 10%er than you can convert back to 100%. So you will never win, You will simply be attacked by the left in every way but you will not have emotions and so it may bother you for a moment but them you will forget it and not forgret it. Every day is a new day on the battle field. You forget all of your loses of the past and you start all over. You are going to get slaughtered on a daily basis because the ones on the left in general would never buy they are in neurosis. So you cannot win and that is just fine because you won't be able to feel satisfaction if you did win and you will not feel depressed when you do lose. I can tell a person "You will have great mental cerebral aspects if you condition away from fear", and they will say "Thank you, that's wonderful I will do it.", and then they will use elementary logic and talk their self out it and the next they see me they will say "You are insane you need medical help." That is as close to a win as you will ever get. You may perceive you are winning at times but that is an illusion you underestimate the neurosis. The Buddhists takes on one student at a time. This is so they can focus all their energy on that one person . I am attempting six billion at a time and with infinite books. I may assist one and if not that is okay because I will convince myself that zero for six billion is a sign my strategy is perfectly flawed. If I tried I would destroy myself. Some suggest it is quality of what you say not how much you say. That is a losing strategy. They are going to drive their self nuts because they are attempting to make rules. So these rules prove they are not really conscious. They need a new teacher. They underestimate the neurosis and it destroys their efforts. They give up. The log in my eye is that I had an accident and woke up to the fact nearly the entire herd called our species is totally asleep mentally and when I try to be honest they say I am crazy and when I try to lie and trick them they still don't get it, they think I am just like they are. So I focus on my log because I can't even touch their log because if they cannot get their log out of their eye I certainly can't. Here is me telling the truth. "Try to have a near death experience and when you think you are going to die do not call for help." That's what I am saying. Go sit in the most haunted scary freak you out into insanity place you can find at night all alone with no chance of getting help and no matter what happens stay there until morning. To one on the left that is insanity to one on the right that is a piece of cake. So everything is relative to which side of the brain you are on. One on the right understands that suggestion is clarity and wise and ones on the left suggest that suggestion is insanity and dangerous and both are right at the exact same time. Relativity is a law. Everything essentially the ones on the left say to me is insanity and everything essentially I say to them is insanity, but we both perceive what we say is sane, and we are both right at the exact same time.

Here is how I see it. Freud, Einstein and Jung were on the right, and they made a bet to see who could fuck up "society" the most and Einstein won. You can write infinite books about how that could not be possible but that is exactly what happened. It is a no brainer who fucked society the most with their ideas. He sent the whole science community into a search for nothing. They will discover nothing at the end of their searching. They will find the smallest particle is nothing. That is how clever or sinister Einstein was. Why wouldn't he be like that, he could be like that and he was like that. Look at the picture of Einstein sticking his tongue out, that is Einstein. That is the true Einstein. He is sticking his tongue out at society as a whole. So I am in competition with Einstein. I will make him wish he was me. I am not arrogant I simply understand I will. I understand he did not go the full measure. The big fish go the full measure and that is usually an accident. There is simply too much ground or stages one can achieve, once they get to the right just like on the left. Mozart was very creative and called a prodigy. He was not a prodigy. He was simply a child that stayed in right brain or the script and math did take hold or fuck him up. He is what all the children should be like and all the adults should be like. Prodigy my ass. Messiah my ass. God my ass. Supernatural my ass. Human beings that avoided or negated the script and math side effects is more accurate. Granted this entire book is extremely out of context. - 10:30:59 AM

Look at this way. Lets pretend. We explore the entire universe and find new life forms and new species and vast amounts of treasure, new civilizations and vast wealth beyond comprehension. Then what? What does that mean? What would that mean? Would it make you feel like you accomplished something? Would that make you feel whole? Would that make you feel happy? Is that what this species is only concerned with is to feel happy or feeling like they accomplished something? Happiness and accomplishment are relative only to ones on the left so they are not absolute sensations but only sensations that are possible at all to ones on the left brain who have radically altered perception in contrast to ones in extreme right brain. So what is the goal? Is it to make everyone live as long as possible? If we could live forever stuck in left brain we would all just be running around jumping off the sky way into the rocks and not being able to die. That cannot be our goal to live forever because there are 14 years olds who lived far too long and so they kill their self.

C R (14) committed suicide after being cyber-bullied

So this being is educated in script and math and then the education system did not condition them properly away from fear and then someone said something to this being and they became shy, embarrassed, regretful, depressed.

Gen 3:11 " cursed is the ground for thy sake; in sorrow shalt thou eat of it all the days of thy life;"

This is what we are as a species. It does not matter if aliens came down and showered us will wisdom. We as a species are cursed.

This C R (14) committed suicide after being cyber-bullied = "in sorrow" and the script and Dena did it because the "educators" are "in sorrow" also so the fruits are "cursed".

This is the fruit of the "cursed ground" = C R (14) committed suicide after being cyber-bullied

If there is a single human being in the universe who wishes to test me, I beg you to test me. I live for you to test me.

This is what my chances are

[00:02] <KarenJ> Lestat I perceive you are mentally ill and need help very badly

[00:13] <+KarenJ> I'm reasonably well educated but that one is nonsense as near as I can tell

* You were kicked by KarenJ (Blacklisted- false doctrine lectures)

My strength is that I understand that is what my chances are. I am post suicide. You will judge my fruits but you will not affect my fruits. To clarify. I am this person, C R (14) committed suicide after being cyber-bullied , but my physical body has not caught up to that fact yet. That is why I am strictly on a vengeance mission. To clarify that, I would be pleased to go home now. To clarify that Buddha said "Health is important." To clarify that, "Take the pain and stay." To clarify that, "I love gnashing of teeth." To clarify that, the hottest coals make the strongest steel. To clarify. I draw in your sand.

I need to run all of that through my parser. - 11:33:43 AM

In summation: Just about every single thing the ones on the left believe is truth and righteous I do not.

What that means is there is one hell of battle going on and I wish I had to try. One wise being says "forgive and forget" and then ones on the left say "never forget" and the truth is the ones on the left can never forget. They are controlled by all these past misdeeds they perceived happened to them. They are mentally unable to forgive because they can never forget. Their memory will not allow them to forget. I forget like an absent minded professor and to reinforce that, I have no emotions so I don't care, so I have no stress. I don't care. Ones on the left can say they don't care into infinity but they can never really not care, in fact they boast that they do care. They love infinitely too much. They love everything to death so it is not love at all it is control. The ones on the left have no idea what love is and they never will and they never mentally can because they are on the left. I will repeat they can never ever understand what love is because they are "in sorrow.. all the days of thy life;".Ones on the left can suggest they love and all they are really saying is "I control this." I am not capable of love I am in the void.

I am not capable of kindness I am in the void. I am not capable of anger I am in the void. I can only give off illusions of these emotions. Void is absence of emotions. I am lifelike.

C R (14) committed suicide after being cyber-bullied

M C (14) took her own life after being constantly bullied

K A (14) allegedly took her own life for unknown reasons

K O(14) took her own life by an unknown method

M D (14) allegedly took her own life by an unknown method

V S (14) allegedly took her own life

B Bl (14) committed suicide by hanging

This is the fruits of your labor. You pass the laws to enable education. You do not suggest fear condition to counter the education. You allow it to happen. You encourage it to happen. You do this day after day and then walk around and say, you love and you are wise. You say "I care about the children." You say "I only want what is best for them", You say "Our children are our future." Right now you have two options in your mind. You can suggest I am totally insane and wrong and in that case you will just laugh at me and mock me and go on "collecting your fruits" and that is perhaps wise because if you mentally understood what I am saying is absolute truth, you would perhaps kill yourself from the grief. I am going to keep pumping out books showing you who you are until you beg god to take all your emotions away. If you jump off into the rocks, I care not. I will go play my video game and ponder when I will start getting medieval your ass. - 12:13:17 PM

Maria H (12) committed suicide after being bullied at school

What I find rather funny is you kill 12 year old children and you perceive I am not going to have your god dam head on a pole. That is hilarious. I am all about blood baths baby. I am compelled to suggest there is going to be a blood bath you would be wise to understand there is going to be a blood bath. I simply type what my fingers suggest. One might suggest the fingers don't lie. I blame it on the rain. Your fear of that will not change it. I will now discuss something valuable.- 12:23:03 PM

This song will sum everything I have said up to this point in the thick pamphlets.

Forgret - http://www.youtube.com/watch?v=461FbCu9XUU

They speak of unconditional love then they suggest they hate people who do not believe what they believe.

They suggest they hate pornography and hate people who cuss and hate people who are uneducated but they do not have a clue what education is. They only understand education is what the retards say education is. "They" means the "cursed above cows", "darkness' "The blind", "infidels". I have compassion and just called them brain dead mole crickets.

Heimdall is a score keeper. As of now the game score is :

The Lefters: Infinity   The Righters : Negative infinity

It is still anybody's game.

1:58:14 PM – Two days ago I thought for a moment this was going to be a good book but now it is all hate and rage and anger and attacks and I am not upset about that but I am aware it is. Then I remind myself I am not warmed up. I am in the machine state but the emotions are still twitching. So once you go into extreme right brain even after you get the "ah ha" sensation it is going to be many months until the emotions stop twitching. At first you are going to think something is very wrong mentally but that is natural. You are literally going from 10% cerebral activity to 100%. So you are going to feel very different mentally. Not just a little different. The mind itself is going to do the work for you so you just let it do its processing and warm up. You are going to start to become aware of things and notice things you never noticed before and this is what is going to create this mental "rage". You are in fact going to be very upset with things once you wake up. That is natural. If you wake up enough you are going to declare war. You are going to be obligated to do what you can to "correct things". You are going to be aware and understand what I understand you are going to find it is very difficult to get anywhere with the "lefters". You might want to write books or you might want to have a group or have speaking events. I took door number three and I am going for waking up six billion at one time, so I am a total idiot because I bite off way more than I chew but that's how I like it.

I am going for broke. You have to get use to the fact you can never win so quantity is what matters. Once you wake up you have to avoid trying. Just let it all out. If you really wake up you do not have to try, you just say what is on your mind and the ones on the left will respond. I do not mean in good way or bad ways I mean they will just respond. That is why the experimentation aspect is important. Have a mindset of a scientist. I hedge my bets. I am aware certain people get it easily and then certain people attack it, but the reality is, the words are not even important. The words are not even real. You can spend much time trying to sound perfect or under rules like proper things to say and rule to follow to speak with the ones on the left but then you are going to fall into traps. There is a catholic sayings that says "Do not ever try to reason with demons" this is in relationship to casting out demons. A demon will try to say things that make you think they are on your side or make you think you are making progress. They will say you are their friend and then you will try to go deeper and they will attack you. So if you have a mindset of winning you are going to become very upset and angry. Your blood pressure is never going to rise over 120/80 but your mind is going to start thinking things like "How dumb can people be." It is not they are dumb, it is because they are in the "other world." So if your mindset is, I can reason with them you are going to lose. If our mindset is that of a scientists running experiments, then you can never lose, you just understand better methods. You will start to read them from a few sentences they say, and then adapt. Some are religious, some are not religious , some are depressed some are happy. You have to experiment and see which train you need to apply to each person. I am horrible at this strategy. I can read people and then I end up believing the words they say and then I get very rageful and end up attacking them. I have not fully grasped that they are illusion in my mind. I forget I am running experiments. I hang myself often but then I ponder what I did and try to adjust a bit, and that is what it is all about. Getting into a "perfect strategy" mindset is dangerous because there is no perfect strategy. Simply put some are not ready to come into the light. Getting good at determining that takes many experiments. I am going for broke so I prefer to hit hard with the understanding people far into the future will read what I wrote. Before the accident I was so depressed and I could relate to everyone. Many of my friends were depressed. The whole attitude of life itself was it just sucks. People I knew who were happy were miserable. The happy ones were miserable and the depressed ones were suicidal. Everybody was just doing enough to convince their self to hold on another day. It was like everything rested on this little tiny thin string. Any second they could snap, I could snap, any second for any reason. The ones who appeared most controlled were the most dangerous ones. They dressed well, and said everything right, and had a nice house and a nice car but when it came down to it the slightest abnormality would turn them into a rage and then they would assume that was proper. The truth is the ones who never do drugs are the most dangerous because they seldom see the right aspect of the mind, this is suggesting when they are not in nirvana or in the right aspect of the mind, so they are in extreme left brain. They never visit the light so to speak. Flat out they are the most dangerous. They are the "holy rollers". They are like KarenJ. They spit venom and they usually have friends to back them up. They will suggest flat out, "You are wrong and evil and stupid."

[00:13] <+KarenJ> I'm reasonably well educated but that one is nonsense as near as I can tell

[00:46] <whomasect> when Maya gets ANGRY we know we are making progress ok ?

[00:45] <whomasect> whatever SHE says, is anti-truth , and luring away

So this is a victory. Maya is simply one on the left. It's the darkness. In Adam and Eve Maya was called a female but that is simply contrast. Not a literal female. This is not about physical this is all about cerebral. Try to just forget all about physical. Nothing I talk about is physical because the neurosis is strictly mental. If I could just raise an army and win the war I already would have. So it is not physical. If you are on the left you may perceive I am calling you the devil. I am not. It's simply contrast. I live on contradictions and paradox. It's all cerebral. It is simply hard to explain the complexity. Sometimes my words seem harsh and sometimes they seem funny and sometimes they seem wise but the truth is, the thoughts are none of those things because they are cerebral or unnamable or without labels. My main strategy is to keep pumping out books into infinity. Makes no difference to me if the books are good or bad, I go for quantity. I suggest all the wise beings wish they were me because I am not an idolater. I have no idols in my mind and so I have no attachments. I do not look up to anything. That is along the lines of assume everyone else is crazy and that mindset will help you deal with being attacked by Maya. You are not going to be able to hold a grudge when you are on the right so you will get insulted and attacked often but that is expected from the Maya. At first you are going to get attacked and it is going to hurt you mentally but the ponder machine will help you learn from that and most importantly you will start to detect your emotions better but eventually you are going to simply became "salt" or turn to stone. That is because you are going to be aware of so many things that are improper that you will have to turn to stone or they will destroy you. Once you condition the fear away the heightened awareness starts and it increases and increases until you are in a situation you are aware of the Maya and you will become somewhat of a racist but in a weird way. You will be mindful of the Maya and also mindful you want to "bring them into the light." So you hate them and care about them without the words hate and care. If you really cared in the absolute definition or were able to care, you would destroy yourself because it would be too painful mentally, so you have to disassociate yourself mentally and understand you are dealing with rabidity, that way you can mentally look at the situation differently. "They" are going to say things to attack your mindset. That is why you must be careful not to reason with them. They will suggest you are bad because you don't do this. They will try to make it seem you are just like them. You will speak with them and then speak with them again and have to start all over again because they won't remember anything. There short term memory is very good but they have no long term memory. They hold grudges in long term memory. They remember well who they hate and that's about it. The script has turned them into monsters mentally. Many on the right go into chat rooms and just observe to try to figure out something to say but I prefer to just drive into the shark waters. I prefer to get banned within the first five minutes, permanent bans.

* You were kicked by KarenJ (Blacklisted- false doctrine lectures)

#christian unable to join channel (address is banned)

That is my proof that I am getting somewhere. It is universal for me. I get banned from every chat room. There are not many chat rooms in this world that I am not banned from. I get banned from LSD chat rooms for being on drugs. That is good to me. That is my motivation. That is my drug.

[00:46] <whomasect> when Maya gets ANGRY we know we are making progress ok ?

It is like the exorcist movie. Rules do not matter, morals do not matter, proper comments do not matter. Maya is going to attack you no matter what you do, so it is best to piss Maya off and that proves you are making progress, not winning, making progress. The trick is, never relent. Never allow Maya to get the best of you. Mindset is they are illusions. That is the wining mindset. They are not real they are rabidity. The rabid ones use physical weapons to fight wars and they do not follow rules in the wars, you are going to fight your war cerebrally and you are not going to use rules. All is proper in war and love. Your sword is doubled edged. You have true love which means you are attempting to assist others in the species to wake up from the neurosis and that is true love and you are in a war because they do not perceive they are in neurosis. They perceive they are "normal". Once you wake up, others that have woken up will make their self known to you. This will be automatic. You will start finding others that woke up. The heightened awareness will make it obvious. So you will become aware of this "invisible" world. The main reason I remain a lone wolf is because I do not want to be biased. I prefer to be the announcer and not on one side or the other.

"Heimdall is the guardian of the gods and of the link between Midgard and Asgard, the Bifrost Bridge. Legends foretell that he will sound the Gjallarhorn, alerting the Æsir to the onset of Ragnarök where the world ends and is reborn." WIKIPEDIA.COM

I am the link not one or the other. So the old world "left" will end and the new world "right" will begin. But the reality is I cannot tell if that is really going to happen because then I would be on a side. I am the link. I am the messenger between the two sides. I am a lone wolf, an accident. I try to talk with many on the right but many do not talk to me because they understand they are not allowed to. Many on the left or the Maya do talk to me because they have silenced awareness and are not able to understand they are not allowed to talk me. It is not an ego trip, the logic is, contact. Anything anyone says to me, I use. I may get the wrong definition they aid to me but someone said Maya to me and now I pondered and I understand it and now I am using that word.

I was found by a little girl by the river and the leaves in the forest behind me suggest that. Do not assume just because someone says they are on the right they are on the right. There are many illusions.

There are many who suggest they are "righteous" but then they insult one of the wise beings or another and that proves they do not understand it fully. They still have labels. They hate one wise being and like two. They suggest Moses was wise and Buddha was an idiot. They suggest Jesus was wise but Hindu's are evil. They are still trapped in the labels. Your only guide is going to be your heightened awareness. You are outnumbered six billion to one essentially. There are a few on the right but they are lone wolfs. They are running their experiments. I prefer six billion to one because to me the hottest coals make the strongest steel. If my mindset is I always lose then I forget what losing is and I just do. I cannot even use the language anymore so if I had a mindset to win, I would destroy myself mentally. I proof read my books and it all looks good to me. In reality to ones on the left they will not be able to come up with a proper description of how retarded I must be to not be able to write better in relation to syntax and rules of grammar. They simply believe if you can't spell cat properly you are retarded, but the truth is if you care if someone can't spell cat properly you are retarded because neurosis is the inability to tolerate misspelled words. Misspelled words kill Maya so she attacks the ones who misspelled words. It is like a cross to a vampire. Maya has no complex logic abilities so when you say things Maya starts assaulting because Maya cannot grasp complexity. Maya is what is known as a viper. Maya cannot see so she makes up for it by spitting venom and attacking everywhere. Maya is simply a generalization because Maya is like saying the devil but the devil has many faces. This of course is contrast and cerebral not literal. It is complex because even the faces of Maya are not absolutes. Some have several aspects of these many faces. They are considered multiple faces. Some are just one face. The reality is you cannot reason with any of the faces because they are all faces of Maya. You are going to see them as perfection and you are going to want to love them all. You are going to want to attach to them. You are a lone wolf. You will destroy yourself if you start to reason with Maya. Simply put you are going to blow it if you reason with Maya. You are going to have cerebral power and have the world at your finger tips and you are going to have to fight that urge to settle on luxury. You are going to try to talk yourself into luxury. You are going to think about isolation so you do not have to face Maya. You want to seek the hottest coals and not run from them. It is not about you and it is not about me.

Joh 15:13 "Greater love hath no man than this, that a man lay down his life for his friends."

Mindset is going to be if Maya doesn't kill you, aren't talking enough. This is the war. Your mindset is you dive into the shark frenzy. Your expectation of living a humble life and pleasing life are delusions. Expectations of the future, considering you are diving into a frenzy of sharks are quite foolish.

These faces of Maya or the Devil so to speak are all on Wikipedia.com.

"Avestan 'angra mainyu' "seems to have been an original conception of Zoroaster's." In the Gathas, which are the oldest texts of Zoroastrianism and are attributed to the prophet himself, 'angra mainyu' is not yet a proper name.[In the one instance in these hymns where the two words appear together, the concept spoken of is that of a mainyu ("mind", "mentality", "spirit" etc[]) that is angra ("destructive", "inhibitive", "malign" etc)."

Forget the religions connotations because the names are different but they are all in relation to the same thing, the psychology of the Maya. I was very close to this face because I was a self harmer. I was very angry and I harmed myself because of that anger. People who starve or are suicidal or get lots of plastic surgery these are forms or faces of this demon aspect. They are angry and they tend to take things out on their self. This is not an absolute though, they will attack others and that tends to harm them also. I have shades of this anger still and that is an indication of how deep this neurosis is. I no longer harm myself I lost my ability to hate and love so I lost my ability to harm myself. This self harm is not about ones who use drugs or smoke. One can use logic like if you drive a car fast you are a self harmer or smoke you are a self harmer. That's not what this face is, destructive mind in relation to self hate. This face is actually a mild face because these people usually can be reached because they are starting

161

to wake up. A self harmer is meek. They are trying to find the light or the right but the signals in the mind are making them harm their self physically. They perceive they are unworthy. They are meek and mild mentally so they are open minded they are still on the left and are heading down to find the right but they tend to kill their self before they find the right. They go all the way down the slide and then they determine they cannot go on and they usually kill their self in some way but not at the spur of the moment, it is a long slide.

"In demonology, Aim (aka Aym or Haborym) is a Great Duke of Hell, very strong, and rules over twenty-six legions of demons. He sets cities, castles and great places on fire, makes men witty in all ways, and gives true answers concerning private matters. He is depicted as a man (handsome to some sources), but with three heads, one of a serpent, the second of a man (to some authors with two stars on his forehead), and the third of a cat to most authors, although some say of a calf, riding a viper, and carrying in his hand a lit firebrand with which he sets the requested things on fire." WIKIPEDIA.COM

This is from Christian theology. This would be like a very wealthy person who appears wise but in the physical world or worldly ways and has many friends 26 legions. Many people on the left idolize this face. They tend to be very wealthy and witty but at the core they are harsh and spiteful. They won't let you get close to them mentally speaking. They perceive they are a cut above because of their physical assets. They tend to hold their physical assets as a medal of power or proof they are better. This of course is in the extreme. Their physical wealth is what makes them handsome to ones on the left. Many seek them for advice on worldly matters but they are not very wise on cerebral matters. There mindset tends to be that their wealth proves they are wise and so they tend to assist others to be wealthy and materialistic and so ones on the left tend to idolize them and "want what they have" and so they also encourage envy and are typically full of pride. Essentially they would harm people for a dollar. So the serpent denotes at his core he is prideful and has no charity, the man with two stars denotes he has credentials or physical things that he shows openly and so anyone near him will see he is powerful and the cat denotes he is witty and quick witted or he jokes a lot to make people perceive he is happy go lucky but the viper he rides is his core aspect. He is a viper at the core. He wears the stars on his head so everyone will know he is powerful. This is like a person who has mansions and nice cars and flaunts the wealth and makes sure everyone knows it and has the credentials and everything they do is a sort of exhibition to show the ones on the left how powerful they are. They would die for their wealth because their wealth is greater than they are. This face is so far to the left they essentially have no concept of cerebral aspects it's all about the high and mighty material things. Strong Ego is the operative word. I go fiddle. - 4:14:39 PM

Fear separates the bright from the night.

"(CNN) -- Barely an hour's drive from the casinos of Las Vegas, a group of unassuming buildings have become as important as the trenches were to WWI. The big difference? Today's warriors are fighting without getting in harm's way, using drones to attack targets in Afghanistan and Pakistan."

So now we can kill people without killing people. So now we praise our great wisdom that we can kill people with robots as if that is some sort of great accomplishment worthy of a news story. These buildings are important because they created a robot that can kill people and we don't have to kill people on our side and we can kill people on their side. We are so wise we can kill people without having to get people killed. That is brilliant, imagine the minds behind that stroke of genius. Why don't we launch all the nukes in the world up into the sky and I will keep track of the bodies I stand upon. Why don't I just see how many people I can kill with my words and then your wise robots will understand who god is because I have given up on the cursed ones, they can all rot in their misery. You keep publishing your wisdom articles and I will keep hanging the world with them. The species is cursed so I assume everything is expendable. I have no preference who's blood it is, I am more concerned with the quantity of blood. I prefer oceans and streams of blood. I will show you how that is done and then you will have something to write about.

Talk about toying with the mice. I draw in your sand, you can't understand.

6:05:49 PM – I experimented today in the depression room and this guy came in and said

* Neur0ticism (~g) has joined #depression

<Neur0ticism> I want to die.

I gave him my words and he said

* Neur0ticism nods

<Neur0ticism> I will think on it

So you see he is aware something is wrong. He wants to die but is aware that won't solve it so he is trying to work it out somehow and what that means is in many cases they end up killing their self to stop the strong emotions. A pill may never help someone wake up. Fear conditioning is the only method and that is complex but it is absolute fact. Everything you fear from words to music to porno to other people to ghosts is in fact all in your head and proof of the neurosis and it is nothing else. It is not your conscience it is your delusions.

7/24/2009 6:23:19 AM – My experiment in depression chat room works well with females but males tend to not like it. I perceive males are more "proud" and females are more "open minded". Of course if you are female you understand that.

7/24/2009 2:24:08 PM – Traditional mammals tend to work in harmony or achieve harmony with the environment and that is true with humans . A good example would be the American Indians before the "white man" they were in fact in harmony with their surroundings, they did not kill all the buffalo for example, they only killed what they needed. The point here is they did not have planned written language or math as we know it. So the ones "the white man" who did have math and planned language came over and saw the Indians and determined they were less civilized and "fixed them" so to speak. This is the proof the planned language has done something to the human beings who "are under the influence of it". American Indians are the same exact species as the "white man" yet they lived in harmony for many years perhaps thousands and then the white comes and they are alien in contrast to the American Indians. The only difference is the white man has the planned language and math education. That means the white man so to speak, went very far to the left brain and that is the controlling aspect and the "only see's parts" and not the "whole" so they found a lot of ambiguity in the Indians and determined to "fix them." Simply, you have two "groups" of the exact same species, one gets the "knowledge" education and one does not. One is very intolerant to ambiguity and one is not. One is in harmony with everything and one is not. It has nothing to do with genes, it has to do with the planned language and math and the fact the people who get it do not use the remedy which is "fear not" which is condition away from fear. I can use language and its not big deal in many respects, but I have no fear and my concentration is perhaps what one may suggest is, heightened. Whatever you hate you are afraid of. You should like all music, so if you hate a certain kind of music you listen to that music until you are pleased with it. The song you hate the most is the one you want to listen to over and over until you are pleased with it. That is what "Neurosis is the inability to tolerate ambiguity." means. If you hate certain words you need to say those even out loud alone. If you hate nudity you need to look at nudity. That is what self control is, doing something you do not want to do. If you hate certain religions you go in their chat rooms and talk. No matter what you hate that is abnormal and a symptom of the script and math. You should be pleased with everything. You should be able to find wisdom in everything. Love your enemy is simply suggesting, you should not hate anything because you should be in right brain and see everything as a whole or as one thing. It is about the fact, hate itself is not real, it is a symptom of the neurosis. Everyone hates some kind of music if they have strong sense of time and strong emotions. "They" also are unable to listen to even a song they say they love for more than a couple hours at a time. A right brain person can listen to the same song all day and all night until it no longer is a song but just a back ground noise. I may not explain this word for word correct but the spirit of what I am saying is accurate. Intolerance of hearing a song for 12 hours is a symptom of the neurosis the demotic and Dena create in the mind. I am aware it is hard to grasp because you may think, "No I hate country music." But in reality you just cannot handle things that are different and repetition. The definition of ambiguity is needs clarification because it mostly suggests "doubtfulness". Others word saying "perhaps" a lot. Some religious people could not ever say a "perhaps there is a god." They are so frozen mentally they are afraid to say a word. That is not mentally healthy.

Gen 3:11 And he said, Who told thee that thou wast naked?

Who told you to be afraid of words?

Who told you to be afraid of nudity?
Who told you to be afraid of music?
Who told you to be ashamed?
Who told you to be embarrassed?

The language we invented had a side effect on our minds that made us all of these things. We as a species told ourselves to be afraid accidentally with the invention of Demotic and Dena because they have a lot of rules and they encourage sequential thought patterns and that is strictly left brain. It just like penicillin. It was a great invention and saved many lives, but there is a problem, unpredictable adaptation or impermanence. Some bacteria have built up an immunity to penicillin and are deadly now, because we invented penicillin and at the time penicillin looked like it could do no wrong. But, with impermanence or, nothing stays the same, or things adapt to any situation, now we have bacteria that didn't use to kill people but now they can because penicillin made them adapt. Our invention of language made us adapt mentally and totally changed us from a docile and "be at peace with everything" to a very violent, take over everything state of mind, because we didn't grasp conditioning away from fear is what is required to use that language invention without have bad side effects. In penicillin doctors are not using it as much now, to counter the fact some bacteria are adapting and becoming to immune to it. So there is a certain give and take here. Every good inventions usually creates a countering bad invention. Every great invention requires a great deal of maintenance. So now we have this great language and math, you are going to have to face reality that some seriously great fear conditioning is required if you want to get back to 100% heightened awareness. If you want some candy, you will be so creative everything you touch will turn to gold. That's very accurate. If you paint, if you're a programmer, if you make music, if you are an inventor, if you are a scientist, no drugs required you have to get that fear log out of your eye yourself. Only you know what you fear and hate. I submit I do not perceive I have written anything that would reach me, how I was in my depressed state, so I am failing and I must get better and I must find some way to say it better. - 2:55:10 PM

Relative truth is easy to discover, absolute truth may be impossible.
The deeper the wisdom the greater the truth.
The value of a law is relative to the number of people it serves.

9:10:22 PM – This is a deep one I just realized. In extreme right brain the creativity or heightened awareness or imagination is go great one can easily mimic the people they are around, this is along the lines of a person on the left becoming like the ones they hang around but on a much strong and swifter level. I understand when I go into a chat room and talk, after the first few comments from ones in that chat room I can detect whether they are hostile or happy about what I suggest. So I mimic it but since my emotions are essentially gone, I cannot tell what is too much so I mirror what they do. If I go into a chat room and they are "pleased" with what I say I am happy go lucky but then if one person attacks me I attack them. It is like I am a mirror and this is along the lines of this contact suggestion. It's like peer pressure but on a lightning scale. It is just like if someone insults you and you insult them back but in extreme right brain ones can over react because their emotions are nil. So the only solution is to be very humble and light or use very strategic words to make sure no one attacks because if they do, one on the right will attack back as a mimic. This would explain why many on the right go to temples and do not tend to hang in other forums and some even remain in silence.

166

I know a few on the right already who never speak. I am aware of them some add me on twitter and they never speak. I can tell by their "ways" they are on the right but they never speak. So one might be able to see how self control would be very important. Combined with heightened awareness and the ability to mimic those you speak with. I understand in person it is different though because the feeling through vision aspect tends to make me a jokester or I keep it very light. I understand for example the disciples were certainly attacked verbally for what they said and they perhaps certainly were not docile. This is like the shaolin monk in Kill Bill 2 the movie. He is very "tough love" and if someone insults him he reacts with 10 fold the punishment or he overreacts like when he plucked that girls eye out because she said an unkind word. That's was a huge overreaction, but one in extreme right brain/nirvana has silenced emotional capacity so they either come back with great anger or they walk away. This does not mean they have strong emotions it is just because one in nothingness is able to assume any identity. They are nothing or absent of ego, so they can be any ego. So now this mindset I try to keep in mind that everyone is an illusion is a form of self control. I simply ignore the comments many make and keep on my train of thought. This is perhaps why young children can see their parents fighting and then they become an angry child. They are great mimics. If they are in a happy home they become happy and if they are in a angry house they become angry. There is a comment in the Bible that where the disciples are told to "mingle with the "left" and be like they are to get the message to them. This is another example of the mimic. Blend in with the ones on the left. Granted this will sound supernatural; but I am aware what is on people's minds. When I read a new article and I detect anger in it I tend to write about it and I get angry. When I read something and detect wisdom I mimic that wisdom. So this extreme right brain is a mimic or mirror to whatever it see's. So left brain is sequential based and in relation to anger or happiness the increments are also sequential, Tit for tat kind of situation. So in extreme right brain it is just the opposite. Full tilt. Ones on the left love certain people and hate certain people. Ones on the right for example love everyone and at times hate everyone. So this is the extremes. Right brain see's everything as one thing. I go into a hostile chat room and I perceive everyone is against me. I go into a friendly chat room and I perceive everyone is for me. This is in relation to "for me or against me" and also in relation to ones on the left not wanting to hang around depressed or negative people but on the right the situation is greatly magnified. So I understand the left brain is perhaps more of a subtle aspect of the right brain. It is somewhat like the left brain has a small amount of the effect of the right brain. Left brain is capable of concentration but right brain is multitudes greater, same with creativity and imagination and awareness. In contrast to left brain right brain is a magnification glass. So it is not so much right brain is so "good" it has greatly magnified aspects so it is accurate to suggest it is the powerhouse of the two but not some "Mr. Morals" kind of thing it is simply the greater of the two in respects to processing power and capabilities. Left brain kind of personality has the same traits as a right brain personality but greatly silenced in some respects like concentration and creativity and more pronounced traits like strong emotions in relation to duration but not magnitude. So the concept of strategic words is perhaps not so much about saying only "good things". An angry word can produce a good outcome and a kind word can produce an unwanted outcome. This is why the words are simply grunts.

General Patton was known to be rather angry with his troops but they produced when it counted. So it all comes back to understanding what to say and when to say it and that is strictly relative to the observer or relative to ones awareness of the situation and awareness varies from brain to brain on every level. Apparently I am skipping back now, a person on the left gets angry at a sequential or step by step basis and when they hit the breaking point they remain angry for perhaps long period and even get physical. This does not mean they have short tempers as much as they have slower progression to the anger. One in extreme right brain become angry very swiftly and then it passes very swiftly. Perhaps I know a lot about the mind although some have suggested I am out of mine. - 10:08:46 PM

7/25/2009 5:48:09 AM – Here are some advantages of having silenced emotions and the ability to have a mindset with paradox. I have no sensation of accomplishment so I have no sensation of failure. I have no purpose in mindset when I write so I have no way to feel like I have no purpose or I am worthless, I don't feel worthless but I also don't feel valuable. A person on the left can feel like they are at a dead end job and thus feel worthless and that creates stress. A person on the left can also feel they are valuable and that creates stress to not let the team down, so to speak. So a paradox on the right in relation to this is, my mind or mindset is I have no purpose yet I do have purpose because I am pumping out books. So my mind is telling me or believes "You have no purpose" yet I am getting things done in reality, so I do have purpose but it is not acknowledged mentally, so I can accomplish a great deal although I cannot register it as accomplishment. So one can imagine how 5000 years ago, the "elite" would be very happy to have all these right brain slaves who never complain and are in a slight sense drones that work till they drop. And one can imagine when Moses said "Let my people go.", suggesting the elite are simply taking advantage of these people. Imagine a professional football player getting paid 20,000 dollars a year and not being able to perceive they are valuable to the team yet doing a great job on the team and never asking for a raise. Imagine an employee that works 12 hours a day and has massive concentration powers yet never asks for a raise and is accepting minimum wage for their entire career. My point is, one can see how a person in this mindset can be very easily taken advantage of by the ones on the left who are all about winning and losing. I am not about winning or losing so I have no stress. My mind does not register a win or a loss, some suggest "I just do." But on the left that is not really possible, because the mind still registers progress and then labels it good or bad progress, and then label's mistakes and failure. This is also in relation to the "anti" mindset of the left. Whatever the left brain person has in mindset the right brain extreme person does not. It is almost as if, I cannot have a carrot in front of my nose meaning I cannot be bought off because that is simply an accomplishment. So Judas was bought off and that denotes he was in left brain. The money is not what the point is in that story, the point is a person on the right cannot be bought off in general because that would denote purpose. Nothingness denotes no purpose in mind set yet still purpose in reality, so this is how the "no stress" is accomplished. So I am not charitable by giving my books freely, it is just my mindset is "no purpose". So one on the left might suggest but you do have purpose because you write books and that is true but that is not true in relation to my mindset. My mindset does not acknowledge I have written one single book, I cannot even remember them in details, so I have no sense of stress as in ,"I have written six books and now I have progressed and its getting tougher."

So a person on the left has this progression mindset. So then there is a whole society with this "Always get a little better or always make more than you did last year." So society itself is in general is setting up for failure because one cannot progress constantly, and so there are times of failure. Everybody in society is looking to better their self, but that an illusion. Getting paid more money than one did last year does not mean one has progressed but one on the left perceives that is the "carrot" that lets them feel like they have progressed. They have not in fact progressed, their mind perceives things that indicate progression. That's the nature of left brain, sequential and linear. "Little bit better than I use to be." When in fact they are not better except on created scales of what indicates better, and when these scales are not met they perceives they are getting worse. So a person on the left works at a job for 5 years and progresses then gets laid off and feels all that progress was cancelled out and gets very depressed and perhaps takes some rash physical action when in reality, they never progressed so they also never digressed. It's all in their head and in relation to these "benchmarks" of progression, like better wages. I get this sensation I am talking about things a person on the left cannot even believe. I was always aware this mental "progression" was taking me so far to the right I would not even be able to discuss things that a person on the left would even believe is real or true at all. If you are on the left you should be saying after reading some of this stuff, 'This is all lies." I am just in a totally different world in relation to mindset or mental state, totally alien in contrast to ones with a strong sense of time and strong hunger. I have in fact taken a "chariot to heaven." so to speak. Although understanding that does not bother me at all. Perhaps it could be worse. I could have huge horns growing out of my head and be like this. That would be worse. I understand this "evil good" "darkness light" statement in religions was not about supernatural but simply a contrast statement. The ones on the extreme right are anti to the ones on the extreme left and that is all those comments mean. Just two totally opposite mental mindset worlds. Both alien to each other would be the better way to look at it. I am not good and they are not bad we are just contrary in mindset and mental characteristics. I understand I am losing my "rage" and just going into the machine state. Total machine state, but I can laugh and crack jokes but all other emotions are so silenced they are for all practical purposes gone.- 6:31:37 AM

The ability to breathe is a difficult health care system to compete with. Overpopulation is a symptom of lack of planning not progress. The one aspect that separates humans from all other animals is a quite simple one yet makes all the difference. Humans can communicate ideas to each other but more importantly human can communicate behavior conditioning ideas that in fact can alter the how the mind operates. I suggest if you condition away from fear from many angels in relation to your behavior you will in fact unlock or condition your mind into the extreme concentration heightened awareness state of mind not for a moment but it will be permanent. This goes far beyond the realms of what a drug can do, yet the communication itself is not tangible. It is a grunt but an understood grunt by many. So with words I can in fact alter indirectly the mindset of anyone who subscribes to these suggestions of conditioning away from fear, permanently. That in turn means that the people who do the fear conditioning will also understand the value of fear conditioning and in turn suggest it to others and so everything can potentially change but not because of a physical aspect but because of properly arrange group of words. Two words "fear not" can change everything yet "fear not" is not a tangible thing it is a grunt. If one does not know the language then "fear not" is simply a grunt and means nothing, if one does know the language "fear not" can totally change their cerebral capacity permanently. So since a word or sentence is simply a grunt I am not doing anything tangible. A word's is simply air going through the vocal chords that creates a vibration and that is enabled by the mind or thoughts. That again is intangible. So if the entire world conditions their self away from fear and into this "Einstein" state of mind because of words I have suggested, I have not done anything but simply arranged words into a fashion others can understand the ideas my thoughts suggest. That is the power of the "word". It is not the words there self, it is how they are arranged that matters. It is not a matter of whether they are spelled properly, it is a matter of them being arranged in such a fashion to convince the reader or listener to take action. Buddha suggested strategic wording and Jesus suggested "the word" but they are the same idea. I have no fear but that does not mean I have no common sense to avoid danger. I use the word fear because I am aware ones on the left perceive fear and can relate to what fear is, if I suggest that word. - 8:34:22 AM

"Fear not" or conditioning away from fear is the way to the truth and the light of the "right"/right brain. Everything else that was suggested in the ancient texts was simply details explaining why "fear not" is important.

10:07:38 PM – The best form of defeat is cooperation. A grudge often takes revenge on the holder of it. Nothing is more frustrating than a peaceful war. Mental peace is achieved through defeating fear in the mind, physical peace is achieved through mental peace. Mental peace cannot be achieved but can be attempted. Doubting your own convictions requires courage. A mental victory is understanding when and where to wage the next mental war. A physical war is often the result of a mental surrender. I am far less concerned about what others are going to do than understanding their motivations for their current deeds. An enemy will often surrender once he understands you won't. Fear is an indication of ignorance in the mind. Ignorance is being afraid to admit you misunderstood.

The entire premise of accepted education has nearly nothing to do with intelligence and nearly everything to do with who can follow rules the best. Someone invented planned language based on rules. Planned language is essentially many rules that must be applied based on the assumption that one who does not follow these prescribed rules is dumb or stupid or a failure. Then you have teacher and they are masters at following the prescribed rules. They are then deemed to be able to detect what students are following the prescribed rules and what students are not. So the best students are in fact the best sheep and the worst students are in fact ones who think for their self, so are bad sheep and thus are punished. Bad sheep are punished for trying to think for their self. ". This component of the brain(right brain) is not concerned with things falling into patterns because of prescribed rules." So in society the ones who are intelligent and able to achieve complexity are in fact deemed stupid and forced into remedial jobs and have a very harsh life because they are deemed stupid by the good sheep that are all about rules. The "good sheep" cannot think without rules that someone else imposed on them so they are unable to handle uneasy ground, or they cannot think out of the box or handle change or instability. These "good sheep" are regarded for falling in line by following all of these rules with an easy life and good pay, and acceptance into the herd of "good sheep" and the "bad sheep" become outcasts and problems in relation to the herd. It is all based on elementary logical deduction. If you cannot follow the rules you are bad or evil or stupid in relation to the rules on planned language. It is impossible to determine ones intelligence based on their ability to follow rules because the "complex" aspect of the mind is against following rules." is not concerned with things falling into patterns because of prescribed rules." So acceptable education in fact makes people dumber with all of it rules. I will repeat, accepted education makes people dumber. All of mankind is in fact dumber because they force so many rules onto people it literally kills the right complex aspect of the mind. It is not a maybe or perhaps, it does, it in fact does. How many rules are there in English and math and in school in relation to "no chewing gum in class", "No cussing", No passing notes" and then you have many rules on top of those rules and that is not even rules that are against the law. You have tax laws and under those tax laws are millions of laws on what you should pay taxes for and not. Then you have rules in the group of people you associate

171

with. Then you religious rules. There are so many rules that people are encouraged to follow to be accepted, many have silenced their right brain to such a degree they no longer have any creativity or ability to think out of the box. They have none. That aspect of the mind is dead and it is dead because the fear of not being accepted if one does not follow all of these rules, kill's it. "He must increase as I decrease" The more rules you have to follow and rules you subscribe to the dumber you get. You can believe whatever you want but that is reality. The only remedy to school or education is to change all these rules and call them humble suggestions and never grade a child or student if they do not follow them, simply because if you grade a student by not following "rules" you are making that student more left brained and thus less complex and creative. You are simply killing their right brain aspect. You do not even want to believe what I say is true because you have so many emotions it may harm you. You may harm yourself if you eve grasped what I say is in fact absolute truth. Your whole world would collapse around you. All of the little petty rules you have followed all of your life so you would perceive you are important have in fact made life miserable for you because they have hindered the complex aspect of your mind. The moment you start to understand that is absolute truth is the moment a mountain is going to appear in front of you and beg for you to climb it. You cannot expect to just understand these things and go on with life. You have to climb a mountain to get out of where you are at mentally. The mountain of understanding is steep and where you are at is safe and warm.

When a student is in a class and they are aware if they do not follow all of these rules in for example language class, they know they will be punished for by the teacher with a bad grade, then by the students who will mock them for failing or getting a bad grade, then by their parents who will punish them for getting a bad grade, and so this education has nothing to with intelligence it only has to do with creating fear in that students mind. Education has nothing to do with intelligence it is merely fear tactics to make a person conform. You can either have rules and ignorance or complexity and creativity but you do not get both for long. All you will get with all of these rules and fear is a mind that is best described as a mind that is cursed above a cow. You can get a doctor to replace your brain with a cow's brain or you can start letting go of these rules and thus fear in your mind, both approaches are acceptable. I am not asking you to dig a hole I am asking you to climb out of one. I am not asking you to follow more rules I am asking you to try and let go of the millions you already follow. I am not asking you to be more afraid I am asking you to try to let go of your fear. Fear kills you when you are unable to understand you must let go of it. The love of rules and control destroys complexity and creativity. Some love me, some hate me, and a few tolerate me.

Here is a complex paradox.

(1)If you are compelled to do something and when you do not do it, that is self control.

(2)If you are compelled to not do something and when you do it, that is self control.

Here is an example of (1). A person insults you badly and you are compelled to hit them but you do not. Here is an example of (2). A person is in a house that is on fire and you do not want to risk your life but you do anyway in the off chance you can save them from the fire. Another example of (1). You get a great deal on an item and find out your friend will buy it for a far beyond value that you paid for it, but you only charge him the price you paid for it instead.(2) A soldier dives on a grenade in combat to save his buddies.

The point here is ,self control can be achieved through doing some things you do not want to do and some things you do want to do. Self control is a very vague concept. Following rules is not self control if you love rules. Breaking rules is not self control if you hate rules. Since there is no absolute self control it all comes down to a decision of the observer. There are at least fifty comma rules and so if you do not know and follow those fifty comma rules you may be considered stupid. That logic is not even in the realm of sanity. If you do not spell a word properly you may be considered stupid. That logic is not even in the realm of sanity. You can either use a comma flawlessly and spell every single word flawlessly every single time or you are stupid and dumb and a failure. That's were that "follow these rules or you are dumb" logic leads. There is no human being than can spell every single word flawlessly every single time, so every single human being is stupid, dumb and a failure. There is no such thing as varying degrees of stupidity. So these language rules set a person up to perceive they are a failure and they are automatically a failure because they can never live up to the rules. Everyone can win when the rules sometimes apply and sometimes do not apply. When you are driving at 3AM and drive through a red light because no one else is on the roads at that time, you break the law, yet you do not turn yourself in, so you are criminal. So everyone is a criminal and also a dishonest criminal because they break the law and then do not feel guilt because if they felt guilt they would atone for it or turn their self in. This means laws are geared towards certain kinds of people. They do not pass laws against crack because white people are smoking it. It's all just a scam and the laws are geared towards controlling certain people. Many smoke pot and they feel like they are bad because the law says they are bad, so the laws are simply fear based and make people feel bad, when in reality they are not bad. Many of these drugs laws are based on the premise of "morals". A moral is a law or a rule, so people who have lots of morals and lots of laws in their head have slight right brain creative open-mindedness brain function. So essentially they are dangerous control freaks. They pass laws and lock their own fellow citizens in jail and then think they are righteous and proper, when in fact they are simply control freaks and they get off on the suffering of others. I do not do drugs since the accident but if I had any intelligence I would slice the heads off of these controls freaks for no reason at all. I would cut all their heads off for no reason at all and when I was done and standing on a mountain of heads, I would feel no remorse and no regret, and I would write about it my book. I would feel no satisfaction and thus no dissatisfaction. So you may be able to understand what self control is. A person with fear would never write these things in a book and then publish them. Some people did but they lived 1500 years ago. Many people with fear in their head use their elementary logic and talk their self out of saying what is on their mind. It tends to come down to the final conclusion. "If I say that I may get in trouble and I am afraid of that." They create this "boogie man" in their head. I killed my boogie man when I was convulsing after taking the pills and I said "I am no longer afraid of you boogie man."

Gen 3:11 And he said, Who told thee that thou wast naked?

Who told you to be afraid, ashamed, embarrassed, shy, scared? I try to tell you to not be afraid and shy and embarrassed so it's not me. You have to ask yourself, who told you to be afraid and shy and embarrassed and ashamed? You have factually nothing to be shy, embarrassed , ashamed or afraid about ever, into infinity, you just believed whoever told you should be these things. Whoever said you should be afraid and embarrassed and shy is in fact mentally damaged goods and you should look at them as illusions and never take what they suggest with anything more than a grain of salt. If your god suggests you should be shy, embarrassed and afraid you tell that god to get behind you. You tell that god to come see me.-7/26/2009 3:46:17 AM

The majority of me is me. There is a line in the sand. I have decided to use my words to suggest to many that they are perhaps in mental cages because of so much fear in their mind. That is my goal and that is what I am compelled to do. Any being that attempts to hinder or block or stop that goal I have, will die. I do not play games. I do not feel remorse. I will not fuck it up like the others did. I understand there are ones that are not pleased with my words. I understand they will attempt to attack my words. I am only able to humbly suggest to them, I have already been deemed insane by my peers before the accident, so all of their judgments against me are powerless. I have no side I am on. I have no group I associate with. I have no attachments. I have no grounding you can attack away with your assaults. You cannot burn my books. You cannot take away that which is not yours. You are in a position that you cannot do anything of value that would delete the words. You have simply been outmatched. I do not cast stones in a war I understand is already over. I am fiddler on the roof watching the mice scurry. You may perceive you have fight left in you, but I assure you the battle is over.

This battle in the mind once one reaches slight sense of time and slight hunger is infinite. There are moments I feel like I have nothing left to say. That is the illusion. My mind is telling me "You cannot say it any clearer so just rest and take a break." I have to be very careful to hang myself in my books and scare people away from wanting to talk to me or meet me because I am to gullible. I will marry three billion women if given the chance. That is my problem and my weakness. I like everything and everyone and so anything and anyone can destroy my goal of writing infinite books. I will rest when I feel fatigue but I never feel fatigue. I cannot rest because my mind suggests I have not started yet. I am waiting for mental overload but it never comes. I am waiting to be speechless but it never comes. I have no concept of start so I have concept of stop. I cannot mentally tell what is enough. I cannot mentally tell how many words is enough. The final word tends to lead to the next final word. Somehow I am just a writer or a long winded poet. I have creativity and I could invent things and maybe even create works of art, but I am trapped as a writer and I do not perceive that is creative. In extreme right brain the creativity is so intense there is a mindfulness of effortlessness. I perceive the ideas I discuss are elementary but that is an illusion. The concentration in extreme right brain is so intense in contrast to one in left brain but relative to me, it is normal. My mindset is to make sure my books have many flaws because I already want to give up. If I leave flaws in my books, there is room for another book. I always have to leave room to clarify one more point with the understanding there will never be a final clarification. The creativity is what gives off the illusion of intelligence. I am not certain what intelligence even is but with enough creativity one can achieve things that give off the impression one must be intelligent. Einstein could not spell every word known to man but he could come up with some theories using creativity that screwed up everyone's mind. Look at some painters they have some painting that are very creative that catch a person imagination and that's the same with music and other arts and some books as well. That is not about intelligence it is about creativity and that is the domain of the right brain. I use to write music and it would take eight hours to go from nothing to finished product and sometimes take a few hours just to get the music down. Now I tend to be able to write a whole song in about 30 minutes to an hour and there is very few "takes". That is because everything sounds good. So it is not the music or my books are factually good on the scale of absolute good, but they are good to me. I have errors in my books, relative to people who believe language syntax denotes one is intelligent or dumb. I can't win that battle. I would have to rely on others perceptions and I cannot do that because then I deny my own perception. If I perceive its good, it is good, because everything is relative to the observer. Everything is not relative to the majority because that would suggest the majority has identical perception and that is not possible.

When Einstein first started to submit theories, the physics community said he was insane and crazy and what he suggested was crazy. It's absolutely true, then Eddington doubted what the majority was suggesting and gave Einstein's ideas a chance and now everyone loves Einstein and assumes they would detect him again if a new Einstein arrived, but the truth is , they would not, they would at first assume he was crazy and insane. That's a symptom of beyond understanding. Do not ever assume I am suggesting I am Einstein because if he understood what I understand he certainly would have suggested it by now. Perhaps he overlooked clarifying all the religious texts. I highly doubt that, it simply was beyond his ability. It took the ones on the left a while to grasp the extreme creativity of the right. I understand Einstein was very reserved because he was not a natural US citizen and he understood if he got to radical in his comments he would simply be deported. I have the luxury of being a US citizen so I won't be getting deported but I may change everything. If I get deported, I prefer you deport me to your worst enemy. If you try to lock me up for my words I will side with your worst enemy. If you try to harm me for my words I will become your worst nightmare. I am open minded about all possible outcomes. If worse comes to worse I will feign insanity.

I understand there are Buddhists who do not see the western religious founders as "wise" but I also understand some do. There are very few western religious people who find Buddha was wise. This is an indication of the fear. The fear has to be gone to gain the extreme right brain that denotes being able to understand this oneness or having the concentration to grasp everything is one thing or a whole. You are simply going to have to scare yourself straight and the sooner you get use to that reality, the sooner you can start to ponder how you are going to do that. I don't want to hear a person with a strong sense of time and strong hunger suggesting they are not afraid, because in fact they have to piss when they even get nervous, so clearly they are out of their mind with fear. In relation to fear conditioning, you are either hardcore or you are not even at the door. A mind that is afraid of a word or a ghost is an infinitely weak mind. A person that fears intangible things like these is mentally unstable by nature. They are unpredictable by nature. There is no pill that will make you not afraid or words and ghosts permanently. One simply has to go through the fire to make it permanent. You may go insane because your fear is so ingrained you will lose your mind.

You may have the imagination to understand what it is going to mean being all alone in old cemetery far out on a dirt road and watching your friends driving away. You can see their taillights fading on a moonless night. You have no chance to get help if something goes wrong. You cannot run fast enough if something goes wrong. You are all alone by yourself and you are surrounded by old tombstones. There are many corpses just under the surface of that ground. You are surrounded by them and your mind is already starting to suggest logical reasons you should never go to that cemetery. That is why you are your own worst enemy. You perceive your judgment is sound and your logic is sound, but that is a delusion. You are in fact sacred out of your of your mind with fear, and that fear makes you come to irrational conclusions. Your mind convinces you everyone needs fear to be alive. That is a delusion. You are making assumptions that are not based in reality at all. You are believing hallucinations in your mind and thus you are mentally unstable. You are a threat to yourself and to those around you at all times because you believe logical deductions that are not logical. You hear the words "fear not" and you assume it is not an absolute ideal. Your intuition when in the left state of mind tends to be wrong but you perceive it is right so you have to deny it and "go for broke." Your mind will tell you not to sit in the dark after watching a scary move because certainly that monster in that movie drove over to your house and is waiting for you. That is total insanity and not even in the realm of possibility, yet your mind is telling you it is fact. It is not fact it is simply the side effect that this Demotic and Dena education has instilled in your mind. I would not tell you that if it was not absolute fact. The fear in your mind is hindering your mind and you will still attempt to believe fear is natural. Fear and common sense is not the same thing. Fear in fact discourages common sense. Many of the things you believe are backwards. Whatever you are afraid of you should not be afraid of, yet you are. I am not afraid of anything, yet I have enough common sense to stay away from you. I am not afraid of you, but I have common sense enough to understand what you are. I can relate better to depressed and suicidal people because they are aware something is wrong. People who are happy about everything are perhaps far too gone mentally. They are afraid of a bad haircut. I am not happy I am tolerant. I tolerate all music, I tolerate ghosts in cemeteries at night, I tolerate a society that mentally damages children and then when the children kill their self society suggests "Reason unknown." or suggests "they were mentally ill". If I was not tolerant I would be up to my neck in rivers of blood right now. Don't kid yourself. I prefer rivers of blood, but I have self control. I say what I think because I do not answer to anyone anymore. Ones may perceive I have to answer to someone, but I understand they misunderstand. They may get me down here, but I get them up there. I have no idea what that means, but my fingers suggested it.- 6:04:51 AM

"The trouble with being poor is that it takes up all your time." Willem de Kooning
This comment simply suggests ones with slight sense of time or ones in Nirvana or on the right tends to not like material things because they are cerebral focused. Poor in material wealth sometimes means rich in cerebral wealth. The physical and cerebral tend not to mix. But to clarify, I did not reach extreme right brain because I had no money I defeated my fear of death accidentally.

This one is complex.
Mar 3:23 And he called them unto him , and said unto them in parables, How can Satan cast out Satan?
"said unto them in parables" this is because in extreme right brain things are all cerebral so ideas and concepts can only be explained in parables. Moses, Jesus, Mohammed, Buddha all used parables. I may use parables but I am experimenting with actualities for a while. There is enough medical knowledge now that I can say right brain and left brain instead of light and dark, and good and evil.
"How can Satan cast out Satan? " This is saying how can a person under the influence of the Demotic or with fear in their mind or one on the left, explain how another person on the left can go to the right? The answer is you cannot, they have to wait until someone "wakes up" usually by accident and then they can explain to a person on the left how to get to the right, and I suggest fear conditioning and there are many aspects to that. Simply put "fear not."
I understand many of these words are simply contrast words. Demotic sounds a lot like demonic. I do not think anyone is Satan I think some people are on the right hand and some people are on the left side, and I understand that is not exactly because they wanted to be, but an

indirect side effect of the "education". So the whole concept of everyone has a choice, is in reality more like, almost no one had a choice or "Suffer the children" and that is also deeper because it means, suffer everyone, everyone essentially was ripped from how they were as a child by the education and so they are still children mentally but have been "blocked out" by the education, accidentally. You can take the most hardcore violent person in the universe and let them condition to the right extreme, and they will become wise lambs. It's a characteristic of the right.

Mar 3:24 And if a kingdom be divided against itself, that kingdom cannot stand.

This is simply saying. The kingdom is the right brain and when the education side effects kick in one becomes left brain, but they are right brain naturally, so they are divided mentally, they are injured mentally. They cannot stand means they cannot think properly. They are at 10% power instead of 100% power. As Moses suggested, they suffer for the rest of their days. The empty feeling and the need to fill it, is that 90% loss of mental power. So everyone on the left feels that and they want to fill it with various physical things but they never can because it the right side that wants to get out but it cannot with the anomaly fear in the mind.

Mar 3:25 And if a house(mind) be divided against itself, that house cannot stand.

This is just a repeat. I am glad I never repeat what I say more than once.

Mar 3:26 And if Satan rise up against himself, and be divided, he cannot stand, but hath an end.

If a person on the left tries to heal himself or go right brain, yet still has fear in the mind, it wont work. This is a nice way of saying money is not going to condition away your fear. Praying is not going to condition away your fear. You have to apply "fear not" and to an extreme, because it is deep seeded. You may even fear me, that's how deep seeded your fear is.

Mar 3:27 "No man can enter into a strong man's house, and spoil his goods, except he will first bind the strong man; and then he will spoil his house."

This is a nice way to say, Once a person is in extreme right brain there is no way another person can make them go left brain so they have to kill them "bind them" to stop them. One might suggest they did a little binding of Jesus and that stopped him from breaking up their slavery party. "spoil his goods" denotes that but that will kill him and then he cannot wake others from the neurosis or the left brain, so it ruins the whole thing, because the one on the right to the extreme is the one who can assist the ones on the left to get to the right in relation to ""How can Satan(left) cast out Satan(left)? "

Mar 3:28 Verily I say unto you, All sins shall be forgiven unto the sons of men, and blasphemies wherewith soever they shall blaspheme:

This is a twofold slightly biased comment. First off it is saying "sins shall be forgiven unto the sons of men" sins are simply characteristics of the left brain. Lust for example, I can feel lust in fact way to easily but I cannot maintain a state of lust. I am pleased with every women I see but I am literally unable to sit home and lust for more than a couple minutes, the "machine" is pondering things so swiftly a mindset of lust is not possible. Now in left brain one can spend days dreaming of a woman or man, and it can fester in their mind, and they will reach a state of lust mentally and absolutely. But what this is saying is, there are no sin's that are not forgiven or a big deal, because "they know not what they do" , they were put into the left brain as a child as a side effect of demotic and Dena education, and so, he is saying, I cast no stones on anyone. How can he, it is not anyone's fault, it was an invention that has unintended consequences. He is saying whatever you do, do not feel shame because the shame and shyness and the embarrassment is a symptom or characteristic of the education, so fear not. I understand these wise being are not saying more rules they were saying less rules and the ones who were the slave masters killed them for saying that. Moses broke the ten commandments on the rocks. I do not know any way to say it clearer than that.

Right "brain is not concerned with things falling into patterns because of prescribed rules." One simply cannot be creative and open-minded and have tons of rules because rules block open-mindedness. It is that simple.

This is an early suggestion of the right hand or right brain.

Gen 48:17 And when Joseph saw that his father laid his right hand upon the head of Ephraim, it displeased him: and he held up his father's hand, to remove it from Ephraim's head unto Manasseh's head.

Gen 48:18 "And Joseph said unto his father, Not so, my father: for this is the firstborn; put thy right hand upon his head." (This comment is suggesting make sure the first born are condition first because if they get to far into learning language and math they will go left brained. Its saying do the Abraham and Isaac fear conditioning on the first born because if you wait to long and they learn language they will go left brain."

Which happened earlier in this book

Gen 22:2 " And he said, Take now thy son, thine only son Isaac, whom thou lovest, and get thee into the land of Moriah; and offer him there for a burnt offering upon one of the mountains which I will tell thee of."

This is simply saying, your son Isaac learned language and has fear and is on the left so you are going to have to make him think you are going to kill him so he will get over his fear and go to the right.,

Gen 22:7 And Isaac spake unto Abraham his father,and said,My father :and he said, Here am I, my son. And he said, Behold the fire and the wood: but where is the lamb for a burnt offering? (This is Isaac being concerned about who is going to be killed so Isaac is afraid and fearful, so that shows Isaac is on the left, and that is why he has to have the fear conditioning done.)

Gen 22:8 And Abraham said, My son, God will provide himself a lamb for a burnt offering: so they went both of them together.(So this is Abraham lying so that his son will not run off, because a person with fear does not like to be scared. You are going to want to run to a light switch after you turn off the lights after you watch as carry movie. Isaac would have ran away to, that does what fear is all about, and that is why Abraham, had to condition it out of Isaac.)

Gen 22:10 And Abraham stretched forth his hand, and took the knife to slay his son.(This is the conditioning, Isaac thought Abraham was going to kill him and Isaac thought he was going to die, so Isaac did not "try to save himself so he found himself." And went to right brain from the conditioning.

Gen 22:11 And the angel of the LORD called unto him out of heaven, and said, Abraham, Abraham: and he said, Here am I.(Here AM I, AM denotes in the now, or no sense of time , so the fear conditioning worked. Its also oyt of sequence "here I am is "proper" in relation to left brain sequence)

Gen 22:12 And he said, Lay not thine hand upon the lad, neither do thou any thing unto him: for now I know that thou fearest God, seeing thou hast not withheld thy son, thine only son from me.(This simply says, you do not have to take a handful of pills or starve yourself for 39 days to face fear hardcore. You have to be in a situation to be afraid and fight that fear but not in an absolute situation that may cause bodily harm, and that is relative to each person.)

7/27/2009 4:43:26 AM

Mar 3:29 "But he that shall blaspheme against the Holy Ghost hath never forgiveness, but is in danger of eternal damnation"

Holy Ghosts/Spirit is one who "woke up" and the ones on the left assume they are "drunk" or "mentally ill" because of what they say or because of the complexity in what they say in relation to.

Act 2:15 For these are not drunken, as ye suppose, seeing it is but the third hour of the day.

And in relation to "<+KarenJ> I'm reasonably well educated but that one is nonsense as near as I can tell" and "[00:02] <KarenJ> Lestat I perceive you are mentally ill and need help very badly." So the one on the left in general, should perceive I am very different, but mentally ill and on drugs, perhaps they wish I was.

"never forgiveness, but is in danger of eternal damnation:" This is simply saying, one on the extreme right is the only kind of person who can wake up ones on the left because """"How can Satan(left) cast out Satan(left)? " So If a person on the left attacks one on the right or kills that one, then the chances of others being woken up decreases and thus the species remains "Gen 3:14 ... cursed above all cattle, and above every beast of the field; upon thy belly shalt thou go, and dust shalt thou eat all the days of thy life:" and be "Gen 3:10 ... I was afraid, because I was naked; and I hid myself.(embarrassed, shy, ashamed,= way to strong emotions and thus not very good at concentration and creativity) so they will be "Gen 3:17 in sorrow shalt thou eat of it all the days"

Translated , if the ones on the left hinder the ones who woke up from the script neurosis they are only harming their self because they will remain on the left with their strong emotions and thus be mentally in sorrow for the rest of their lives.

Mar 3:30 Because they said, He hath an unclean(left brain extreme as a result of script education) spirit. Ones on the left assume if you say something bad about the "holy spirit" as in the word holy spirit that you are cursed or bad simply because they fear words, they never grasped the two words "Fear Not", they perceive a word is going to harm them because there mind is so full of fear they also think nudity is bad and evil, and words and they are simply in "in sorrow shalt thou eat of it all the days". They are the lost, they are blind, they are the dead, mentally. I am not suggesting if one on the left stands in my path they will be eternally damned but on the other hand I have not yet determined how these wise beings understood they were on the right hand in relation to which aspect of the brain was dominate in them. Perhaps it was simply because they had heightened awareness far beyond my understanding.- 4:58:32 AM

Gen 3:11 And he said, Who told thee that thou wast naked?(should be ashamed and afraid and embarrassed of these things)

Learning requires memorization (left brain), understanding requires concentration (right brain).

It is easier to understand how to learn than to learn how to understand.

To clarify, I can suggest condition away from fear and you will go extreme right brain and you will have extreme concentration and the ability to learn swiftly on the other hand if you are on the left you are not capable of extreme concentration so all learning will be a struggle. Learning from mistakes denotes remembering the mistakes understanding your mistakes denotes you apply that lesson into your strategy. Many can memorize history yet very few can understand it. The main problem with my books is, I understand them. I want to be something that appears as nothing for a change.

7/27/2009 2:15:27 PM – Perfectual is a state of mind where one uses assumptions of safety on false scales to assume everything is perfect or safe. Some examples would be "My house is not burning down so everything is good"."My child got straight A's in school so he is perfect." Used in a sentence. After Bill was told of his pay raise his coworkers could tell from his face he was perfectual. Perhaps I am just the new found leader of crazy people and it gives me a great deal of perfectual.

The point is, either I accidentally conditioned away all my fear and became totally insane or a vast majority of the population with their fear is insane. I am open minded and pondering both aspects in order to keep my sanity or what is left of my sanity depending on which side of that pondering coin you are on. I have never heard this interpretation of the "ancient texts" and I certainly have great doubt I am capable of interpreting these ancient texts with such ease so perhaps I have misunderstood the Adam and Eve parable and the "knowledge tree" is something other than language and math and so whatever that tree may represent, it perhaps completely escapes me if it is not math and language. Falling on one's own sword is most difficult because it tends to be the sharpest. A self inflicted wound may never be avenged and is difficult to forget.

Rev 15:4 "Who shall not fear thee, O Lord, and glorify thy name? for thou only art holy: for all nations shall come and worship before thee; for thy judgments are made manifest."

This comment is not actually translated properly. What it means to say is, Whoever shall not have fear or condition away all the fear will be "holy" in relation to "sound drunk in their words" to the ones on the left because they will become extreme right brained, and many will seek their council because they use the complex /wise aspect of the mind and make "proper" judgments. A proper judgment is in relation to how Jesus treated the prostitute. A judgment that is absent of ignorance is a judgment that takes into account "we" invented language and math and that made us use short term memory and many rules and accidentally made us go left brain dominate to such an extreme "we" gained all these strong mental side effects such as greed, lust, envy, fear, coveting and the list goes on. Few can even ponder that reality let alone understand it. - 9:26:44 PM

7/28/2009 6:33:23 AM

Gen 15:1 "After these things the word(how to get back to right brain) of the LORD(lord of the mind the complex right brain) came unto Abram in a vision(Abraham pondered or used his extreme concentration of right brain to figure out how to get back to extreme right brain), saying, Fear not(is how it is accomplished, fear conditioning), Abram: I am thy shield, and thy exceeding great reward.(your regard is heightened awareness and extreme concentration and some telepathy thingy and feeling through vision and you won't be so prone to violence or physical focused yet more cerebral focused)

This next bit is will prove why Einstein was in fact extreme right brained or in Nirvana to at least a degree. "One of Einstein's great insights was to realize that matter and energy are really different forms of the same thing. Matter can be turned into energy, and energy into matter.

"different forms of the same thing" denotes he noticed the whole or one thing in relation to "The right brain looks at the whole picture and quickly seeks to determine the spatial relationships of all the parts as they relate to the whole." And contrary to that left brain "excels in naming and categorizing things". So essentially left brain is good at creating categories or parts, and that tends to complicate what is in reality a simple thing. There are many examples. There is a food, food is not really food, it is simply atoms. So ones on the right say you need food to survive, but what they are really saying is you need atoms to survive. All food is/are atoms. So we are atoms and we use atoms to remain animated. A person on the left tends to turn that simple reality into a complex situation or tends to turn a mole hill into a mountain. They have food, then various kinds of food and then various kinds of each of those foods. One reason there are so many classifications of food is because ones on the left tends to like and dislike certain foods. I no longer like or dislike any food because I essentially no longer taste food in contrast to how much I tastes food before the accident, so "any way the wind blows doesn't really matter to me." Right now there are many physicists attempting to categorize atoms and parts of atoms and find this "god particle", but they miss the point Einstein was suggesting. Everything is one thing. One can attempt to categorize red dirt, brown dirt, black dirt and come up with all of these theories about the various kinds of dirt but in reality they are all the same dirt and deeper still they are just atoms like all other atoms. Essentially the left brain tends to make one make a mountain out of mole hill. They left will suggest there are Americans and British and Chinese and Japanese and perceive these are valid categories when in fact they are not valid categories , they are just people. It does not matter of one suggests they are not just people they are categories of people because that is the nature of the left brain. It tends to create many categories and then it uses is less than complex sequential concentration to make sense of it, and it cannot. Left brain creates complexity with categorizing things yet is unable to handle complexity and is only capable of simplemindedness or narrow-mindedness. Left brain tries to create these categories to appear smart yet it is unable to deal with the categories so it reveals it's self in the end. It simply cannot hang with the big fish, right brain. Another way to look at it is, left brain tends to make things much harder than they really are. That is what this comment is suggesting

Gen 3:17 " cursed is the ground(mind) for thy sake(because of what you did which is learned the language and math and didn't condition away from fear to remain in right brain); in sorrow(making mountains out of mole hills) shalt thou eat(easy things will be difficult things) of it all the days of thy life(for as long as you are in left brain);"

This may appear as a simple fear conditioning putting but the truth is, the Abraham and Isaac techniques suggests that may be the only way to go the full measure, which is, condition away from fear of death.

Not that I ever get off topic, but, the problem with suggesting things are moving is determining what movement is. Movement denotes a measurement. Time denotes a measurement. The only accurate way to suggest movement is to first determine what environment this movement is taking place in. There perhaps cannot be movement in infinity and there perhaps cannot be time in infinity. Time and movement are measurements and one is unable to measure in infinity or in an infinite vacuum unless they create artificial measurements. If the universe is infinite where exactly are these things being measured moving? Are these things being measured moving up, down, left, right, in an infinite universe? This also requires artificial scales to determine which way things are moving. One may announce a meteor is heading towards the earth. Which way is towards the earth? Is that north , south , east or west? So this all comes back to the assumption the universe is not infinite but finite. That all goes back to the assumption that because we can see with the Hubble, galaxies before they were well formed, there must be a "big bang" that started everything. The problem with that assumption is you cannot get something (mass) for nothing or from nothing. You cannot have nothing and then have something you can only have nothing and then have more nothing that may appear to be something if one creates artificial scales to categorize these "more nothing" as something. The moments before the big bang it is understood there was no time and no mass and no energy and not even a location and then all the sudden there was time and mass and energy and a location so there is perhaps really only one explanation without defying e=mc2. What appears to be "real" is not real but only a very convincing illusion. It is easy to create a convincing illusion if one wants to believe it is real. Helen Keller suggested something along the lines of "Death is simply going from one room to another except in my case I will be able to see."

"Death is no more than passing from one room into another. But there's a difference for me, you know. Because in that other room I shall be able to see. "

Helen Keller

What this suggesting is nothing is really happening only illusions that give off the impression something is happening. Helen Keller had very little "contact" in relation to she was not "manipulated" by the comments or suggestions of others simply because she could not see and could not hear. Someone could yell fire but Helen would not become afraid. Someone could yell terrorists and Helen would not sign away her freedoms. She could not hear, so she was not susceptible to fear tactics. She could not see so she was not afraid of the dark or boogie men, so her mind was very sharp. If you see where the train went, call. This is because she had extreme concentration because many of these outside influences were taken away or not possible. That is why Buddha suggested "contact". If ones turns off sight, hearing, taste, smell, touch the mind is forced to increase its "concentration" abilities because it adapts. So when all the fear is conditioned away that is like another sensory perception that is turned off and thus the mind takes all the energy used to achieve fear or energy it spends on fear, and uses it for other things.

In a combat situation a commander who has great fear cannot think properly and a commander who has little fear tends to think more properly. This is because the one with slight fear mind is not consumed with fear and so they have more "energy" to think clearly. Fear is relative to concentration, but fear itself is not an absolute. Fear itself is an anomaly in the mind. A person is not afraid of ghosts a person that is afraid of ghosts has to much of this anomaly and it is hindering their minds ability, so they tend to do things that are not logical. I recall before the accident I would walk from my isolation chamber to the bed room at night and halfway there I would "feel" ghosts or scary things my mind suggested were real, and I would end up running the rest of the way to the room. So I was running from hallucinations my minds was suggesting were real. I was hallucinating and thus delusional because I was running from the dark when there was nothing in the dark. I was not seeing ghosts with my eyes I was thinking there were ghosts and my minds was suggesting there were ghosts and that made me run to the bedroom. I was reacting in a physical manner to hallucinations created in my mind. So in reality I was in "sorrow" because my mind had this anomaly called fear and it was making me do things because it was making me believe these "fear" things were real. They seemed very real, but they were not real, it was all in my mind. So being afraid at all is essentially the mind that is in a state of hallucinations. This is far more complex than just being afraid of the dark. Being afraid of guys in sandals and signing all your freedoms away is the exact same thing. Passing a law to lock up people because you are afraid drugs are bad is the exact same thing. Giving a small child psychiatric drugs because you are afraid they are mentally different than what you perceive they should be, is the exact same thing. The fear is making you hallucinate and those hallucinations are making you do physical things that are not logical but delusional. So I am now in a position of pondering why am I going to pander to a person who is hallucinating, and making delusional decisions because their mind is full of a mental abnormality called fear. I am certainly not going to allow rabidity to determine my fate. The point is, if you have fear in your mind the last thing in the universe you are is an authority on anything because you are prone to hallucinations. Translated you are a person hallucinating and you assume I am going to believe what you say and agree with laws you say, and agree with your arguments. I am fully aware you are hallucinating because I use to be hallucinating. I understand I am not hallucinating to the degree a person with strong hunger and strong sense of time I hallucinating. I am not going to subscribe to the babblings of one who is hallucinating no matter what they suggest. All of their conclusion are essentially based on hallucinations. They suggest I am bad or evil if I drink a beer, smoke a joint, look at porno or say certain words. They are in fact totally out of touch with reality. They are delusional to the extreme. A person that is hallucinating cannot be trusted because they know not what they do.

"The whole religious complexion of the modern world is due to the absence from Jerusalem of a lunatic asylum. "

Thomas Paine

Either I am insane because I believe a person is not evil or bad because they smoke a joint, drink a beer, cuss a little or misspell a word or you are veil and bad because you believe a person is evil or bad if they smoke a joint, drink a beer, cuss or misspelled a word. There is no other option here. IF I am not evil because I understand these things do not determine if a person is bad or evil then you are bad or evil because you have determined person is bad if they do these things. Perhaps you are still able to comprehend elementary logic. I would not suggest a child is a failure because they misspell a word on a spelling test but you hang children by the bus load every single day in every single way, when they misspelled a word on a test. Do not assume I am without judgment when I have suggested I am on a vengeance mission. You do not have enough mental function to avoid my wrath, I assure you of that. Thomas Paine is explaining they(ones on the left) killed Jesus(one on the right) because they assumed he was crazy.

[00:13] <+KarenJ> I'm reasonably well educated but that one is nonsense as near as I can tell

I make no sense to ones on the left so then they use their elementary logic and then they conclude: [00:02] <KarenJ> Lestat I perceive you are mentally ill and need help very badly.

KarenJ just wants to help me because she is unable to grasp the only one in all reality that needs help is her. The ones on the left got sick of Jesus and helped him up on the cross and the last thing you need to ever suggest is it was a certain race or gender of people, it was on the ones on the left and if you have a strong sense of time and strong sense of hunger and strong emotions, you are on the left and that is a fact beyond all reality no matter what you may try to suggest, ever, into infinity. You may perceive I am mentally ill, but before it is all over, I am going to convince you, you are mentally ill, and then you will understand who I am.

"What can you do against the lunatic who is more intelligent than yourself, who gives your arguments a fair hearing and then simply persists in his lunacy?"

George Orwell

I keep pumping out books and you may perceive I am a lunatic, yet I keep pumping out books. I am pumping out books and you are perhaps trying to use your elementary logic to conclude what I am, but I am still pumping out books. This is the seventh book in seven months. Can I be a lunatic when you cannot do that? You cannot do that so I cannot be a lunatic unless you are an infinite lunatic. Either I am conscious and you are not or you are conscious and I am not. I am mentally the reverse of you. You cry over dead people, I do not. We are anti in contrast to each other. Perhaps you should find one sentence in my books that does not make sense to you, so you can suggest I am a lunatic, and that way you can continue on with your mindless specter existence. I do not pander to what I own.- 8:45:03 AM

"Griswold depicted Poe as a depraved, drunk, drug-addled madman and included Poe's letters as evidence."

<KarenJ> Lestat I perceive you are mentally ill and need help very badly.

"the right brain seems to flourish dealing with complexity, ambiguity(doubt) and paradox."

"Act 2:15 … not drunken, as ye(ones on the left) suppose"

"The lunatic, the lover, and the poet, are of imagination all compact."

William Shakespeare

Maybe I am just a lover and a poet and not a lunatic, maybe I will be anything you want me to be although I understand I am nothingness and thus can assume any role.

BellucciMonicaJust wondering: what is my best role yet?

Lestat9@BellucciMonica Your Mary role, of course.

The illusion in my books is that I am making progress and making a convincing argument and everything is going to be better but that is simply a perfectual mindset. It is not reality. I am making no progress. It is not going to be better. I cannot ever win because the neurosis in the ones I attempt to communicate with is far beyond my verbal ability to reach. I am cannot make a convincing argument to a person that perceives their mental state and their fear is a natural condition and not a abnormality and symptom of neurosis. I cannot convince a person their strong sense of hunger and time is a symptom of neurosis and simply an anomaly in their mind. An insane person does not perceive they are insane. A blind person does not perceive blindness is blindness if they have been blind all their life. The blindness simply becomes normal and is thus accepted as normal in that persons mind. One can eventually become use to sorrow and assume sorrow is just a part of the package. Although I have won the battle in my mind I cannot win the battle of their mind. They assume these things their mind suggests are reality so they are trapped and thus cursed by their own perception and their own mind.

This is a comment by a "Buddhist" and she has disliked me from the beginning because she perceives because I am not a Buddhist I must not understand anything. She perceives Buddhism is the only path and the other western religions are not valid, so she is in fact trapped in narrow-mindedness. She is unable to see everything is one thing so she tends to attack me and suggest I am unknowledgeable because she is unable to grasp who I reached nirvana. She suggests I am a liar when I explain I am simply a failed suicide attempt. So she has difficult with ambiguity, she cannot doubt herself so she doubts me.

I will lay her comment to me out in my books and give it a fair shake.

<Lestat9> I have published the first 6 books and am nearly finished with the seventh so my fish heads are eagerly awaiting your first book, sunshine.

*This comment I make is my way of telling her she needs to publish books and not be afraid to put her thought son a world stage. That is a very powerful fear conditioning aspect and it has worked with some I have suggested this to. The logic is, first off you should not be afraid to write things down and have others read them. Once you pass that simple fear conditioning aspect you should not be afraid to publish them and let the whole world read them. The worst thing that will happen to you is you will die, and that is already and eventual fact.

<jnana> i dont know enough

*Now she retorts with "I do not know enough" and that seems like she is humble but that is an illusion. She is arrogant because she bans me from all the Buddhists channel because she says I know nothing about Buddhism and I should not be allow in Buddhist channels. So she know something she assumes I am bad and I am evil, because I speak of religions even Christian and Jewish religions and in her "control freak channels" and she says that is not what this channel is about and if you speak about Buddha you do not know about him so you get banned. She is what is known as Maya. That's her state of mind. She proclaims to be a teacher but if anything goes out of her realm of understanding it is evil and bad and she must kill it, as in ban me. She is trying to have rules and morals but that is only keeping her in left brain. It is not making her more "enlightened" it is turning her into a control freak.

<Lestat9> perhaps that is because you are banning ones who do know enough from your channels.

*This is my little jab at her because every Buddhist channel on Mirc she has gotten me banned from. I have never banned one person and I have never forced a person out of a room. I go to a #spirit chat room and when someone comes in I give them "ops" so that they can ban me if they wish, but I do not ban people for any reason because that's is my mental conditioning away from control which is left brain. My goal is not to control anyone my goal is to assist people with letting go of all the rules and controls. The complexity is, one has to let go of the rules and morals in order to get to the right and once they are in the right brain their fruits are docile and they do not have the characterics of the "seven deadly sins". Coveting is control. It can be as simple as "You live under my roof so you do as I say." To "You are in my channel so you do as I say." Both are simply trying to control another person with a scare tactic. "Do as I say or else" is a scare tactic. "Get good grades or you are a loser in life and I will punish you." That is the worst scare tactic because it is done to a child. One is better off killing their self than to mentally harm a child like that. I do not care what your god says about that comment.

<jnana> besides i'm not trying to catch fish

*This is an inside joke, but this is also a symptom of her misunderstanding. If she is not trying to catch fish, then why is she banning me and suggesting I am not knowledgeable about religions. It all comes back to one thing, she thinks I am a liar when I suggest I reached nirvana by accident as the result of a failed suicide attempt, and she perhaps doe4s not grasp that is why a Buddhist teaching about going to a cemetery at night to face one fears is in fact what I did, except I faced more than a ghost I faced my fear of my death, accidentally and lost all fear. I pulled an Abraham and Isaac and she cannot grasp that and if I suggest Abraham and Isaac she will say, that is not Buddhism and your are not a Buddhist so I will ban you if you speak again. This is a good example of everything is relative to the observer. She perceives I am evil or bad because she perceives she is good or righteous, because we do not see "eye to eye".

<jnana> you dont know buddhism, it is a Buddhist channel

*Here she says , "you do not know Buddhism" so she knows enough to know I do not know Buddhism. That is very dangerous. Apparently she is Buddha of the age and perhaps God himself because she can tell who knows Buddhism and who does not. She is trapped in the labels. There is no Buddhism or Christianity or Islam or Judaism, they are simply labels created by ones on the left to explain mental conditioning concepts. And those mental conditioning concepts can be summed up in two words "Fear not". One cannot build a religion around two words unless they are on the left and want to make a mountain out of a mole hill. This is all a symptom of the left brain person trying to categorize things and making this huge issue out of a non issue. One who goes the full measure with fear not will lose the seven deadly sin fruits of their thinking and gain the seven holy virtues mentally and that is it. There is no need for religion, everyone knows what "conditioning away from fear to achieve the complex right aspect of the mind." means. I do not need to build a worship temple or church to explain that to people. There is nothing left to say after that aspect of the doctrine. One either applies it or does not apply it. But then ones on the left who are all about "greed" will turn that simple comment into a money making opportunity or an opportunity to achieve "control", and that is how one can tell the wheat from the chaff. "I am your religious teacher give me money." That is what the ones on the left do. "I need money to continue my complicated and vast explanation of the two words "fear not"." The left brain tends to categorize things and the more categories the more complex and the left brain is unable to deal with complexity, so it defeats itself. Left brain is simply self defeating. Right brain is so creative and imaginative it will conquer any complexity eventually and rather swiftly. I do not need to run an experiment about what I understand.

<Lestat9> your rules and your morals are your worst enemy perhaps

*This is where I attempt to suggest "right brain/nirvana" is against rules and so she should try not to have so many rules.

<jnana> having such difficulties with my morals shows that you really do not understand a thing and need to go back to the beginning, if you can, the problem is you cant, your stuck in "know it all syndrome" which means you cant learn, you only know, which is the greatest obstacle of all

    *This is where she goes back to her assumption, I am a liar that I achieved nirvana or extreme right brain from a failed suicide attempt. She cannot grasp that is the reality. She assumes I need a teacher. She assumes I certainly need some assistance. She assumes I am arrogant. She assumes I am ill when she is the one who bans me and tries fear tactics on me." <jnana> you dont know Buddhism" Her mind is already locked on this because I tried to explain to her from the start how I reached this state of mind that she tries so hard to reach, because of a failed suicide attempt and I accidentally conditioned away all my fear. She assumes that is a lie. So she assumes I am evil or bad or wrong. She judged herself perfectly ", your stuck in "know it all syndrome" which means you can't learn". Her mind is so closed she cannot believe I reached Nirvana because of a failed suicide attempt. That is beyond her current mental states ability to believe, so she assumes I am a liar and need much work. There are ones who are "Buddhist" who totally agree with my conclusions but it does not do any good to mention that to her because she will just assume they are evil and bad and in need or more help. I would never ban her from a chat room no matter what, yet she bans me because she is in fact "stuck in "know it all syndrome"" So never assumes I am any of these religions I certainly am not. I am a lone wolf. I will not associate with people because it always comes back to one thing, relativity. According to her I am evil and bad and need much help just like KarenJ suggests. If it not them then it certainly must be me. They know they are not wrong so they assume I certainly must be wrong. They are using classifications. They cannot just let things be. They cannot let me sit in their channel and talk about anything on my mind, they have to try to stop it or control it and if they cannot they kill it or ban it. That's elementary logic. "You do as I say or I ban you and this is my channel, and it is mine, and I know it is mine, and you are not like me so you are evil because I know I am good." The thing is some monk somewhere told Jnana she is wise and now she perceives she is the end all be all, "having such difficulties with my morals shows that you really do not understand a thing", perhaps it is moral to scare people with fear tactics in attempts to control them. I have difficulty with control freaks. One has to be proper and one has to be improper. Is a slave master proper or is one who likes freedom proper? When one is born are they a slave or are they free? She suggests "shows that you really do not understand a thing"". I do not understand a thing. That's a compliment from my point of view. I understand nothing not something, but I am aware she is suggesting I need more schooling because she cannot grasp I am the school. This one is a Maya and many I know who are in nirvana understand she is Maya. If she had heightened awareness she would not be so attacking towards me. She would be aware but instead she goes out of her way to let everyone know I am not a Buddhist and so I am not allowed in Buddhist chat rooms. So she has a grudge. You may perceive I have a grudge against her by adding this to my infinitely poor thick pamphlets but in reality, I have to write about something. I will not even remember exactly what I wrote about this when I start the eighth book so I have no grudge I am just aware of one who is on the left when I see it. All I can do is act natural and suggest how I feel and if I am the genuine article my thick pamphlets should be full of contradictions, ambiguity(doubt) and paradox. If I was consistent, logical and unwavering in my convictions that would prove I am not the genuine article." right brain seems to flourish dealing with complexity, ambiguity and paradox " This translates as, the more crazy and illogical I sound to ones on the left, the more extreme into the right brain or subconscious I in

fact am. Perhaps Jnana has assumed I am here to be a moralistic crusader and in turn neglected to grasp I am here on a vengeance mission. I have to write about something.- 1:03:54 PM

"The place where optimism flourishes most is the lunatic asylum."
Havelock Ellis
"The place where optimism most flourishes is the lunatic asylum."
Henry Ellis

A lunatic tends to be optimistically certain about their own state of mind; A sane person doubts they are sane. Hallucinations are the only things that flourish in the mind of a lunatic.

A lunatic is a person who is very reckless not in relation to words they suggest but in relation to actions they take as in physical actions. One cannot be considered a lunatic or insane because of words they say because words are relative to the observer. One cannot suggest one is a lunatic because of what they look at. So the line in the sand is what a person does physically. Ones on the left tend to kill each other over grains of sand and tend to kill their self when they do have enough money. The definition is very vague and thus complex. If Washington was here today and tried to negate all of these laws and rules against freedom of speech with physical actions he would be tried and convicted as a terrorist and perhaps killed. One must first find a way to determine who the tyrant is. If California has no problems with people in that state growing pot and the federal government goes in that state and arrests people growing pot, who is the tyrant? Is a state more powerful than the federal government? If a state is not more powerful or a state law is not more powerful than a federal law then that state is not a state but a device under the control of the federal government, one has to be dominate over the other. The state in turn becomes a puppet of the federal government but the federal government has no master of it. A state cannot enforce its will on the federal government or it would be deemed a terrorist. If a state resists the federal government it is also deemed a terrorist or a radical or right wing by the judgment of the federal government then apparently the federal government is more powerful than all of the states combined because the states cannot control the federal government but the federal branch can control all the states. The federal government is not a place it is an ideal. A state is a place. Whoever is more powerful automatically denotes the other one is the slave. There is no such thing as equal power sharing if the federal government can go into a state and wield its power regardless of what the state suggests. It makes sense the federal government wants the states to fear it because the federal government is afraid if the states do not fear it, they will do as they wish, and if the states do as they wish, the federal government becomes obsolete, and all that power the federal government has is worthless. If a bully does not keep everyone scared they will become meaningless as a bully. So it is important for the federal government to enforce its will on states to let all the other states know who the bottom line is. So one can look at it like there are 50 kids , the states, and this one bully, and all that bully has to do is torment one kid to keep all 50 kids in line. It is a simple combat strategy. You attack a small village and let a few people go, and they go to a big city and suggest how "evil" or dangerous that army is, and that word gets out and that big city surrenders to the will of that army. It is simply scare tactics. Even if California legalizes pot the federal government will still go into that state and arrest people, so what is the point of the state at all when it is not even in control over its own destiny.

"Profane language" includes those words that are so highly offensive that their mere utterance in the context presented may, in legal terms, amount to a "nuisance."

This is nothing more than censorship. "So highly offensive" I do not even know what the fuck that means. Maybe what they meant is, it is offensive to a person with left brain who pisses their self when they get nervous or signs away their freedoms when someone yells wolf. "mere utterance" denotes saying a word is bad, because the people who believe that never could grasp "sticks and stones may break my bones but words will never harm me." I bet they are trying to protect the kids. They are so righteous they perceive they have reached the top of the mountain and now they can start to instill in others their great and vast wisdom and morals and laws. They must be god himself. They have determined they are able to determine what is highly offensive on all scales and under all circumstances no matter whom the observer is, and they do it to protect everyone from the "evil words". I like that because I prefer a blood bath. - 1:51:55 PM

Waking up is not the problem, tolerating the lunatics you will find yourself surrounded by is.

It is this time 2:17:41 PM and I was up at 6AM and it feels like I have been writing for an eternity. I recall yesterday I thought to myself, I have nothing left to say, yet now I have typed all of these words today and I do not feel I got anywhere. I feel like I am doing these things but I have no ability to perceive accomplishment or satisfaction. I run to the left and run to the right and I end up back in the middle on the fence where I live now. I am compelled to write infinite books and I try to get through them as fast as i can. Perhaps I will write one sentence of wisdom by the infinite book, perhaps not.

I found an interesting contradiction by Buddha. So this is a symptom of the ambiguity/doubt one experiences in the extreme right brain.

"Hatred does not cease by hatred, but only by love; this is the eternal rule."
Buddha
"He who loves 50 people has 50 woes; he who loves no one has no woes. "
Buddha
So you see he says love is the eternal rule but then he says don't love anyone. He is saying don't have attachments. Love is an attachment and when one is on the left is a controlling attachment. A desire to control. You only get two things. You get emotions and controlling mental states or you get the machine state. You simply do not get both. I do not know what he means by hatred. Maybe the people who insult me are right and so they do not insult me they are righteous in their judgments of me. He is trying to communicate complexity with words and it ends up with many contradictory statements. The bible talk about true love or real love, and that is simply a non controlling love. A love without strings attached. It is in a sense indifference I look at it like the machine state. I don't cry over a corpse. I don't cry when I get kicked in the teeth. That's indifference or the machine state. The extreme concentration costs emotions like fear and anger and bitterness and envy and lust and greed. "he who loves no one" is the machine state of the right brain. That again is indifference. That is good not bad. That means when a child gets a word wrong on a test you do not say they are a failure, you just let it go. That means when your boss insults you, you do not go home and get a gun

190

and start shooting people. That means when someone near you dies you do not go into months of depression. You are indifferent to loss and suffering. That is the machine state. So Buddha had some language training and then he had to nearly starve to death to get over his fear and then he went into extreme right brain after he purged the fear. It is not so much you go to right brain it is more like when you get rid of the fear you revert back to your natural mental state which is right brain dominate. That is why "education" is in fact a conditioning tool to negate your natural right brain tendency. Maybe no other being on the planet understands that or maybe the "powers that be" understand that and want that to continue. Granted one may suggest that is quite a conspiracy theory, but the truth is, it is happening every day and there is no mention of fear conditioning so maybe the whole world is so weak minded they cannot even grasp this or maybe someone wants this. If everyone had extreme concentration and had heightened awareness they would not tend to be suckers and fooled easily with fear tactics, that's a fact. So you see this left brain conditioning is very much geared to make people prone to being fooled by fear tactics and being prone to the herd mentality. When people are afraid they like to huddle into masses. I do not know what that logic is but maybe it along the lines of, "If I am going to die, you are coming with me."

"It is a man's own mind, not his enemy or foe, that lures him to evil ways."

<u>Buddha</u>

This is a nice way of saying the kingdom is within, or the mind is within. A mind with fear is a mind on the left and the side effects are lust, greed, envy etc and a mind without fear is a mind on the right and it is in the machine state. I am not charitable because I give my books freely I am in fact indifferent to money. Ones may perceive I am charitable but that is not how I see it at all. Wealth has a lot to do with satisfaction. In the machine state satisfaction is not really possible and so dissatisfaction is not possible. "The more money you have the better you are", is a symptom of this satisfaction. That's a left brain "emotion". One is simply never going to reach the extreme concentration and heightened awareness if they try to hold onto emotions. "As he increases I must decrease." This whole concept about "You should have some emotions" is an illusion, one either has no emotions or too many emotions. I understand I had much rage even at the start of this month but now I have nearly no rage. I am not trying to achieve this right brain dominate state, I accidentally lost my fear of the big one, death and everything went down the drain with it so to speak, in relation to emotions. I am not suggesting you should do anything. I am not suggesting I am good or righteous, I am suggesting if you condition away the fear your emotional baggage is going away. There is no test or experiment you need to worry about, you will understand that is fact if you do condition away the fear. I have moments I wish I could go back to the left and feel satisfaction and maybe a little lust, and maybe a little greed. They are absent in me so I have moments I wish I had them. There are people on the left who wish they had fewer emotions, less lust, less greed, less envy, less anger. I am the opposite of that. I do not feel better than anyone else because feel better is a symptom of ego. I can say words that makes one perceive I feel emotions but I am suggesting that is an illusion. My mind simply cannot maintain emotion, any emotion. So at times I feel like I want to get out of this, because I went into it so fast I mentally struggle to get out at times. I feel like I am in a balloon and I ponder how long one day lasts and I ponder how long my life is going to be even if I live another year, and I want to go back to the left, but I am vain, because I understand I cannot go back to the left because I purged the big fear by accident, my fear of death. I am not use to fear being gone, and I am not use to the machine state. One cannot suggest one mental state if better than the other but one can certainly suggest one mental state is more complex and has more cerebral features. My sense of time is so slowed down now, one day is far too long for me to handle. My sense of time is slowing down faster than I can mentally get use to but I cannot stop it, so I just have to take it. I keep writing because I am getting pulled under so fast that the writing tends to help me focus on something else. It do not even care what I write about anymore. I am using the language to try to get back to the left in some ways. I understand the language is how one goes so far to the left so I am trying to learn the language again in hopes it will slow down this progression. Anyone on the left can condition away from fear because there are many things they fear, nearly everything, but how can one regain fear once all fear is gone is the problem. The answer is perhaps you cannot ever regain fear. Maybe someone will show up at my house and threaten me and I will all the sudden be afraid again and go back to the left a little or slow down this progression a little, but I am aware that's not the trend , the trend is I am still in the progression into the right away from emotions. It's the reverse thing again. This is all about the ambiguity or the doubt in this state of mind. I have moments that I doubt this state of mind is good. I have doubts that understanding all these things I understand is good. Some I speak with suggest it is good, but I still doubt, and that is the ambiguity kicking in. It's a little late for me to have doubt about publishing my books. Doubt is not the same as emotions. Doubt is simply a questioning or pondering and that is healthy for the mind because it gives it something to do. Some suggest what I am doing is proper but they do not grasp I cannot process praise. I take praise the wrong way because I am very open minded and sometimes I assume they are sarcastic and insulting me. Not that I can be insulted but anything someone says to me I ponder it heavily "I think too much" but that is the nature of the complex aspect of the mind. That is what complexity is, the ability to not take everything on face value.

"Peace comes from within(right brain, the cerebral aspect of the mind). Do not seek it without.(left brain is physical based or physical mindset)"
Buddha
Mat 6:33 "But seek ye first the kingdom(right brain) of God, and his righteousness(right brain); and all these things(telepathy, extreme concentration, feeling through vision, cerebral mindset) shall be added unto you."
"Do not seek it without" is perhaps a bit preachy, but what it is suggesting is, one can never satisfy the mind with a physical thing. This is along the lines of "Do not drink wine for it is excess" which means you can reach right brain with some physical techniques like drugs but it is never going to be permanent so you are never going to be filled up, so to speak. Many have suggested my comments prove I am "full of it." but perhaps I misunderstood what they meant.
There is wisdom in your words equal to the beauty in your eyes.
In the depths the shallows appear as folly thus I pray for ignorance.
I am letting go of this book on 7/29/2009 7:05:44 AM
It is difficult for me to cast stones on this demotic induced neurosis matter because I find it quite interesting that we as a species could do something like this to ourselves, and still perhaps doubt we have done this to ourselves.

It is done. Tis well.